Celebrating

Compiled by
Sanctuary Hospice House
Established 2000

Mission Statement:

The Sanctuary Hospice House seeks to provide compassionate care to the dying in response to God's call to serve one another.

Sanctuary Hospice House, Inc.
P.O. Box 192
Tupelo, MS 38802
662/844-2111
FAX 662/844-2354

www.sanctuaryhospicehouse.com

email: office@sanctuaryhospicehouse.com

The proceeds from *Celebrating Hospice-tality* will be used to aid in the day to day operations of the Sanctuary Hospice House, Inc. of North Mississippi.

First printing 5000 August 2004

ISBN: 0-9746693-0-X

For additional copies, use the forms in the back of book or order online from the website noted above.

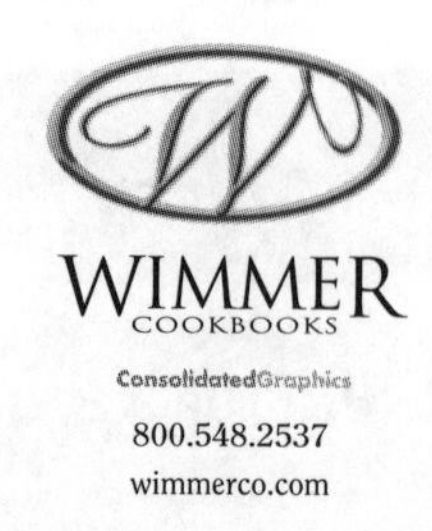
WIMMER
COOKBOOKS
ConsolidatedGraphics
800.548.2537
wimmerco.com

Table of Contents

Celebrating Hospice-tality

Comfort, Cuisine and Reflections from North Mississippi

This unique publication promises a bestseller with "*Celebrating Hospice-tality—Comfort, Cuisine & Reflections from North Mississippi.*" Its popular affirmation offers a long selling life as a classic cookbook, and pages of cooking and storytelling are a winning combination, a prized collection for cooks and readers.

Whether people enjoy cooking or reading – or both – dyed-in-the-wool cookbook collectors will find space for a new copy of "*Celebrating Hospice-tality*" on their bookshelves. Sure to be a treasure, the book will grow with value through time and time again, and handed down through generations.

An elegant book, a quality spiral notebook with pages and pages of tested and retested recipes, the hallmark of good taste in every sense is the culmination of many volunteers working on a fundraising project to support Sanctuary Hospice House.

The Sanctuary Hospice House is its own story, and volunteers bring the dream to reality, and with additional volunteers, give vision, time and hard work in publishing "*Celebrating Hospice-tality*". The Sanctuary Hospice House draws support from nineteen counties around the hub of the Sanctuary Hospice House in Tupelo – so does an excellent cookbook reach a wide market.

From sideboards to dining tables, from breakfast nooks to patios, food is celebrated with family and friends. Formal seated dinners for a dozen, simple suppers for two or more, brunches and breakfasts and teas are treated to any number, buffets add a few or many diners with food and conversation, informal picnics on the patio gather adults and children together, a traditional barbecue serves scores of guests for memorable times: a welcome that means hospitality.

Southern cookery is a varied mixture drawn from many states and regions, and always has belied a standard style of cuisine, because one definition is among twelve states that fall south of the Mason-Dixon Line. As one mere example, French flavors and Creole tastes add ingredients as times change, but regional cooking comes from many regions.

Deltas and hills and valleys, Mississippi or the Deep South is no longer isolated. Changes have welcomed businesses and industries and professions, and people move to the Tupelo area to contribute a new meld: cosmopolitan, cities, villages, towns, country farms, and a mixed history of lifestyle and food. The background of regional or local cooking, and styles of entertaining will hold its own from the cotton farms to the boardroom.

The history of food is no longer restricted to an area, or the food that can be grown in season, or homegrown food preserved for the remaining year. Supermarkets display fresh asparagus or strawberries hauled from one coast to another – and specialty items are an available array.

"Kicked up a notch" and "elegant but easy" are two statements repeated by those who work on the "*Celebrating Hospice-tality*" cookbook. They reach across wide interests for cooks who will be able to choose a menu for any occasion. Seven chapters are arranged in appetizers, beverages, bread, breakfast, brunches, soups, salads, sandwiches, side dishes, entrees and desserts.

Enjoy "*Celebrating Hospice-tality—Comfort, Cuisine & Reflections from North Mississippi.*" Read it and try recipes for family, friends and special occasions, because you'll find the best of all combinations suited to your own family and friends. Choose recipes, present a menu that you serve with pride, cooked and served with all the many ways of good taste.

~Phyllis Hawkins Harper
Tupelo, MS

Phyllis Hawkins Harper

In the words of Phyllis Hawkins Harper, "Writing a food column was only a sideline that we expected to fill a few hours, anchoring our new food section, and for years was printed under the kicker *"Now We're Cooking."* She covered a news beat, wrote a personal column, *"Seems To Me,"* and became Northeast Mississippi Daily Journal's features editor. Now semi-retired, Mrs. Harper writes a Sunday column and in addition does some free-lance writing.

Recipes from many sources were featured in the Daily Journal food column. With college, marriage, and moving to several other areas around the country, Phyllis Harper became interested in fine food – from cooking and serving family meals to entertaining guests. In her writing of the food column, an interest grew among Daily Journal readers with requests for recipes, which culminated in a successful book, *"Country Cooking With JUST A SPOONFUL Of Sophistication."*

Mrs. Harper's philosophy of creative cooking – haute cuisine – may be a simple recipe or an elaborate menu. As Mrs. Harper states, "Good taste deserves being served elegantly, either in simple pottery or fine china. A spoonful of sophistication can turn cold potato soup into vichyssoise."

Acknowledgments

Our cookbook was one of the original fund-raising ideas conceived when we began our journey in bringing the Sanctuary Hospice House to reality.

We would like to acknowledge the following people for their continued support in completing this worthwhile project.

Special thanks to Phyllis Hawkins Harper for the Introductory Article.

Sanctuary Hospice House

2004 Officers

Sanctuary Hospice House

Board of Directors

Sanctuary Hospice House

Regional Board

In Memory of Felix Black

My wife, Edna, and I met Felix and Ruth Black in 1988.

Luke writes of Barnabus in Acts 11:24, "He was a good man, filled with the Spirit and of great faith." This is the way I remember Felix. He was a good man. The best man I have ever known. His goodness and kindness permeated all his activity. Kindness is one of the great qualities of the Christian life. Felix was the kindest man I have ever known.

He was filled with the Spirit. He never yawned at life. With his Spirit filled life, he believed miracles would happen and they did happen through him and his efforts. He was a man of faith. Early in life he accepted God's gift of love and his faith made him a leader in his church, in his community, and across the state.

Felix accomplished much in life and he made others believe in themselves and in God. For forty years, Felix visited every Monday night in the evangelism program of St. Luke United Methodist Church. Felix was a true friend. I loved Felix Black.

~Tom Cupit
United Methodist Minister
Tupelo, MS

Sanctuary Hospice House Cookbook Committee

Joanne Golebiowski, Chairwoman
Holly Temple, Co-Chairwoman

Lori Anger
Audra Armistead
Kathy Aycock
Betty Barnes
Lottye Betts Beasley
Sheryl Blackburn
Marty Massey Brown
Charlotte Busby
Betty Cayson
Nancy Collins
Becky Cook
Alice Virginia Daniels
Lela Finney
Whit Grace
Trip Hairston
Jane Hammond
Jo Anne Harris
Pat Hazel
Merrie Hughes
LaNelle Lacey
Nell Lamberson
Jackie Massey
Posey McGraw
Allison Spencer
Cathy Wikle

Thanks to the past and present officers of the Sanctuary Hospice House Auxiliary for their support of this project. We also wish to thank the Sanctuary Hospice House Auxiliary members for their efforts in contributing and testing recipes. Without their support the three-year effort to bring this cookbook to publication would not have been possible.

Special thanks to Jackie Massey for the Cover Art and her other artistic contributions. We also thank Debi Caldwell, Lucie Gaines, Carolyn Thompson for their art work. Thanks to Cheryl Hale and Kim Long for their help with artistic efforts.

The Chairwomen also add a special thanks to all of the Committee Members who worked so tirelessly over many months to collect recipes, stories, distribute and test recipes. We apologize for the increase in their waist lines due to many delicious testing sessions!

Our sincere appreciation to all who submitted recipes. We regret we were unable to include all of them because of limited space and similarity. The names of all recipe contributors are listed separately.

Arbor de la Vita Hospice

(This seed of hope germinated in Mexico)

It is a Friday morning in August 2000. Our First United Methodist Church medical mission team has had a tiring but extremely rewarding week. We have visited several of the poorest areas of Mexico City – a city of 22 million souls overwhelmingly composed of poor neighborhoods – and we have seen more than 200 patients each day. But now we are in our van, heading for our final destination. As we get nearer, the neighborhoods perceptibly change. The buildings, already poor, become even poorer. Streets narrow and are more unkempt. Old cars seem even older. Residents trudge through the dirty streets with their heads down. Finally, we are there – the Arbor de la Vita Hospice.

The Arbor de la Vita is a rarity in Mexico. Families provide almost all of terminal care in Mexico. The residents here either have no family or have been abandoned, and they are destitute. There are no government funds available. The benefactor of this place is a recovering alcoholic. One day, in the midst of his despair, he promised God that if he recovered, he'd give his life to help the poor.

He did indeed recover, and he wrote a book about his experiences. It became a best seller, and the money from the book funds this place. Still, there is never enough money. There is food, loving care, and one blanket each, but very few medicines. The owner's daughter tells us, "We depend on God for even our day to day needs." This is my second year to visit, and as before, the sights and smells overwhelm me. There are 40 residents on single beds in two large rooms – one for men and one for women. Every inch of space is utilized. A few residents have managed to purchase their own coffins, and they are packed with their personal belongings, much like a footlocker.

There is a man with no legs. The year before, when I did his exam, I asked him how he lost his legs. "I don't know," he answered. I am an alcoholic. I got drunk one night. Two weeks later I woke up in the hospital with no legs. No one ever told me what happened." A 23-year-old is dying of AIDS. There is no AIDS medicine, but she has pain. We leave her our only remaining 1,000 Tylenol, and she thanks us profusely.

A middle-aged man is paralyzed from the waist down, and he is dying. A tube runs from his bladder out through his abdominal wall. It has not been changed in two years. He was sent to the government hospital, but doctors there told him it was not possible to change his tube. At no more than a glance we see that it is horribly infected. Fortunately, John Elliott, a retired urologist, is a team member, and through maximum effort he is able to remove the tube. And – miracle of miracles – there is a single replacement tube on site. We irrigate the wound, replace the tube, and give the one dose of IV antibiotic pills for another two weeks, and we move to the next patient. We have given this gentleman an extra year of life. After everyone is seen, we leave all our remaining medicines and all our remaining money, and we board the plane and fly to Tupelo.

But Nancy Collins is a nurse on this trip, and the idea of a hospice house is strong in her mind. She later shares her thoughts with Louise Harris (also on the trip) and Carol Elliott. And out of the squalor of the Arbor de la Vita, and through the vision of Nancy Collins, Tupelo's Sanctuary Hospice House is born.

~Joe Bailey, MD
Tupelo, MS
Sanctuary Hospice House Board Member

The Beginning

"How do you say it?" asks Gilda in English. She is interpreting a Spanish speaking patient's complaint of painful toes. "You know," she says, pointing to her own toes. "She hurts in her feet fingers." Everyone laughs. Nine medics and helpers lead by John Sudduth, a Methodist minister and Joe Bailey, a physician, are in Mexico City holding medical clinics in needy areas. The place is "El Arbor De La Vita" (The Tree of Life), a hospice house for the poor. This is where the "Sanctuary Hospice House" story begins. This is the day that the seed was planted, September 6, 2000.

As the group walks through the open male and female dormitories, all the patients appear well clothed. All the bunk beds have a clean, white sheet and a wool blanket. The nights are cool at five thousand feet. There is a patient whose bones ache, a stroke patient, a schizophrenic, a patient with AID's, several patients whose bodies have outlived their minds, and then there is Juan, the paraplegic. He is lying quietly with his eyes closed, so he is passed by until Elena, the director, speaks. "Juan has put nothing through his catheter bag for two days. We nurses have tried, but without success. He was taken to the hospital, but they refused to see him." On closer exam, there is a huge, lower abdominal abscess, which the medics drain after reestablishing urinary flow. The nurses administer injectable antibiotics and hope for the best. Two days later the group returns to find Juan much brighter eyed and sitting in his wheel chair. He has lived.

That was the medics' last visit to "The Tree of Life". If one day, the group returns, Juan will likely not be there. He will be in another place of clean, white sheets and nice, warm blankets – where wounds heal without suppuration and disease leaves no disability. Although death was not defeated, only postponed, each one in the group was thankful for the opportunity to serve, to care, to show compassion, to make a difference.

On the way home, it seemed to all that if it could be done in Mexico, it could be done in North Mississippi. Later Nancy Collins, RN, contacted Carol Elliott, RN. Both were hospice nurses that were thinking about the need for a hospice home. They, along with Louise Harris, RN, began to organize the community effort that has resulted in plans to start construction on "The Sanctuary Hospice House" in the Spring of 2004. Along the way, there have been many mini-miracles.

~John Elliott, MD

Tupelo, MS

Am I My Brother's Keeper?

Am I my Brother's Keeper? A Dream – two women – prayers. Sanctuary Hospice House! Three women - more prayers - trials. Thirty member board – many prayers – much faith. Celebration Village! More dreams – many trials… And a growing certainty that God wants The Sanctuary Hospice House to become a reality… a non-profit, incorporated ecumenical Christian Ministry for the terminally ill.

Our Mission Statement: The Sanctuary Hospice House seeks to provide compassionate care to the dying in response to God's call to serve one another.

This is our miracle story, which began because of the greatest miracle of all. Indeed, it has been as if there was a Star that guided us and there have indeed been Hosts of people - helping, giving, sacrificing and bringing about our miracle.

The idea began years ago as I heard hospice nurses saying there was a need for a hospice home for the dying without an able caregiver – young or old, rich or poor. Surely, I thought, someone would build one – and maybe there would already be one if it were assured that there would be a profit. A mission trip to Mexico City. A hospice home for the poorest of the poor. People with no families or homes. Lovingly cared for by human hands that had become the Hands of Jesus. If the people in Mexico could do this, couldn't we in this great land of plenty? An idea was birthed. It was fed. It grew as one by one people from different walks of life would come and say, "Have you ever thought of building a hospice home here?" A friend, whose sister died in a metropolitan hospice home, said it. A priest said it. There was Joyce Riley, who on the eve of Jack's death said, "God told me to help build a hospice house for those who did not have someone to take care of them." Memories of those long gone, say, "Do it!"

The nuts and bolts of organization stagger us, as we look backward. Office space was donated. A lawyer, volunteer office manager, and a volunteer bookkeeper all donated their time. Seed money of $15,000 from First United Methodist Church, Tupelo, Mississippi, and the first patient room was donated by a couple in Ripley, Mississippi. Corporations opened their hearts and billfolds.

We have learned to go to Washington, D.C. and appeal for a lifting of regulations that hinder rural hospice homes from being established in America. Congressman Wicker and Senator Cochran have introduced legislation to that effect. The American Medical Association began to actively help.

continued on next page

Another miracle! Was it a coincidence that at a Sunday church service in Washington, D.C., a retired Congressman from Alabama met us and offered to introduce us to key members of Congress?

October 2001! Forty volunteers start an auxiliary as a part of the Sanctuary Hospice House. October 2002! The Sanctuary Hospice House presents the first Celebration Village! A Christmas Holiday Marketplace with over one hundred (100) vendors. Over five hundred (500) volunteers. A labor of love. A huge success! An annual event that will help ensure the operating costs of the Sanctuary Hospice House every year.

How can we say thank you to the Volunteers, the Tupelo Furniture Market, the people who donated food, the school children who sang, the hospitals who support us? In unison, we say, "Glory to God in the Highest!"

What is our status now? $1.7 million has been raised to build our home. Plans are for it to be opened February 2005. Located on a beautiful tract of land west of Tupelo, Mississippi, on Highway 6, the Sanctuary Hospice House will accommodate sixteen (16) patients in private rooms with a truly homelike environment. There will be family meeting rooms, a chapel, and an accessible kitchen and out door gardens. The Sanctuary Hospice House will neither appear nor function like a hospital or nursing home, yet it will have the professional staff, volunteers and equipment necessary for providing palliative care and other services for the terminally ill and their loved ones.

Our national legislation was used to craft a National Demonstration Project included in the Medicare Package, signed into law by President George W. Bush in late 2003. Thus, what was originally a local initiative has become an opportunity for others in our Nation.

I applaud North Mississippi for the teamwork, which has served to support the Sanctuary Hospice House. Ultimately, our communities throughout our region are judged not just on their progressiveness but with how they care for their most vulnerable citizens.

I want to say thank you for partnering with us. This is a much greater endeavor than we expected. The Sanctuary Hospice House will be a model; the first of its kind. If our community and faith leaders can accomplish this, it can happen in other places in rural America. Thank you for continuing to help us make sure that there will always be "a room in the inn" for those in their season of need.

~Nancy Collins
Tupelo, MS

The Dream

The Sanctuary Hospice House began as a dream to fulfill the need for a non-profit, ecumenical, Christian ministry to provide physical, spiritual and emotional care for the terminally ill.

In December 2000, a group of retired medical physicians, nurses and community leaders came together with interested community individuals and the dream of a hospice house in Tupelo was realized.

The name "The Sanctuary" was conceived to denote a place of refuge, care and peace, and plans were crafted for a home to shelter 16 patients with family rooms, a chapel and gardens.

The Need

In North Mississippi, there are fourteen hospice agencies that provide excellent care to patients at home. No one agency has the financial resources to provide an in-patient hospice facility for those who can no longer be cared for within their own home. There is no other option for these patients but to admit them into a hospital or nursing home.

Hospitals are curative by nature and cannot offer the service that a hospice patient needs and deserves, and nursing homes are not equipped to care for the dying patient on a short-term basis since their objective is to house and care for the long-term patient. In Mississippi, there is currently an average 18-month waiting period for acceptance into a nursing home.

The Sanctuary Hospice House will serve the specific and sensitive needs of the dying patient and his or her family with a 24-hour health care professional staff trained in pain management and hospice care, emotional and spiritual support, long-term family grief counseling and the comforts and privacy of home living.

Care will be provided for those who have acute symptoms that require a supervised setting, those who require respite care, individuals without able caregivers and those in need of palliative care.

The Costs

Construction costs for this facility are estimated at $1.7 million.

Yearly operating costs are estimated at $2 million.

We will be reimbursed by Medicare, Medicaid and private insurance. The remainder will come from private pay reimbursements, annual fundraisers, donations and grant assistance. No one will be turned away based on ability to pay.

With continued financial support, The Sanctuary Hospice House can serve those leaving the world as carefully and lovingly as they were served upon entering.

The Facility

The Sanctuary Hospice House will be located on Highway 6 West in the Tupelo area and will provide care for needy persons. The House will accommodate 16 patients and be open to families, friends, visitors and pets.

Family rooms, an accessible kitchen, a chapel and an outdoor garden provide the patient with the comforts of home living.

Construction is estimated to be completed in early 2005.

Patients must be referred by a physician or a hospice agency and will be admitted regardless of age, sex, race, religion, diagnosis or ability to pay.

Opportunities for Support

Rooms and Furnishings:

Rooms in the house are $10,000, $25,000 and $35,000 depending on the room. For example, bedroom suites are $25,000. All furnishings are $10,000. A plaque will be placed outside each room designating the persons who bought and furnished the room. The donors may, within certain limits, decide what is to be put on the plaque.

Calendar of Caring:

A 365-day calendar will be built into one wall of the house. A date can be reserved to commemorate a special day or event. There will only be one name per date except in the case of an anniversary. The cost of one day is $1,000. One-third of the amount must be paid within 30 days to reserve the date and the remainder within one year. Please give three (3) dates in order of preference in case one date is already taken.

Physicians Wall:

A wall has been designated for physicians, dentists and their spouses. The title of this wall is "To Cure Sometimes, To Relieve Often, To Comfort Always" which is a quote from Hippocrates. A gift of $1,000 will reserve a place on this wall.

Special Friend of the Sanctuary:

Special Friends is a three-year commitment of $1,000 per year. A special place in The Sanctuary will be designated for donors at this level. This level will give added financial security for the future of the home.

Endowment:

An endowment fund has been set up at Create Foundation, Inc. Bequests in Wills and Insurance Policies are two ways that money can be placed in this fund. An endowment insures income needed for operation. You can get more information on this from The Sanctuary Hospice House, Inc. or Create Foundation, Inc.

Memorials and Honorariums:

Gifts may be made in memory or in honor of someone. An acknowledgement card is sent and you will receive confirmation of the gift.

Other:

Bricks, trees, gardens fountains, benches and other items are available. You may obtain information about these gifts from the Sanctuary office.

Celebration Village:

This will be the major annual fundraiser. It is a four-day market with upscale items from vendors all over the United States. There are four levels of sponsorship: $10,000, $5,000, $2,500 and $1,000. We are asking that you consider making your sponsorship for three years. A personal donation of $250 will provide two passes for all events.

All gifts are tax deductible.

The Sanctuary Hospice House is 501(c) (3)
tax-exempt from the IRS so all checks can be made to
The Sanctuary Hospice House
P.O. Box 192
Tupelo, MS 38802
662-844-2111 Fax: 662-844-2354
www.sanctuaryhospicehouse.com
E-mail: office@sanctuaryhospicehouse.com

Appetizers and Beverages

Grove-ing on a Saturday Afternoon

Sweet Potato Chili, page 83

Patio Beans, page 185

Grilled Hot Dogs and Hamburgers

Southern Black-Eyed Pea Hummus
with Pita Chips, page 22

Delta Cookies, page 211

Artichoke Cheese Bake

- 1 (14 ounce) can artichoke hearts, drained
- 1 (6 ounce) jar marinated artichoke hearts, drained
- 1 (4 ounce) can green chilies, drained
- 1 (8 ounce) package shredded Cheddar cheese
- 2 tablespoons mayonnaise
- Assorted crackers

Chop artichokes and chilies and transfer to a bowl. Add cheese and mayonnaise and mix well. Spoon mixture into a 1½-quart baking dish. Bake at 350 degrees for 25 to 30 minutes. Serve with assorted crackers.

Serves 8-10

Hot Asparagus Dip

- 2 (15 ounce) cans asparagus spears, drained
- 1½ cups mayonnaise
- ½ cup sour cream
- 1½ cups Parmesan cheese
- 1 garlic clove, crushed
- Dash of salt and cayenne pepper
- Dash of white pepper
- ⅛ teaspoon Tabasco sauce

Mash asparagus in a bowl. Add mayonnaise, sour cream, Parmesan cheese, garlic, salt, cayenne pepper and Tabasco and mix well. Spread mixture into a 2-quart baking dish. Bake at 350 degrees for 20 to 30 minutes.

Serves 10-12

Bacon-Tomato Dip

- 1 pound bacon, cooked, drained and crumbled
- 3 large ripe tomatoes, seeded, drained and chopped
- 1 cup mayonnaise
- 1 tablespoon Dijon mustard
- ¼ cup chopped green onions
- ¼ cup chopped fresh parsley
- 6 drops Tabasco sauce
- Assorted crackers

Combine bacon and tomatoes. Gently mix in mayonnaise and mustard. Add onion, parsley and Tabasco. Transfer to a serving dish and refrigerate. Serve with assorted crackers.

Serves 8-10

Southern Black-Eyed Pea Hummus

The two most popular varieties of parsley are curly leaf and Italian or flat leaf parsley.

~from The New Food Lover's Tiptionary

- 1 (15 ounce) can black-eyed peas, rinsed and drained
- 2 tablespoons tahini
- 2 tablespoons olive oil
- ¼ cup fresh lemon juice
- 2 garlic cloves
- ½ teaspoon salt
- ¼ teaspoon ground cumin
- ½ teaspoon freshly ground black pepper
- ⅛ teaspoon cayenne pepper
- 3 tablespoons water
- Olive oil (optional)
- Chopped fresh parsley (optional)
- Pita crisps

Process peas, tahini, oil, juice, garlic, salt, cumin, black pepper and cayenne in a food processor until smooth. Gradually add water and process until desired consistency. Cover and refrigerate for 1 hour. Drizzle with oil and sprinkle with parsley. Serve with pita crisps.

Serves 8-10

Substitute 1 (15 ounce) can chickpeas, rinsed and drained for black-eyed peas.

Black Bean Appetizer

- 2 (16 ounce) cans whole kernel corn, drained
- 2 (15 ounce) cans black beans, rinsed and drained
- 2 (4 ounce) cans chopped green chilies, drained
- 2 (8 ounce) jars chopped pimentos, drained
- 1 (8 ounce) package shredded sharp Cheddar cheese
- 1½ cups sour cream
- Garlic salt to taste
- ½ cup chopped fresh cilantro
- Corn chips

Combine corn, beans, chilies, pimentos, cheese, sour cream, garlic salt and cilantro and mix well. Refrigerate until cold. Serve with corn chips.

Serves 8-10

Cajun Queso Dip

- ¼ cup butter
- 1 cup chopped onions
- ¼ cup chopped celery
- ¼ cup chopped sweet red pepper
- 2 tablespoons minced garlic
- 1 pound smoked andouille sausage, diced
- 1 (6 ounce) jar jalapeño peppers, seeded and chopped
- 1 (2 pound) box processed cheese loaf, diced
- 4 cups mayonnaise
- Salt and pepper to taste
- Tabasco sauce to taste
- ¼ cup chopped parsley

Melt butter in a heavy skillet over medium-high heat. Add onion, celery, pepper, garlic and sausage. Sauté until vegetables are tender. Add jalapeños and cook 2 to 3 minutes more. Remove from heat and cool. Transfer mixture to a food processor and blend until smooth. Pour mixture into a large bowl. Add cheese and mayonnaise. Whip with a wire whisk until smooth. Season with salt, pepper and Tabasco. Sprinkle with parsley. Spoon mixture into a microwave safe serving bowl or crockpot. Heat thoroughly before serving.

Serves 8-10

"I am only one. But still I am one. I cannot do everything. Because I cannot do everything, I will not refuse to do something that I can do."

~Edward Everett Hale

Trice's Hot Crawfish

- ½ cup butter
- 1 bunch green onions, chopped including tops
- 1 tablespoon chopped garlic
- Juice of one lemon
- 2 packages frozen crawfish tails, thawed and drained
- 2 teaspoons Creole seasoning
- 3 (8 ounce) packages cream cheese, softened
- Large corn chips

Melt butter in a large skillet. Add onion and garlic and sauté until tender. Add juice and crawfish and cook until hot. Stir in seasoning. Place cream cheese in a large bowl. Pour hot crawfish mixture over cream cheese. Blend with electric mixer on low speed until incorporated. Pour mixture into a 13 x 9 x 2-inch baking dish. Bake at 350 degrees for 25 minutes. Serve with large corn chips.

Serves 12-14

Corn Salsa

When my friends and I cook together, I will prepare a bowl of this salsa for us to enjoy as we cook. Sometimes my children and I along with my husband play "I Spy" at dinner. My children get a thrill at tricking Mom or Dad with a clever observation. My dear friend, Karen Dillard, and I often share meals. She will cook at her home and I cook at mine. We combine the dishes to a great and sometimes interesting meal for our two families to share together.

~Jima Alexander, Tupelo, MS

- **1 (10 ounce) can diced tomatoes with chilies**
- **1 (11 ounce) can shoe peg corn, drained**
- **1 (4 ounce) can chopped black olives**
- **1 (4½ ounce) can green chilies**
- **2 tablespoons vinegar**
- **1 tablespoon olive oil**
- **Tortilla or corn chips**

Combine tomatoes, corn, olives, green chilies, vinegar and oil in a medium serving bowl. Serve with tortilla or corn chips.

Serves 4-6

Feta Cheese Spread with Sautéed Mushrooms

- **½ cup mayonnaise**
- **4 (3-ounce) packages cream cheese, softened**
- **1 (8 ounce) package crumbled feta cheese with basil and tomato**
- **2 garlic cloves, minced**
- **¼ teaspoon dried dill**
- **¼ teaspoon dried marjoram**
- **¼ teaspoon dried thyme**
- **¼ teaspoon dried basil**
- **¼ cup butter**
- **1 pound mushrooms, chopped (combination of portobello, cremini and white)**
- **4 garlic cloves, minced**
- **1 shallot, minced**
- **¼ cup chopped fresh parsley**
- **1 tablespoon chopped fresh thyme or 1 teaspoon dried**
- **1 tablespoon chopped fresh basil or 1 teaspoon dried**
- **1 tablespoon chopped fresh marjoram or 1 teaspoon dried**

Combine mayonnaise, cream cheese, feta cheese, garlic, dill, marjoram, thyme and basil in a food processor. Process until well blended. Spread into the bottom of a serving dish. Refrigerate until serving time.

Melt butter in a skillet. Sauté mushrooms 2 to 3 minutes. Add garlic, shallot, parsley, thyme, basil and marjoram. Cook until mushrooms are tender. (Layer over feta cheese spread.) Serve with crackers.

Serves 6-8

Three Cheese Dip

- 1 (8 ounce) package shredded sharp Cheddar cheese
- 3 (4 ounce) cans chopped green chilies, drained
- 3 cups sour cream
- 1 (8 ounce) package shredded mild Cheddar cheese
- 1 (8 ounce) package shredded Monterey Jack cheese
- Assorted crackers

Preheat oven to 375 degrees. Layer one-third sharp Cheddar cheese in the bottom of a buttered 8 x 8 x 2-inch baking dish. Continue to layer with one-third of each of green chilies, sour cream, mild Cheddar cheese and Monterey Jack cheese. Repeat two more layers of each ingredient. Bake at 375 degrees for 30 minutes or until center is set. Serve with crackers.

Serves 30

Hot Chicken Dip

- 1 (10¾ ounce) can cream of mushroom soup
- 1 (2¾ ounce) package almonds, chopped
- ½ teaspoon Worcestershire sauce
- 1 (8 ounce) package cream cheese
- 1 (5 ounce) can chunk white chicken
- 1 (2 ounce) can sliced mushrooms, drained
- ⅛ teaspoon pepper
- ⅛ teaspoon garlic powder

Combine mushroom soup, almonds, Worcestershire sauce, cream cheese, chicken, mushrooms, pepper and garlic powder in a saucepan or fondue pot. Cook and stir over medium heat until blended and cheese melts. Serve hot with tortilla or corn chips.

Serves 6-8

Beverly's Spinach and Artichoke Dip

- 2 (10 ounce) packages frozen chopped spinach, thawed and squeezed dry
- 1 (14 ounce) can artichoke hearts, chopped
- 2 (8 ounce) packages cream cheese, cubed
- 2 (10 ounce) cans diced tomatoes with green chilies, undrained
- 1 (8 ounce) package shredded Colby Monterey Jack cheese blend
- ½ cup grated Parmesan cheese
- Tortilla chips

Combine spinach, artichokes, cream cheese, tomatoes, Colby cheese and Parmesan cheese and mix well. Pour mixture in a 2-quart casserole dish. Bake at 350 degrees for 20 minutes or until bubbly. Serve with tortilla chips.

Serves 6-8

Garden Fresh Corn Delight

1 large bell pepper
2 (11 ounce) cans shoe peg corn, drained
1 (8 ounce) package shredded Cheddar cheese
½ cup mayonnaise
½ cup sour cream
½-1 cup finely chopped jalapeño pepper
1 teaspoon salt
1 teaspoon ground cumin
1 teaspoon pepper
½ bunch green onions, chopped
Large corn chips or crackers

Combine bell pepper, corn, cheese, mayonnaise, sour cream, jalapeño, salt, cumin, pepper and onion. Refrigerate until cold. Serve with corn chips and crackers.

Serves 8-10

Swiss Cheese and Bacon Bake

1 (8 ounce) package cream cheese, softened
½ cup mayonnaise
1 cup shredded Swiss cheese
2 tablespoons chopped onion
10 slices bacon, cooked and crumbled
Crackers

Preheat oven to 350 degrees. Combine cream cheese, mayonnaise, cheese, onion and bacon, reserving 3 tablespoons bacon. Spread mixture into the bottom of a greased 1-quart baking dish. Crumble about 10 crackers and combine with reserved crumbled bacon. Sprinkle over cheese mixture. Bake at 350 degrees for 15 to 20 minutes. Serve with crackers.

Serves 8-10

Curried Crabmeat Dip

1 (8 ounce) package cream cheese, softened
½ teaspoon salt
Pepper to taste
½ teaspoon curry powder
2 tablespoons minced chives
14 ounces crabmeat, finely shredded
2 tablespoons capers, drained
Potato chips or Melba rounds

Beat cream cheese, salt, pepper, curry and chives with electric mixer until smooth. Fold in crabmeat and capers. Refrigerate. Serve with chips or Melba rounds.

Serves 16-20

Lake Charles Dip

1 cup sour cream
1 (0.7 ounce) envelope dry Italian dressing mix
1 tablespoon mayonnaise
Juice of one-half lemon
½ ripe avocado, finely chopped
½ tomato, chopped
Dash of Tabasco sauce
Tortilla chips or raw vegetables

Combine sour cream, dry mix, mayonnaise, juice, avocado, tomato and Tabasco. Serve immediately or refrigerate. Serve with chips or raw vegetables.

Serves 12-14

Fresh Fruit Fantasy

1 cup sour cream
1 (8 ounce) package cream cheese, softened
½ teaspoon cinnamon
1 apple, peeled and shredded
½ cup chopped nuts
2 tablespoons packed brown sugar
Fresh fruit for dipping

Cream sour cream, cream cheese and cinnamon with an electric mixer on medium speed. Stir in apples, nuts and sugar. Serve with fresh fruit for dipping.

Serves 8-10

Mississippi Sin

1 (8 ounce) package cream cheese
1½ cups sour cream
1 (8 ounce) package shredded Cheddar cheese
½ cup mayonnaise
½ cup browned sausage
⅓ cup chopped green chilies
½ cup chopped onion
Worcestershire sauce to taste
1 Hawaiian bread loaf

Cream together cream cheese, sour cream and cheese. Stir in mayonnaise, sausage, chilies, onion and Worcestershire sauce. Carve out center of Hawaiian bread. Cut center bread piece into cubes. Place mixture in hollowed out bread and cover tightly with foil. Bake at 350 degrees for 1 hour. Serve with bread cubes.

Serves 10-14

Baked Vidalia Blitz

Life is like an onion. You peel it off one layer at a time; and sometimes you weep.

~Carl Sandburg

~from The New Food Lover's Tiptionary

- 2 tablespoons butter
- 3 large Vidalia onions, coarsely chopped
- 2 cups shredded Swiss cheese
- 2 cups mayonnaise
- 1 (8 ounce) can sliced water chestnuts, drained
- ¼ cup dry white wine
- 1 garlic clove, minced
- ½ teaspoon Tabasco sauce
- Tortilla chips or crackers

Melt butter in a large skillet over medium-high heat. Add onion and sauté for 10 minutes or until tender. In a bowl, combine cheese, mayonnaise, chestnuts, wine, garlic and Tabasco. Stir in onion and mix well. Spoon mixture into a lightly greased 2-quart baking dish. Bake at 375 degrees for 25 minutes. Let stand for 10 minutes. Serve with tortilla chips or crackers.

Serves 6 cups

Roasted Red Pepper Dip

- 2 large sweet red peppers, roasted, peeled and seeded or 1 (4 ounce) jar roasted red peppers
- ½ cup sun-dried tomatoes packed in oil, drained
- 2 garlic cloves, minced
- 1 teaspoon ground cumin
- ½ teaspoon salt
- 1-2 pickled jalapeño peppers, chopped
- 1 bunch green onions, white part only
- 2 (3 ounce) packages cream cheese, softened
- Blue tortilla chips or pita bread

Cool peppers and press between paper towels to remove excess liquid. Process red peppers, tomatoes, garlic, cumin, salt, jalapeño pepper, onion and cream cheese in a food processor until smooth. Serve with blue corn chips or pita bread.

Serves 8-10

Smoked Salmon Appetizer

- 1 pound smoked red salmon or canned salmon
- 2 (8 ounce) packages cream cheese, softened
- 2 tablespoons fresh lemon juice
- 4 teaspoons grated onion
- 2 teaspoons horseradish
- ½ teaspoon liquid smoke
- ½ teaspoon salt
- 1 cup chopped pecans, divided
- 5 tablespoons dried parsley, divided
- Stuffed olives and paprika for garnish
- Assorted crackers

Combine salmon, cream cheese, juice, onion, horseradish, liquid smoke, salt, ¾ cup pecans and 3½ tablespoons parsley. Pour mixture into a fish mold, lined with plastic wrap. Refrigerate. Prior to serving, unmold salmon onto a serving platter. Mix together remaining ¼ cup pecans and 1½ tablespoons parsley. Sprinkle over salmon. Use stuffed olives for fish's eyes. Sprinkle with paprika. Serve with assorted crackers.

Serves 10-12

Jalapeño Spinach Dip

- 5 tablespoons butter, divided
- 3 stalks celery, finely chopped
- ½ large onion, chopped
- 1 (6 ounce) can mushroom pieces
- Cayenne pepper (optional)
- 1 (10 ounce) package frozen chopped spinach, thawed
- Garlic salt to taste
- 1 (8 ounce) box jalapeño processed cheese loaf
- 1 (10¾ ounce) can cream of mushroom soup
- Tortilla chips

Melt 3 tablespoons butter in a saucepan. Sauté celery, onion and mushroom and cayenne until tender. Drain and set aside. In same pan, cook spinach in remaining 2 tablespoons butter until no liquid remains. Season with garlic salt. In a separate pan, melt cheese over low heat. Stir in soup until well blended. Add cooked vegetables to cheese and mix well. Transfer to a chafing dish. Serve warm with tortilla chips.

Serves 10-12

Divine Inspiration

In October of 1998 my husband Jack was diagnosed with cancer. The next two years he fought a long and courageous battle but lost the fight November 28, 2000. With the help of family, friends and hospice, we were able to keep him at home surrounded by the things he loved and those who loved him. During his two-year battle, we spent many hours at the Cancer Center. I was deeply touched, especially by the elderly caregivers, many with health problems of their own. I often wondered how they managed at home. I remember one elderly gentleman. He was alone, in dirty blue pajamas and in much pain. He moved my heart in such a way that God led me to be involved in the building of the Sanctuary Hospice House.

Jack loved the game of golf. His friends and family thought, "What better way to help in this project than with a yearly golf tournament in his memory." The proceeds from our first Jack Riley Memorial Tournament went to building the Chapel in the Sanctuary Hospice House. Future funds will be used for other rooms and operating expenses of the house.

During the darkest days of Jack's struggle, the loving care of family, friends and the beautiful hospice nurses gave me the courage to face each new day. This is what Sanctuary Hospice House is about: It will be a comforting place for those in the last phase of their life's journey and for their loved ones who are unable to care for them at home. It will be a way to find peace, love and the support they need during those most difficult times.

Joyce Riley
Tupelo, MS

On a hot day in July, several years ago, an elderly woman with cancer living alone in a run down mobile home without air-conditioning or fans, died alone. She did not have a caregiver. This incident and others like it stirred the hearts of doctors and nurses in this rural community of Tupelo, Mississippi. However, it was not until September, 2000 that the impetus for The Sanctuary Hospice House actually began.

Nancy Collins, Tupelo, MS

Asparagus Party Crisps

12 slices thin white bread
8 slices bacon, cooked, drained and crumbled
2 (3 ounce) packages cream cheese, softened
12 cooked asparagus spears or canned
Melted butter

Trim crust from bread slices. Roll to flatten. Cream together bacon and cream cheese. Spread mixture over bread slices. Lay an asparagus spear on one end of bread and roll up. Place seam side down on a baking sheet. Cover and refrigerate until serving time. Brush each roll with melted butter. Toast in the oven until lightly browned.

Serves 12

Butter Bean Cakes with Creole Sauce

2 (15½ ounce) butter or lima beans
2 tablespoons lemon juice
2 eggs
¾ cups plain bread crumbs
¼ cup chopped green onions
Salt and pepper to taste
Tabasco sauce to taste
1 tablespoon cornstarch
1 (14½ ounce) Cajun-stewed tomatoes, undrained

Mash beans in a bowl. Stir in juice and eggs. Add bread crumbs, onion, and season with salt, pepper and Tabasco. Mix until well combined. Shape into patties. Brown patties in small amount of oil, turning once. Keep warm. In a saucepan, mix cornstarch with 2 tablespoons of cold water until dissolved. Add tomatoes and season to taste. Cook and stir over low heat until sauce is bubbly and slightly thickened. Serve over fried patties.

Serves 6

Warmed Cranberry Brie

⅓ cup crushed cranberry sauce
2 tablespoons packed brown sugar
¼ teaspoon rum extract
⅛ teaspoon ground nutmeg
1 (8 ounce) round Brie cheese
2 tablespoons chopped pecans
Sliced green apples

Combine cranberry sauce, brown sugar, rum extract and nutmeg and mix well. Peel top off of cheese round, leaving ¼-inch rim. Top cheese with cranberry mixture. Sprinkle with pecans. Bake at 500 degrees for 4 to 5 minutes. Serve with apple slices.

Serves 10

Brie en Croûte with Pear and Cranberry Chutney

- **5 ripe pears, cored and chopped**
- **1 (12 ounce) package cranberries**
- **1 large red onion, chopped**
- **3 cups golden raisins**
- **3 cups packed light brown sugar**
- **3 cups cider vinegar**
- **2 tablespoons mustard seed**
- **1 tablespoon whole cloves**
- **2 teaspoons crushed red pepper**
- **1½ tablespoons salt**
- **1 pound whole Brie cheese**
- **½ cup chutney**
- **1 (17 ounce) package frozen puff pastry, thawed**
- **1 egg yolk**
- **2 tablespoons milk**
- **Apple and pear slices**

To make pear and cranberry chutney, combine pears, cranberries, onion, raisin, brown sugar, vinegar, mustard seed, cloves, red pepper and salt in a large non-reactive saucepan. Bring to boil. Reduce heat and simmer for 1 hour, stirring often. Meanwhile, preheat oven to 400 degrees. Scrape the outer white layer off the top of the cheese. Spread chutney evenly on top. Encase entire cheese in puff pastry. Use second pastry to patch as needed. Whisk together egg yolk with milk. Lightly brush over pastry. Use pastry scrapes to make decorative pieces. Arrange on top and brush with egg wash. Bake at 400 degrees for 20 minutes until puffed and golden. Let stand for 15 minutes before serving. Serve with pear and cranberry chutney and apple and pear slices.

Serves 10

Pear and cranberry chutney may be processed in sterilized jars or covered and refrigerated for several weeks.

Grand Marnier Brie with Green Apples

- **¼ cup butter**
- **½ cup packed brown sugar**
- **3 Granny Smith apples, chopped**
- **1 cup coarsely chopped pecans**
- **½-¾ cup dark raisins**
- **½ cup Grand Marnier liqueur**
- **1 (5-inch) wheel Brie cheese, warmed and top casing removed**
- **Crostini or Melba toast**

Cook butter and brown sugar over low heat until sugar melts. Add apples, pecans and raisins. Cook for 3 minutes. Add liqueur. Cook 3 minutes more until apples are crisp-tender. Serve over warmed cheese with Crostini or Melba toast.

Serves 4-6

Blue Cheese Ball

- 1 (8 ounce) cream cheese, softened
- 2 (8 ounce) packages shredded sharp Cheddar cheese, room temperature
- 2 tablespoons milk
- 2 tablespoons finely chopped onion
- 2 tablespoons Worcestershire sauce
- 1 cup crumbled blue cheese
- ¼ teaspoon garlic powder
- Chopped parsley, chopped pecans or cracked black pepper for garnish (optional)
- Assorted crackers

Beat cream cheese, Cheddar cheese, milk, onion, Worcestershire sauce, blue cheese and garlic powder until light and fluffy. Shape into one ball or 3 small balls. Roll ball in choice of garnish. Cover and refrigerate. Let stand 15 minutes prior to serving. Serve with assorted crackers.

Serves 14

For tidy preparation and clean up, use plastic wrap for shaping balls.

Cheese Bruschetta

- 1 cup shredded Swiss cheese
- ½ cup mayonnaise
- ½ cup sour cream
- 1 (0.7 ounce) envelope Italian dressing mix
- 1 loaf French bread, cut into about 40 slices
- 1 small bell pepper, finely diced
- 1 small sweet red pepper, finely diced
- Ripe olives chopped or sliced (optional)

Combine cheese, mayonnaise, sour cream and dressing mix. Spread mixture on bread slices. Sprinkle with peppers. Bake at 350 degrees for 10 to 12 minutes or until bubbly. Top with olives.

Serves 40

North Carolina Chili Cheese Toast

- 1 (8 ounce) package shredded Monterey Jack cheese
- 1 (4½ ounce) can chopped green chilies, drained
- 1 (4 ounce) can chopped ripe olives, drained
- 2 green onions, sliced thin including white part
- ¼ cup mayonnaise
- Cocktail rye bread

Combine cheese, chilies, olives, onion and mayonnaise and mix well. Spread mixture on rye bread. Bake at 400 degrees until hot and bubbly.

Serves 36

Almonds aren't really nuts, but the kernels of the almond fruit.

~from The New Food Lover's Tiptionary

Chutney Almond Ball

- **2 (8 ounce) packages cream cheese, softened**
- **1 cup chutney (see recipe below)**
- **2 teaspoons curry powder**
- **½ teaspoon dry mustard**
- **¾ cup chopped almonds**
- **Assorted crackers**

Blend cream cheese, chutney, curry and mustard. Roll into a ball and place in a small bowl lined with plastic wrap. Refrigerate at least 4 hours. Remove from bowl and roll in almonds. Serve with crackers.

Serves 8

May use bottled chutney if short on time. May substitute coconut or chopped green onions for almonds.

Homemade Chutney

- **2 tablespoons minced onion**
- **1 garlic clove, minced**
- **1 tablespoon olive oil**
- **2 (12 ounce) jars apricot preserves**
- **¼ cup orange juice**
- **2 tablespoons apple cider vinegar**

Sauté onion and garlic in oil over medium heat for 5 minutes or until tender. Add preserves, juice and vinegar. Bring to boil over medium heat, stirring frequently. Reduce heat and simmer, uncovered, for 20 minutes or until reached desired degree of thickness.

Makes 2 cups chutney

Watching my grandmother, Allie, cook in the kitchen was always a joy to me. Even as a small child, I knew her love for cooking was a special gift to our family.

~Jima Alexander, Tupelo, MS

Mardi Gras Cheese Log

1 (8 ounce) package cream cheese, softened
1 tablespoon minced onion
1 garlic clove, minced
½ teaspoon dried dill
¼ cup butter
1 teaspoon Worcestershire sauce
¼ cup packed dark brown sugar
½ teaspoon prepared mustard
1 cup finely chopped pecans
Green onion tops for garnish
Wheat crackers

Beat cream cheese, onion, garlic and dill until smooth. Shape mixture into a log and set aside. Combine butter, Worcestershire sauce, brown sugar, mustard and pecans in a saucepan. Cook, stirring frequently, over low-medium heat until thickened. Cool and spoon sauce over cheese log. Garnish with green onion tops in a decorative row along the log. Serve with wheat crackers.

Serves 12

Curried Cheese Pâté

2 (3 ounce) packages cream cheese, softened
1 (8 ounce) package shredded sharp Cheddar cheese
½ teaspoon curry powder
¼ teaspoon salt
½ teaspoon garlic powder
¼ cup dry sherry
1 (9 ounce) jar chutney, chopped
½ bunch green onions, finely chopped including white part
Assorted crackers

Mix cream cheese, Cheddar cheese, curry, salt, garlic and sherry by hand. Press mixture firmly and evenly into the bottom of an 8-inch pie plate. Refrigerate or freeze. Before serving, invert cheese from pie plate and allow to reach room temperature. Cover top of cheese round sparingly with chutney and sprinkle liberally with green onion. Serve with assorted crackers.

Serves 12

The cheese mold may be made in advance and refrigerated two to three days or frozen 2 weeks prior to serving. Chutney and green onions should not be added until about 1 hour before serving. Any leftover cheese mold may be frozen after scraping off the garnish.

Garden Gate Chutney Spread

1 (10 ounce) package frozen chopped spinach, thawed and squeezed dry
Dash of ground nutmeg
Dash of ground cumin
Dash of celery seed
¼ teaspoon dried oregano
2 teaspoons beef bouillon granules
3 (8 ounce) packages cream cheese, softened, divided
1 medium onion, chopped
1½ cups chopped pecans
1 (8 ounce) package shredded Cheddar cheese
1 (7 ounce) jar chutney
Assorted crackers

Lay spinach on a baking sheet. Bake 400 degrees for 15 minutes or until dry. Mix spinach with nutmeg, cumin, celery seed, oregano, beef bouillon and 1½ packages cream cheese. Set aside. Combine onion, pecans and Cheddar cheese. Layer half of pecan mixture in bottom of 10-inch springform pan. Blend remaining 1½ packages cream cheese and chutney. Spread chutney mixture on top of pecan mixture. Layer spinach mixture over chutney. Top with remaining pecan mixture. Refrigerate overnight. Serve with assorted crackers.

Serves 10

May be prepared in advance and frozen.

Cajun Crab Cheesecake

1¾ cups plain bread crumbs
2 teaspoons plus 1 tablespoon Cajun seasoning, divided
½ cup butter, softened
2 (8 ounce) packages cream cheese, softened
½ cup shredded Parmesan cheese
2 teaspoons horseradish
¼ cup dry sherry
2 eggs
2 (6 ounce) cans crabmeat, well drained
¼-½ teaspoon Tabasco sauce
1 tablespoon diced sweet red pepper
Assorted crackers

Preheat oven to 325 degrees. Combine bread crumbs, 2 teaspoons Cajun seasoning and butter and mix well. Press into the bottom and 1-inch up the sides of an ungreased 9-inch springform pan. In a large bowl, beat cream cheese, Parmesan cheese, 1 tablespoon Cajun seasoning and horseradish with an electric mixer on medium speed until smooth. Add sherry and beat on high speed for 2 minutes. Add eggs, one at a time, beating well after each addition. Gently fold in crabmeat and Tabasco. Pour mixture into crust. Bake at 325 degrees for 50 to 60 minutes or until filling is set. Cool in pan on wire rack for 30 minutes. Cover and refrigerate at least 4 hours or up to 24 hours. Remove sides of pan and place on serving platter. Top with sweet red pepper. Serve immediately or let stand 30 minutes. Serve with assorted crackers.

Serves 16

Ham-Green Onion Cheddar Cake

½ cup plain bread crumbs
3¼ cups shredded sharp Cheddar cheese, divided
6 ounces thinly sliced ham
3 (8 ounce) packages cream cheese, softened
1 cup cottage cheese
¾ cup chopped green onion
4 eggs
3 tablespoons jalapeño peppers, finely chopped
2 tablespoons milk
1 garlic clove, minced
¼ cup diced green onion
Chopped parsley for garnish
Assorted crackers

Butter a 9-inch springform pan. Combine bread crumbs and ¼ cup Cheddar cheese. Sprinkle mixture in bottom of pan and refrigerate. Beat 3 cups remaining Cheddar cheese, ham, cream cheese, cottage cheese, green onion, eggs, jalapeño peppers, milk and garlic with an electric mixer until smooth. Pour over crumb mixture in springform pan. Place on baking sheet and bake at 325 degrees for 1 hour, 15 minutes. Turn oven off and cool cake 1 hour with oven door ajar. Remove from oven and cool completely. To serve, remove sides from pan and place on serving platter. Top with green onion. Garnish with parsley around bottom edge of cake. Serve with crackers.

Serves 15

Baked Garlic Appetizer

4 large garlic heads, unpeeled
2½ tablespoons butter, thinly sliced
¼ cup olive oil
2-2½ cups chicken broth
2 cups sun-dried tomatoes
¾ tablespoon herb seasoning
Pepper to taste
1 (6 ounce) block goat cheese, sliced
Basil leaves for garnish
1 large loaf Italian bread, sliced

Preheat oven to 375 degrees. Slice ¼-inch off tops of garlic heads opposite root end. Remove any loose outer papery skin. Place garlic cut side up in medium baking dish. Arrange butter slices evenly over garlic. Pour oil over garlic. Add 2 cups broth to dish. Arrange tomatoes around garlic. Sprinkle with herbs. Season with pepper. Bake at 375 degrees for 1 hour, 15 minutes. Baste with broth every 15 minutes. Add more broth to maintain liquid in dish. Arrange goat cheese around garlic. Bake 10 minutes more or until cheese melts. Garnish with basil and serve with bread.

Serves 6

To eat, pierce a garlic clove and press to release from the skin. Spread garlic on bread slice and top with tomato/cheese mixture.

My family lived in the Canal Zone the first time I had this dish. We would eat at the Yacht Club restaurant and I would have this every time. The restaurant overlooked the Panama Canal and we would watch the ships go by.

Cheveche (Crabmeat Appetizer)

1½ pounds crabmeat (scallops or white fish)
Fresh lime juice
¼ cup minced onion
¼ cup chopped parsley
¼ cup chopped green chilies
1 large ripe tomato, chopped
3 teaspoons olive oil
Cayenne pepper, salt and pepper to taste
Assorted crackers

Shred crabmeat or cut scallops into thirds. In a large bowl, cover crabmeat with lime juice. Refrigerate for 4 hours. Add onion, parsley, green chilies, tomato, oil and season with cayenne, salt and pepper. Serve with crackers.

Serves 16

Mexican Cheesecake

3 (8 ounce) packages cream cheese, softened
1½ teaspoons Tabasco sauce
1½ teaspoons chili powder
2 eggs
2 teaspoons chicken bouillon granules
½ cup hot water
1 cup finely chopped cooked chicken
1 (4 ounce) can green chilies
1 jar chunky salsa
1 cup finely grated Cheddar cheese
Chopped green onions
1 (4 ounce) can sliced black olives
Tortilla chips

In a food processor, combine cream cheese, Tabasco and chili powder. Dissolve bouillon granules in hot water. Add eggs and bouillon and process. Stir in chicken and chilies. Pour mixture into a greased 9-inch springform pan. Bake at 350 degrees for 30 minutes. Cool 15 minutes before removing sides. Pour salsa on top of cheesecake. Sprinkle with cheese, green onion and olives. Serve with tortilla chips. Best used day it is made.

Serves 20

Egg Salad Mold

- 1 tablespoon unflavored gelatin
- 2 tablespoons lemon juice
- 2 tablespoons cold water
- 8 hard-cooked eggs, chopped
- 1 cup mayonnaise
- Salt and pepper to taste
- 1 teaspoon Worcestershire sauce
- ¼ teaspoon Dijon mustard
- 1 (4 ounce) jar caviar
- Chopped green onion for garnish
- Pumpernickel and party rye rounds

Soften gelatin in juice and water. Set bowl over a saucepan of hot water to melt gelatin. Add eggs, mayonnaise, salt, pepper, Worcestershire sauce and mustard and mix well. Spread egg mixture into a greased 4-cup round mold. Refrigerate until set. Unmold onto a serving platter. Spread caviar around mold and sprinkle green onion over mold. Serve with pumpernickel and rye rounds.

Serves 10-12

Polenta and Wild Mushroom with White Wine Beurre Blanc

- 1 quart water
- 1 teaspoon salt
- 2 cups cornmeal
- ½ cup grated Parmesan cheese
- 1 teaspoon pepper
- ¼ cup butter
- 1 pound assorted wild mushrooms
- ¼ cup plus 2 tablespoons chopped shallots, divided
- 1 teaspoon minced garlic
- ½ cup chopped fresh herbs of choice
- 2 cups white wine
- 1 bay leaf
- 2 sprigs thyme
- Parsley stems
- 1 tablespoon black peppercorns
- ¼ cup heavy cream
- 1 pound butter, cut into tablespoons and softened
- Salt and pepper to taste

Bring water and salt to boil. Very slowly sprinkle in cornmeal while stirring constantly. Add Parmesan cheese and pepper. Cook over low heat, stirring constantly, about 15 to 20 minutes until polenta pulls away from sides of pan. Grease a small baking sheet lined with parchment paper. Spread polenta onto the sheet to form a ½-inch layer. Bake at 350 degrees for 20 minutes. Cool. Cut into diamond shapes. Pan fry in butter until golden browned. Keep warm. Melt 4 tablespoons butter in a large skillet. Sauté mushrooms and ¼ cup shallots until half cooked. Add garlic and herbs and cook until vegetables are tender. Keep warm. To make sauce, combine wine, 2 tablespoons shallots, bay leaf, thyme, parsley and peppercorns in a saucepan. Cook over medium heat, stirring frequently, until reduced to 2 tablespoons liquid. Add cream and reduce heat to very low. Slowly add butter one tablespoon at a time while stirring constantly. Strain sauce through fine sieve. Season with salt and pepper. Serve polenta with mushrooms and sauce.

Serves 36

Life is too short to stuff a mushroom.

~Shirley Conran, British writer

~from The New Food Lover's Tiptionary

Bacon Stuffed Mushrooms

- 2 (8 ounce) containers whole mushrooms
- 1-2 teaspoons butter
- 1 small onion, chopped
- 4 slices bacon, cooked, drained and finely crumbled
- 1 teaspoon salt
- 1 teaspoon pepper
- 1 (8 ounce) package cream cheese, softened
- Buttered bread crumbs mixed with Parmesan cheese

Remove stems from mushrooms and finely chop. Reserve mushroom caps. Melt butter in a large skillet. Sauté chopped mushrooms and onion until tender. Add bacon, salt, pepper and cream cheese. Mix until well combined. Stuff mushroom caps with cheese mixture. Sprinkle with bread crumb mixture. Place in a 13 x 9 x 2-inch baking dish and refrigerate overnight. Prior to baking, add a small amount of water to dish. Bake at 350 degrees for 15 minutes. Serve immediately.

Serves 8

Walnut-Feta Stuffed Mushrooms

- 1 teaspoon olive oil
- 2 teaspoons butter
- 1 small onion, minced
- 1 garlic clove, minced
- 3 tablespoons walnuts, chopped
- 2 green onions, minced
- 3 tablespoons crumbled feta cheese
- ¼ cup shredded Parmesan cheese
- Dash of salt and pepper
- 24 large mushroom caps

Heat olive oil and butter in a large skillet over medium heat. Sauté onion and garlic until translucent. Add walnuts and green onion. Cool slightly. Stir in feta cheese, Parmesan cheese, salt and pepper. Fill mushroom caps with cheese mixture and place on a broiler pan. Bake at 400 degrees for 5 to 7 minutes or until cheese melts and is golden browned.

Serves 12

Charlies (Cheese and Olive)

- **1 (8 ounce) package shredded sharp Cheddar cheese**
- **½ cup butter, softened**
- **½ teaspoon salt**
- **1 teaspoon paprika**
- **Dash of cayenne pepper**
- **1½ cups all-purpose flour**
- **25 large stuffed olives, well drained**

Combine cheese, butter, salt, paprika, cayenne and flour until a dry dough forms. Roll 1 teaspoon of dough into a ball. Flatten ball with thumb and place olive in center. Close dough over olive making a ball. Place dough balls on baking sheet. Bake at 350 degrees for 10 minutes.

Serves 25

May substitute dates for olives.

Olive Pesto

- **2 garlic cloves**
- **2 tablespoons pine nuts, toasted**
- **¾ cup Parmesan cheese**
- **3 cups pitted kalamata olives**
- **½ cup olive oil**
- **Croutons or Melba rounds**

Process garlic, pine nuts, Parmesan cheese and olives in a food processor. With processor running, add oil in a steady stream. Process until well blended. Serve on croutons or Melba rounds.

Serves 8

Great served over penne pasta with Parmesan cheese.

Cafe Le Economie Oysters

- **4 mushrooms, sliced**
- **3 garlic cloves, minced**
- **¼ cup unsalted butter**
- **1 (8 ounce) jar oysters**
- **1 teaspoon ground cumin**
- **1 teaspoon pepper**
- **1 tablespoon soy sauce**
- **Splash of white wine**
- **Dry garlic toast for dipping**

Sauté mushrooms and garlic in butter. Add oysters, cumin, pepper, soy sauce and wine. Cook until oysters begin to curl. Serve with dry garlic toast for dipping in the sauce.

Serves 8

Pastrami and Pepper Roll-Up

- ½ pound sliced pastrami
- ⅓ cup chive and onion cream cheese spread
- ½ cup roasted sweet red peppers, drained, cut into ¾-inch wide strips
- Rosemary sprigs (optional)

Spread pastrami slices with cream cheese. Place pepper strip on one edge. Starting at pepper edge, roll up tightly. Place seam side down onto a plate. Refrigerate at least 2 hours or until firm. To serve, cut each roll into 1-inch thick pieces. Secure with rosemary sprigs or cocktail toothpick.

Serves 40 pieces

This appetizer looks wonderful on a buffet table with the fresh rosemary "skewers".

Pesto Hots

- ½ cup fresh basil, finely chopped
- ½ cup Parmesan cheese
- 1 garlic clove, minced
- 6 tablespoons mayonnaise
- Small loaves French bread, sliced thin

Combine basil, cheese, garlic and mayonnaise and mix well. Toast one side of bread slices under the broiler. Remove from oven and spread mixture on untoasted side. Return to oven and broil until bubbly.

Serves 8

Texas Tortes

- 2 eggs, beaten
- 2 tablespoons all-purpose flour
- ½ teaspoon salt
- ⅓ cup milk
- 1 (4 ounce) can chopped green chilies, drained
- 1 (8 ounce) package shredded sharp Cheddar cheese
- 1 (8 ounce) package shredded Monterey Jack cheese

Beat eggs, flour, salt and milk with a wire whisk until well blended. Add chilies and cheeses. Pour mixture into a well-greased 8 x 12 x 2-inch baking dish. Bake at 350 degrees for 35 minutes. Cut into tiny squares and serve hot.

Serves 96 pieces

Hot Salmon Puffs

1 (7½ ounce) can salmon, drained and flaked
1 tablespoon lemon juice
1 teaspoon grated onion
¼ cup mayonnaise
1 teaspoon horseradish
½ teaspoon liquid smoke
1 (2 ounce) jar capers, drained
Salt and pepper to taste
2 (9 inch) pie pastry shells
Paprika for garnish

Combine salmon, juice, onion, mayonnaise, horseradish, liquid smoke, capers and seasonings and mix well. Refrigerate until cold. Cut pie pastry into sixteen wedges each. Spread each wedge with salmon mixture. Beginning with wide edge, roll up pastry. Place on baking sheet and pierce top with fork. Sprinkle with paprika. Bake at 450 degrees for 10 to 15 minutes.

Serves 32 pieces

Pickling Spice Shrimp

2½ pounds shrimp
¼ cup pickling spice
1 onion, thinly sliced
8 bay leaves
2 tablespoons caper with juice
1¼ cups vegetable oil
¾ cup vinegar
Dash of Tabasco sauce

Fill a large saucepan with cold water. Add shrimp and pickling spice. Bring to boil. Once water has reached a full boil, remove from heat and cover. Cool, peel and devein shrimp. Layer shrimp, onion, bay leaves and capers in a 13 x 9 x 2-inch baking dish. Whisk together oil, vinegar and Tabasco. Pour oil mixture evenly over layers. Cover and marinate overnight in the refrigerator.

Serves 10

Zesty Shrimp Spread

1 (3 ounce) package cream cheese, softened
1 (8 ounce) container sour cream
2 teaspoons lemon juice
1 (0.7 ounce) envelope dry Italian dressing mix
2 tablespoons finely chopped bell pepper
1 (4½ ounce) can medium shrimp, drained, rinsed and chopped
Raw vegetables or crackers

Beat cream cheese until light and fluffy. Stir in sour cream, juice, dressing mix, bell pepper and shrimp and mix well. Refrigerate at least 1 hour. Serve with raw vegetables or crackers.

Serves 1⅔ cups

Shrimp Butter

- ¾ cup butter, softened
- 1 (8 ounce) package cream cheese, softened
- 2 (4½ ounce) shrimp, drained
- 3-4 tablespoons lemon juice
- 1 tablespoon minced onion
- ¼ cup mayonnaise
- Assorted crackers or chips
- Cocktail sauce for garnish

Beat butter and cream cheese with electric mixer until smooth. Add shrimp, juice, onion and mayonnaise and beat until fluffy. Shape mixture into a ring on a serving platter. Refrigerate at least 4 hours. Bring to room temperature before serving. Arrange crackers or chips around ring and spoon cocktail sauce in center of ring.

Serves 8

Peanut Butter Strips

- ⅔ cup vegetable oil
- ⅔ cup creamy peanut butter
- ½ cup sugar
- 8 slices white bread, edges trimmed

Combine oil, peanut butter and sugar in a bowl. Cut each bread slice into 5 strips. Toast strips, edges and 1 whole bread slice at 400 degrees 10 to 12 minutes. Crush edges and whole bread slice into crumbs. Dip strips in peanut butter mixture. Roll in bread crumbs. Let stand to set. Best to use stale bread.

Serves 6-8

A friend in Nashville, Tennessee told me my favorite "food story."

Years ago, at an old elite country club in Nashville, an elderly blue-blooded lady sat at her table waiting to be served. The waiter brought her a basket full of saltine crackers wrapped in cellophane. The lady said, "James, what is this?" He replied, "Well, this is the way crackers come now. All you do is pull the red tabs to open them." The genteel lady said with much exasperation, "James, if I had wanted to prepare lunch, I would have stayed at home!"

~Caroline Harmon, Belden, MS

Party Pecans

1 egg white, slightly beaten
2 tablespoons water
½ cup sugar
½ cup packed brown sugar
1 teaspoon cinnamon
½ teaspoon ground nutmeg
4 cups pecan halves

Whisk together egg white, water, sugar, brown sugar, cinnamon and nutmeg in a large bowl. Add pecans and toss to coat well. Spread pecans on a baking sheet. Bake at 200 degrees, stirring often, until mixture is dry.

Serves 3 cups

Pecans are great as an appetizer or tossed into a green salad.

Savory Prosciutto Pinwheels

2 sheets frozen puff pastry
½ pound thinly sliced prosciutto, divided
3 ounces freshly grated Parmesan cheese, divided
1 (4 ounce) jar sweet-hot mustard, divided
1 egg, beaten with 2 tablespoons water

Thaw puff pastry at room temperature for 20 to 30 minutes. Lightly flour board and roll out one sheet of pastry to about 12 by 15 inches. Spread pastry sheet with half of mustard. Top with half of prosciutto, arranged in single layers. Sprinkle prosciutto with half of Parmesan cheese. Press cheese down with your fingers or a spatula. Roll pastry into a spiral. Brush edges with a little water and press to seal. Using a serrated knife, slice the roll into 1-inch pinwheels. Arrange pinwheels on a baking sheet and compress them with the bottom of a glass or the back of a spatula. Repeat for the second sheet of puff pastry, then refrigerate pinwheels for 15 minutes. Brush pinwheels with egg wash and bake in a preheated 400-degree oven for 10 minutes. Turn and bake another 5 to 10 minutes or until golden brown.

Serves 2 dozen

Roasted Pecans

2 cups water
3 tablespoons salt
2 cups pecans

Bring water and salt to boil. Remove from heat and add pecans. Soak 15 minutes. Drain and pat dry on paper towels. Spread pecans in a single layer on a baking sheet. Bake at 275 degrees for 40 minutes. Cool completely.

Serves 2 cups

(The Original)

Whiskey Speech

As composed and delivered by
N. S. SWEAT, JR.

My Friends:

I had not intended to discuss this controversial subject at this particular time. However, I want you to know that I do not shun controversy. On the contrary, I will take a stand on any issue at any time, regardless of how fraught with controversy it might be. You have asked me how I feel about whiskey. All right, here is how I feel about whiskey...

If when you say whiskey you mean the Devil's brew, the poison scourge, the bloody monster that defiles innocence, dethrones reason, destroys the home, creates misery and poverty, yea, literally takes the bread from the mouths of little children; if you mean the evil drink that topples the Christian man and woman from the pinnacle of righteous, gracious living into the bottomless pit of degradation, and despair, and shame, and helplessness, and hopelessness, then certainly I am against it.

But,

If when you say whiskey you mean the oil of conversation, the philosophic wine, the ale that is consumed when good fellows get together, that puts a song in their hearts and laughter on their lips, and the warm glow of contentment in their eyes; if you mean Christmas cheer; if you mean the stimulating drink that puts the spring into the old gentleman's step on a frosty, crispy morning; if you mean the drink that enables a man to magnify his joy, and his happiness, and to forget, if only for a little while, life's great tragedies, and heartaches, and sorrows; if you mean that drink the sale of which pours into our treasuries untold millions of dollars, which are used to provide tender care for our little crippled children, our blind, our deaf, our dumb, our pitiful aged and infirm; to build highway and hospitals and schools, then certainly I am for it.

This is my stand. I will not retreat from it. I will not compromise.

Reprinted by permission from family.
Corinth, MS

Sparkling Non-Alcoholic Sangría

1 (750 ml) bottle non-alcoholic red wine
⅓ cup sugar
1 orange, thinly sliced
1 lemon, thinly sliced
1 lime, thinly sliced
1 cup sparkling water, chilled
Ice cubes

In a 1-quart pitcher, combine wine and sugar. Stir until sugar dissolves. Add orange, lemon and lime slices and allow flavors to blend for 1 hour. Stir in sparkling water and ice cubes prior to serving. Serve in wine glasses.

Serves 4 (1-cup) servings

No Punch Champagne

1 (750 ml) bottle non-alcoholic white wine, chilled
1 (1 liter) bottle ginger ale, chilled
1 lemon, scored and thinly sliced for garnish
1 lime, scored and thinly sliced for garnish

Pour wine and ginger ale into a 2-quart pitcher. Mix well. Pour into glasses. Garnish with fruit slices and serve immediately.

Serves 7 (1-cup) servings

Southern Mint Tea

6 cups water
2 cups sugar
6 mint tea bags
¾ cup lemon juice
1 (46 ounce) can pineapple juice, chilled
1 (0.5 liter) bottle ginger ale, chilled

Bring water to boil. Add sugar and stir to dissolve. Add tea bags and steep for 15 minutes. Remove bags and stir in lemon juice. Pour into gallon pitcher. Add pineapple juice and ginger ale. Stir well before serving.

Serves 1 gallon

Fall Iced Spice Tea

3 sticks cinnamon
¾ teaspoon whole cloves
½ teaspoon whole allspice
4 cups hot tea
⅓ cup sugar
3 cups orange juice
1 cup pineapple juice

Place cinnamon, cloves and allspice in cheesecloth. Tie ends together to enclose spices. Combine hot tea, sugar and juices in a large saucepan. Drop spice bag into liquid. Simmer for 30 minutes. Remove spice bag. Serve warm or freeze and serve as slush.

Serves 8-10

Lemonade Grape Punch

1 (12 ounce) can frozen pink lemonade concentrate, thawed
4 cups white grape juice
1 (1 liter) bottle ginger ale
Lemon slices for garnish

Prepare lemonade according to package directions. Add juice and ginger ale and stir well. Refrigerate until cold. Prior to serving, garnish with lemon slices.

Serves 16

Tangy Orange Punch

2½ cups orange-flavored drink mix
3 quarts water
2 (46 ounce) cans pineapple juice
1 (6 ounce) can frozen lemonade concentrate, thawed and undiluted
2 (2 liter) bottles ginger ale, chilled
Mint for garnish

Dissolve drink mix in water. Stir in pineapple juice and lemonade. Freeze. When ready to serve, thaw punch slightly and mix with ginger ale. Serve slushy and garnish with mint.

Serves 50

May substitute champagne for ginger ale.

Kathy's Mimosa

1 (6 ounce) can frozen orange juice concentrate, thawed
1 (46 ounce) can unsweetened pineapple juice
2 (750 ml) bottles extra dry champagne, chilled
1 (10 ounce) jar red maraschino cherries

Prepare orange juice according to package directions. Mix orange juice and pineapple juice and refrigerate. Prior to serving, stir in champagne. Serve in wine glasses with a cherry.

Serves 1 gallon

May substitute ginger ale for champagne. Use green cherries for St. Patrick's Day.

Pirate's Punch

2 (46 ounce) cans unsweetened pineapple juice
1 (12 ounce) can frozen orange juice concentrate, undiluted
1 (8 ounce) bottle lemon juice
1 (8 ounce) bottle lime juice
1 cup sugar
1 quart light rum
¼ teaspoon salt
Dash of bitters
2 (32 ounce) bottles lemon lime soda, chilled

Combine pineapple juice, orange juice, lemon juice and lime juice in a large container. Add sugar and stir until dissolved. Stir in rum, salt and bitters. Refrigerate until cold. Prior to serving, add lemon lime soda. Serve over ice.

Serves 20

Delicious, but potent!

Merrie's Cosmopolitan

1½-2 ounces quality vodka, kept in freezer
½ ounce triple sec
1 ounce cranberry juice
Juice of one-half lime, or more to taste
Slice of orange peel for garnish

Combine vodka, triple sec, cranberry juice and lime juice in a cocktail shaker. Strain and pour into a well-chilled martini glass. Garnish with orange peel slice.

Serves 1

Frozen Margaritas

1 (6 ounce) can frozen limeade concentrate
6 ounces tequila
3 ounces triple sec
2 heaping tablespoons powdered sugar
Crushed ice
Lime juice and margarita salt for garnish

Blend limeade, tequila, triple sec and powdered sugar in a blender. Add ice and blend until smooth. Add more ice and blend to reach desired consistency. Wet tops of margarita glasses with lime juice. Coat glasses in margarita salt. Pour margarita into prepared glasses.

Serves 4-6

Plantation Punch

1 (6 ounce) can frozen orange juice concentrate, undiluted
1 (6 ounce) can frozen pink lemonade concentrate, undiluted
¾ cup fresh lemon juice, no substitutions
1 (750 ml) bottle Southern Comfort, chilled
3 (1 liter) bottles lemon lime soda, chilled
Ice ring made from diet lemon lime soda
Several drops red food coloring (optional)

Combine orange juice, lemonade, lemon juice and Southern Comfort in a large pitcher. Refrigerate until ready to serve. Prior to serving, pour juice mixture into a punch bowl. Add lemon lime soda and ice ring. Stir in food coloring if desired. Serve in punch cups.

Serves 32

Chocolate Martinis

2-2½ cups vodka, chilled
1¼ cups chocolate liqueur
¼ cup raspberry liqueur
½ cup half-and-half
Chocolate liqueur or syrup
Sweetened cocoa powder

Combine vodka, chocolate liqueur, raspberry liqueur and half-and-half in a large pitcher or martini shaker. Refrigerate at least 1 hour. Dip well-chilled martini glasses in chocolate liqueur. Coat rim of glasses in cocoa. Pour vodka mixture into glasses. Serve immediately.

Serves 4

Pick's Boys

When Coach Pickens A. Noble came to Tupelo in 1944, the fortunes of the Tupelo Golden Wave football teams improved dramatically. Pick was not only a good coach, but he was one heck of a recruiter. We had many a good laugh through the years over the various outstanding players who just happened to come to Tupelo to finish their high school careers while Pick was coaching. The list included such stalwarts as Bill Plaxico, Bobby Kitchens, Mike Mask and Hilton Collier. There were others, but these were all certainly 'difference makers' to the teams they played on.

I will tell you the story of the best of them all, and Pick's first "conquest". In 1942, '43 and '44 Aberdeen had an outstanding tailback by the name of Chester Henley. Chester was by far the best running back in Mississippi by the time he was approaching his senior year. Many compared him to the legendary "Shorty" McWilliams of Meridian.

In an interesting turn of events, the job of director of the Tupelo High School Cafeteria was suddenly available, and the city fathers offered the position to Chester's mother. She accepted and the rest is history. Chester led the Tupelo Golden Wave to its only Big 8 Conference Championship and was not only named to the Big 8 team but named the most outstanding player in the state. We were going to have a good team in 1945 without Chester, but he was the one missing link that put us over the top.

Coincidence? Hardly. Illegal? Not really. In every case the player and his family were better off by the boy coming to play for Coach Pick. Could you get away with these tactics today? Doubtful. But who cares. Mrs. Henley was happy. Chester was happy. We, his teammates, were happy, and Pick Noble was ecstatic!

By the way, in 1945 Pickens A. Noble was THE coach. He coached football, basketball, baseball and track. He had no assistants and he even drove the school bus to all away games!

~Norris (Piggy) Caldwell
Tupelo, MS

Brennan's Bloody Mary

- ¾ cup vodka
- 3 cups tomato-vegetable juice cocktail
- ⅔ cup canned beef bouillon
- 2 tablespoons fresh lime juice
- 4 teaspoons Pickapeppa sauce
- 4 teaspoons Worcestershire sauce
- 4 dashes of Tabasco sauce
- ½ teaspoon salt
- Lemon pepper seasoning for garnish

Combine vodka, vegetable juice, beef bouillon, lime juice, Pickapeppa sauce, Worcestershire sauce, Tabasco and salt in a large pitcher or shaker. Mix well. Serve over ice and sprinkle with lemon pepper.

Serves 4

Mint Daiquiris

- 2 (6 ounce) cans frozen limeade concentrate, thawed, undiluted and divided
- 2 cups light rum, divided
- ½ cup fresh mint leaves, divided
- Ice cubes
- Mint sprigs for garnish

Blend 1 can limeade, 1 cup rum and ¼ cup mint leaves in blender for 30 seconds. Add ice cubes to bring mixture up to the 4-cup level. Blend until slushy. Pour into a large freezer container. Repeat procedure with remaining ingredients. Freeze until ready to serve. Thaw mixture to desired serving consistency.

Serves 9 cups

Mint Daiquiris may be prepared a month in advance and frozen.

Mother's Punch

- 1 (46 ounce) can pineapple juice
- 1 (32 ounce) can orange juice
- 1 (6 ounce) can frozen lemonade concentrate, thawed and undiluted
- 4 cups sugar
- 1 gallon plus 2 cups water
- 1 (8 ounce) can crushed pineapple
- 2 (2 liter) bottles ginger ale

Mix together pineapple juice, orange juice, lemonade, sugar, water and pineapple in a large punch bowl. Add ginger ale prior to serving.

Serves 40

Bread, Breakfast and Brunch

Bulldog Days of Autumn

Garden Fresh Salad

Swiss Cheese Bread, page 56

Grilled Sirloin Steak with
Asparagus Tapenade, page 117

Cornbread Salad, page 109

Bourbon Pecan Pound Cake, page 215

Sesame Bread Sticks

¼ cup plus 2 tablespoons butter, melted
¼ cup sesame seeds
2 cups biscuit baking mix
½ cup milk
1 tablespoon sugar

Melt butter with sesame seeds in a 13 x 9 x 2-inch baking dish in at 375 degree oven. Combine biscuit mix, milk and sugar in a bowl. Stir until a soft dough forms. Beat until stiff and sticky. Turn dough onto a board dusted with biscuit mix. Knead gently for 10 minutes. Roll into a 12 x 8-inch rectangle. Cut into 32 finger-size strips. Dip each strip in melted butter, turning to coat both sides. Arrange strips in buttered pan. Bake at 375 degrees for 12 minutes.

Serves 32 bread sticks

Age is not important, unless you are a cheese.

~Helen Hayes, American actor

~from The New Food Lover's Tiptionary

Apple Squares

½ cup butter
1 cup packed brown sugar
1½ cups sugar, divided
2 eggs
1 teaspoon vanilla
2 cups sifted self-rising flour
1 tablespoon plus ½ teaspoon cinnamon, divided
1 cup chopped cooking apples, peeled
1 cup finely chopped nuts (pecans or walnuts)

Melt butter in a large saucepan. Remove from heat and stir in brown sugar and 1 cup sugar. Blend in eggs and vanilla until smooth. In a bowl, combine flour and ½ teaspoon cinnamon. Stir in flour mixture, apples and nuts to creamed mixture until well combined. Spread into a greased 13 x 9 x 2-inch baking dish. Combine remaining ½ cup sugar and 1 tablespoon cinnamon. Sprinkle over apple mixture. Bake at 350 degrees for 30 minutes. Cool and cut into squares.

Serves 15

Swiss Cheese Bread

Only dull people are brilliant at breakfast.

~Oscar Wilde, Anglo–Irish playwright

~from The New Food Lover's Tiptionary

1 (16 ounce) loaf French bread, sliced
1 pound Swiss cheese slices
¾ cup butter
3 green onions, chopped
2 teaspoons lemon juice
2 teaspoons poppy seeds
2 teaspoons Dijon mustard
1 teaspoon seasoned salt

Place bread on large piece of aluminum foil. Place cheese slices between each slice of bread. Melt butter in a saucepan and add onion, juice, poppy seeds, mustard and salt. Pour butter mixture between each bread slice. Close foil tightly. Cover with another piece of foil. Bake at 350 degrees for 25 minutes. Remove top foil and bake for 15 minutes until browned.

Serves 8-10

Athens Breakfast Bread

¾ cup chopped bell pepper
¾ cup chopped onion
1 pound ground sausage, cooked and crumbled
3 (7½ ounce) cans buttermilk style refrigerated biscuits
⅓ cup butter, melted
½ cup sharp shredded Cheddar cheese
Chopped olives and mushrooms (optional)

Sauté pepper and onion until tender. Mix vegetables with sausage in a large bowl. Cut biscuits into quarters. Add biscuits pieces, butter and cheese to sausage mixture. Place mixture in a greased 10-inch tube pan. Bake at 350 degrees for 30 minutes.

Serves 8-10

May substitute bacon or ham for sausage.

Mrs. Elaine Hancock's Coffee Cake

- **½ cup vegetable shortening**
- **1½ cups sugar**
- **3 eggs**
- **2 cups sifted cake flour**
- **1 tablespoon ground nutmeg**
- **1 teaspoon baking powder**
- **1 teaspoon baking soda**
- **1 cup buttermilk**
- **½ teaspoon vanilla**
- **7 tablespoons butter, melted**
- **5 tablespoons evaporated milk**
- **¾ cup packed brown sugar**
- **1 cup flake coconut**
- **1 cup pecans, chopped**
- **Pecan halves for garnish**

Cream shortening and sugar, one-half cup at a time. Add eggs, one at a time, beating well after each addition. Sift together flour, nutmeg, baking powder and baking soda. Add to creamed mixture. Pour in buttermilk and vanilla and mix until smooth. Batter will be thick. Pour batter into a waxed paper lined 13 x 9 x 2-inch baking dish. Bake at 350 degrees for 30 minutes. While cake is baking, combine butter, milk and brown sugar. Add coconut and let stand for 3 minutes. Stir in pecans. Spread topping evenly over cooled cake. Broil cake 8 to 10 inches from heat source until coconut is toasted. Garnish with pecan halves.

Serves 15

From kindergarten, my closest friend was Lauren Hancock Patterson, therefore I spent many countless hours in the Hancock home. I learned so many wonderful things from Mrs. Elaine Hancock-from cooking to needlework, canning, preserving, to flower and vegetable gardening. It was a resourceful and fun place to visit and grow up in with the Christian morals, principles and basics she taught us by example.

~Emily Raspberry Barber, Belden, MS

Granny's Apple Muffins

- **4 cups diced Granny Smith apples**
- **1 cup sugar**
- **2 large eggs, room temperature**
- **½ cup corn oil**
- **2 teaspoons vanilla**
- **2 cups all-purpose flour**
- **1 teaspoon salt**
- **2 teaspoons baking soda**
- **2 teaspoons cinnamon**
- **1 cup raisins**
- **1 cup chopped walnuts or pecans**

Combine apples and sugar in a large bowl. In a small bowl, whisk together eggs, oil and vanilla. In a separate bowl, combine flour, salt, baking soda and cinnamon. Stir egg mixture into apples. Gradually add dry ingredients and stir until just moistened. Fold in raisins and nuts. Spoon into greased muffin cups. Bake at 325 degrees for 25 minutes.

Serves 24 muffins

As a child, my Grandmother always had a chocolate cake baked for my cousins and me on the days we went swimming in the lake in her pasture. We had to run the cows out of the water on the really hot days or beat them to the pond. It was as if she knew when company was coming because she always had something special for everyone. I try to carry on the tradition with my family except my grandchildren swim in the Tennessee River at Pickwick with no cows to beat to the water!

Banana Bread Loaves

- **1 (18 ounce) package yellow butter cake mix**
- **1 teaspoon baking soda**
- **3½ ripe bananas, mashed**
- **1 cup canola oil**
- **4 eggs, room temperature**
- **1 (8 ounce) package cream cheese, softened**
- **½ cup butter, softened**
- **1 (16 ounce) package powdered sugar**
- **1 cup chopped pecans, additional for garnish**

Preheat oven to 350 degrees. Grease and flour three 8-inch cake pans. Beat cake mix, baking soda, banana and oil with an electric mixer. Add eggs, one at a time, beating after each addition. Pour batter into prepared cake pans. Bake at 350 degrees for 20 minutes or until cake tester comes out clean. To make icing, beat cream cheese and butter with mixer. Gradually beat in powdered sugar until smooth. Stir in pecans. Spread icing over top of cake layers. Sprinkle with chopped pecans for garnish.

Serves 12-15

Fig Cake

- **1¼ cups buttermilk, divided**
- **1 cup vegetable oil**
- **3 eggs, room temperature**
- **2 teaspoons vanilla, divided**
- **2¼ cups sugar, divided**
- **2 cups all-purpose flour**
- **1½ teaspoons baking soda, divided**
- **¼ teaspoon salt**
- **1 teaspoon cinnamon**
- **1 teaspoon ground cloves**
- **1 teaspoon ground nutmeg**
- **1 cup pecans, chopped**
- **¾ cup fig preserves, chopped**
- **¾ cup butter**
- **1 tablespoon light corn syrup**
- **Powdered sugar for garnish**

Whisk together 1 cup buttermilk, oil, eggs and 1 teaspoon vanilla in a bowl. In a large bowl, combine 1½ cups sugar, flour, 1 teaspoon baking soda, salt, cinnamon, cloves and nutmeg. Gradually mix liquid ingredients into dry ingredients. Mix until well combined. Add pecans and preserves. Pour batter into a greased and floured 13 x 9 x 2-inch baking dish or Bundt pan. Bake at 300 degrees for 55 minutes or until cake tester comes out clean. To make glaze, combine ¼ cup buttermilk, ½ teaspoon baking soda, ¾ cup sugar, butter, corn syrup and 1 teaspoon vanilla in a saucepan. Bring to boil, stirring constantly. Cook until sugar melts. Pour over warm cake. Cool completely. Sprinkle with powdered sugar before serving. Cut into 1-inch squares.

Serves 16

Date Nut Bread

- 2 eggs, beaten
- 1 cup sugar
- 1 cup all-purpose flour
- 1 (10 ounce) package dates, chopped
- 1 pound pecan halves
- ½ teaspoon salt
- 1 teaspoon vanilla
- ¼ cup milk
- 1 teaspoon baking powder

Combine eggs, sugar and flour and mix well. Stir in dates, pecans, salt, vanilla, milk and baking powder. Batter will be very stiff. Spread batter into a 9 x 5 x 3-inch loaf pan. Bake at 300-325 degrees for 1 hour or until browned and toothpick inserted in center comes out clean. Cool completely. Slice with an electric knife.

Serves 10-12

This bread freezes well.

For every family gathering, my mother, better known as Mimi, was asked to bake her date nut bread. This is a favorite of her children, grandchildren and great grandchildren. After her death, Mimi's Date Nut Bread was featured in Mississippi Magazine and was selected as a Reader's Favorite in the 20th Anniversary edition of Mississippi Magazine. Someone in my family still makes Mimi's Date Nut Bread for every special occasion.

~Jane Hammond, Tupelo, MS

On this day—
Mend a quarrel, search out a forgotten friend.
Dismiss suspicion, replace it with trust.
Give a soft answer. Encourgage youth.
Manifest your loyalty in a word or deed.
Keep a promise. Find the time. Forego a grudge.
Forgive an enemy. Listen. Apologize if you were wrong.
Try to understand. Flout envy.
Examine your demands on others.
Think first of someone else.
Appreciate. Be kind. Be gentle.
Laugh a little more. Deserve confidence.
Take up arms against malice. Degree complacency.
Express our gratitude. Worship your God.
Gladden the heart of a child.
Take pleasure in the beauty and wonder of the earth.
Speak your love. Speak it again.
Speak it still once again.

~Carolyn

Easy Yeast Rolls

2 packages active dry yeast
½ cup warm milk (100 to 110 degrees)
1 cup milk
½ cup sugar
½ cup vegetable shortening, melted
2 large eggs, beaten
1 teaspoon salt
5½ cups all-purpose flour
½ cup butter, melted and divided

Combine yeast and warm milk in a 2-cup measuring cup. Let stand for 5 minutes. Combine yeast mixture, milk, sugar, shortening, eggs and salt in a large bowl. Gradually add 1 cup flour, stirring until smooth. Stir in enough flour to make a soft dough. Place dough in a well-greased bowl, turning to grease top of dough. Cover and let rise in a warm place for 1 hour or until doubled in size. Turn dough out onto a floured surface and knead 5 or 6 times. Divide dough in half. Roll each half to ¼-inch thickness. Cut dough with a 2-inch round cutter. Brush rounds with melted butter and fold in half. Place rolls in three lightly greased 9-inch round cake pans. Cover and let rise for 1 hour or until doubled in size. Bake at 375 degrees for 15 to 18 minutes or until golden browned. Brush with remaining melted butter.

Serves 36 rolls

Broccoli Cornbread

1 (10 ounce) package frozen chopped broccoli, thawed and well drained
3 eggs
¾ cup cottage cheese
1 small onion, chopped
½ cup butter, melted
1 teaspoon salt
1 (8½ ounce) corn muffin mix or 2 cups self-rising cornmeal
1 cup shredded Cheddar cheese

Heat a large well-seasoned cast iron skillet in the center of a 450 degree oven. Combine broccoli, eggs, cottage cheese, onion, butter, salt, cornmeal and cheese in a large bowl. Remove skillet from oven. Quickly pour cornmeal batter into skillet. Bake at 450 degrees for 20 to 30 minutes.

Serves 8-10

Easy Cheesy Muffins

1 cup self-rising flour
6 tablespoons butter, melted
1 cup sour cream
1 cup shredded Cheddar cheese

Preheat oven to 350 degrees. Combine flour, butter, sour cream and cheese and mix thoroughly. Spoon batter into lightly greased muffin cups. Bake at 350 degrees for 25 to 30 minutes. Cool in muffin tin.

Serves 12-15

Mammy Jane's Shrimp Cornbread

- **2 eggs**
- **1 medium onion, chopped**
- **½ cup vegetable oil**
- **1 package Mexican cornbread mix**
- **1 cup shredded Cheddar cheese**
- **1 (15½ ounce) can cream-style corn**
- **1 pound shrimp or crawfish**

Combine eggs, onion, oil, cornbread mix, cheese, corn and shrimp in a large bowl. Pour batter into a greased 13 x 9 x 2-inch baking dish. Bake at 375 degrees for 30 minutes. Cool slightly before cutting into squares.

Serves 8

This recipe can be doubled.

South of the Border Bread

- **2 cups self-rising cornmeal**
- **2 eggs**
- **1½ cups milk**
- **⅓ teaspoon salt**
- **Dash of pepper**
- **Dash of garlic powder**
- **1 cup shredded sharp Cheddar cheese**
- **2 tablespoons minced onion**
- **3 green onions, chopped**
- **2 tablespoons chopped pimento**
- **3 tablespoons picante sauce**
- **2 medium jalapeño peppers, seeded and chopped**
- **1 (11½ ounce) can Mexican corn, drained**
- **1 tablespoon vegetable oil**

Preheat oven to 450 degrees. Heat a greased 8-inch cast iron skillet in the oven. Combine cornmeal, eggs, milk, salt, pepper, garlic powder, cheese, onion, green onion, pimento, picante sauce, jalapeño peppers, corn and oil in a large bowl. Mix until well blended. Pour into hot skillet. Bake at 450 degrees for 20 to 35 minutes or until browned.

Serves 10

Celebration is a high form of praise, of gratitude to the Creator
for the beauty of God's creation…Celebrate all that is in your life.
Celebrate all that is good. Celebrate you.

~Melody Beattie

"Miss Nelle" and Her Strawberries

Stories about the legendary Mrs. Rex Reed are quite numerous around the area and many have been told over and over. I would like to tell you a story that may not have been made public. I was involved so I can vouch for the accuracy.

Better known as "Miss Nelle" to all who knew her, Mrs. Reed invited many members of my high school senior class to a special party at her family estate on West Main. Her home was located on the hillside overlooking the lake where Ballard Park is now. It was a beautiful, yet unusual looking home that was a showplace on the western side of the city.

I can't remember who the party was for and I could possibly have been one of the honorees. It was a beautiful day and we played some outdoor games before the main event. "Miss Nelle" had a large strawberry patch behind her house on the land that is now occupied by the soccer fields. It was a very large field and would have been quite a task for someone to go in and gather all the ripening strawberries. Well, "Miss Nelle" solved two problems that day. She came up with a good, friendly competition for the party attendees, and solved her crop gathering problem at the same time.

I can still see her in her bright yellow dress and ever present wide brimmed hat, standing on her back steps shouting instructions for the upcoming event. We were all given empty baskets and instructions to enter the field and start picking strawberries. The person who gathered the most strawberries in the prescribed time would win the prize. In my mind, I could see a new Spalding football or a portable radio. I am sure the girls had their own ideas about what would have been a special prize. As over fifty eager Tupelo High School seniors entered the field the strawberry picking was furious. In less than an hour the field was picked clean and the Reed back porch was covered with overflowing baskets of bright red berries.

Mary Jane Nethery was deemed the winner. As "Miss Nelle" presented Mary Jane with her prize we all looked at each other and grinned. "Miss Nelle" had fulfilled her obligations to many friends by having such a grand party and she had gathered her crop all in one afternoon. I am sure Mary Jane enjoyed her box of ice cream sandwiches which, as I remember, she had to immediately share before they melted.

Great small town American fun and another special memory of a very special lady.

~Norris (Piggy) Caldwell
Tupelo, MS

Rio Grande Grits

2 teaspoons salt
7 cups water
2 cups quick grits
1 cup butter
1 (6 ounce) roll garlic cheese
1 (6 ounce) jar jalapeño processed cheese
4 eggs
½ cup half-and-half
1 teaspoon salt
1 teaspoon white pepper
1 pound mild or hot sausage, cooked and drained
1 pound bacon, cooked and crumbled
2 (4½ ounce) cans chopped green chilies
1 (12 ounce) package shredded sharp Cheddar cheese
1 (8 ounce) package shredded Monterey Jack cheese

Add salt to boiling water. Add grits and cook, stirring often, over low heat for 20 minutes. Add butter, garlic cheese and jalapeño cheese. Stir until butter and cheeses melt. In a bowl, blend eggs, half-and-half, salt and pepper. Add to grits mixture. Stir in sausage, bacon and green chilies until well combined. Pour grits mixture into a greased 13 x 9 x 2-inch baking dish. Top with Cheddar and Monterey Jack cheeses. Cover and bake at 350 degrees for 40 minutes. Uncover and bake an additional 20 minutes.

Serves 10

For a great holiday gift, divide the grits mixture among three 8 x 8 x 2-inch foil round cake pans. Cook, uncovered, for 30 minutes.

~Lisa Springer, Cleveland, MS

Raisin Pecan Baked Apples with Southern Seasoning

1 cup packed dark brown sugar
2 teaspoons lemon juice
2 teaspoons cinnamon
1 teaspoon ground nutmeg
1 teaspoon ground cloves
½ teaspoon salt
⅔ cup pecans, chopped
½ cup golden raisins
½ cup bourbon
2 teaspoons vanilla
3 tablespoons butter
10 apples, cored

Combine brown sugar, juice, cinnamon, nutmeg, cloves and salt in a saucepan. Cook, stirring often, over low heat for 2 minutes or until sugar melts. Add nuts, raisins, bourbon, vanilla and butter. Cook, stirring frequently, for 3 minutes. Using a slotted spoon, fill apple centers with nuts and raisins. Place apples in a 13 x 9 x 2-inch baking dish. Brush apples with sugar glaze. Bake at 350 degrees for 1 hour. Baste apples with glaze three times during baking.

Serves 8-10

Caramel Apple Breakfast Pudding

- 2 large Granny Smith or Jonathan apples, peeled, cored and sliced
- ¼ cup water
- ¼ teaspoon cinnamon
- ½ cup packed brown sugar
- 2 tablespoons light corn syrup
- 2 tablespoons butter
- ¼ cup chopped pecans
- 3 eggs, beaten
- 1¼ cups milk
- 1 teaspoon vanilla
- ¼ teaspoon ground nutmeg
- 8-10 (½-inch) slices of Italian or French bread

Combine apple slices and water in a saucepan. Bring to boil. Reduce heat and cook, covered, over medium heat for 5 to 7 minutes or until apples are tender. Drain and place in a bowl. Add cinnamon and gently stir. Set aside. In same saucepan, combine brown sugar, corn syrup and butter. Cook and stir until mixture just comes to boil. Remove from heat and pour into a 8 x 8 x 2-inch baking dish. Sprinkle pecans over caramel sauce. In a bowl, whisk together eggs, milk, vanilla and nutmeg. Arrange half of bread slices in dish. Spoon cooked apples evenly over bread layer. Layer remaining bread slices on top. Slowly pour egg mixture over bread, pressing bread down to completely moisten. Cover and refrigerate for 3 hours or up to 24 hours.

Bake, uncovered, at 325 degrees for 40 to 45 minutes or until tester comes out clean. Remove from oven and run a knife around the edge to loosen. Cool for 15 minutes. Carefully invert pudding onto a serving platter. Spoon any caramel mixture from dish to top of pudding. Cut into triangles. Serve warm or room temperature.

Serves 8

Chocolate Chunk Scones

- 2 cups all-purpose flour
- ⅓ cup sugar
- 1 tablespoon baking powder
- ½ teaspoon salt
- 5½ ounces bittersweet or semi-sweet chocolate squares, coarsely chopped
- 6 tablespoons cold unsalted butter, cut into cubes
- ¾ cup heavy cream
- 2 large egg yolks, slightly beaten
- 1 large egg, slightly beaten
- 1 tablespoon milk
- 1-1½ teaspoons sugar

Preheat oven to 400 degrees. In a large bowl, combine flour, sugar, baking powder and salt. Add chocolate and toss to coat with flour. Cut in the butter until mixture is the size of peas. In a small bowl, blend cream and egg yolks. Add this all at once to flour mixture. Stir with a fork until ingredients are combined. Continue to knead the mixture with hands until a soft dough is formed. Do not overknead. Shape dough into a ball and place in center of a parchment paper-lined baking sheet. Flatten dough into a 1-inch thick round and 7-inches in diameter. With a sharp knife, cut round into eight wedges. Separate wedges. Whisk egg with milk and brush over scones. Sprinkle with sugar. Bake at 400 degrees for 18 to 22 minutes or until deep golden and tester comes out clean. Slide parchment paper onto wire rack and cool scones for 10 to 15 minutes.

Serves 8

Crusty Cheese Bread

- 1 package dry active yeast
- ¼ cup warm water (115 to 120 degrees)
- 3 cups sifted all-purpose flour
- 1 teaspoon sugar
- 1 teaspoon salt
- ⅔ cup mashed potatoes, warm or cold
- ⅓ cup butter, melted
- 1 cup shredded sharp Cheddar cheese
- 2 eggs
- ¼ cup scalded milk, cooled to lukewarm

Sprinkle yeast into warm water. Stir until dissolved. Sift together flour, sugar and salt. Combine potatoes, butter, cheese, eggs and milk in a large bowl. Mix until well blended. Add yeast mixture and dry ingredients to potato mixture. Mix thoroughly. Turn dough onto a well floured surface and knead for 8 minutes or until satiny and smooth. Place in a greased bowl and cover. Let rise for 1 hour in a warm place until doubled in size. Punch down and knead for 2 minutes. Divide in half and place each into a greased 9 x 5 x 3-inch loaf pan. Let rise for 30 minutes or until almost double in size. Bake at 375 degrees for 25 to 30 minutes.

Serves 12-15

This bread is best when toasted. This cheese bread has been a tradition in the Poland family for many, many years. I make it for our three children and their families before Christmas each year. I must say that they are very selfish about sharing it.

~Alma Wright Poland, Tupelo, MS

Sour Cream Coffee Cake

- 2 cups sugar
- 1⅛ cups butter, softened and divided
- 2 eggs
- 2 cups all-purpose flour
- 1 teaspoon baking powder
- ¼ teaspoon salt
- 1 cup sour cream
- 1½ teaspoons vanilla, divided
- 3 tablespoons packed brown sugar
- 1 teaspoon cinnamon
- 1 cup chopped pecans
- 2 cups powdered sugar
- 2 tablespoons heavy cream or milk

Beat sugar and all but 2 tablespoons butter until smooth. Add eggs. In a separate bowl, combine flour, baking powder and salt. Add flour mixture and sour cream, alternately to creamed mixture, starting and ending with flour. Add 1 teaspoon vanilla. In another bowl, combine brown sugar, cinnamon and pecans. Pour half of batter into a greased and floured 10-inch tube pan. Top with half of pecan mixture. Repeat layers. Bake at 350 degrees for about 50 minutes. Cool in pan for 10 minutes. Invert onto serving platter. To make icing (optional), cream together 2 tablespoons butter, ½ teaspoon vanilla and powdered sugar. Add cream or milk as needed to reach desired consistency. Drizzle icing over cake.

Serves 15

This coffee cake is just right for a special brunch. Very moist and easy to prepare. Cake freezes well also.

~Barbara Vaughn, Tupelo, MS

Christmas Morning Pie

Great for a brunch or with a green salad for a "ladies" light lunch on the veranda.

- **1 pound sausage with sage, cooked, drained and crumbled**
- **1 cup shredded Swiss cheese**
- **1 cup shredded Cheddar cheese**
- **2 (9-inch) pie shells, unbaked**
- **6 eggs, slightly beaten**
- **1 cup milk**
- **½ cup chopped onion**
- **⅓ cup chopped sweet red pepper**
- **⅓ cup chopped bell pepper**

Combine sausage and cheeses. Divide and spread mixture on the bottom of two pie shells. Mix together eggs, milk, onion and peppers. Pour half egg mixture into each shell. Bake at 350 degrees for 55 to 60 minutes or until knife inserted in center comes out clean. Cool 5 minutes before cutting.

Serves 16

May substitute maple-flavored sausage for sage sausage. The recipe may be halved for one pie.

Quiche Medley

This quiche is excellent with a fruit salad for lunch or light dinner. May store in refrigerator and reheat in microwave.

- **1 (9-inch) pie crust pastry**
- **1 cup shredded Monterey Jack cheese, divided**
- **1 (4 ounce) jar sliced mushrooms, drained**
- **6-8 asparagus spears**
- **3 eggs**
- **1¼ cups half-and-half**
- **Zest and juice from one lemon**
- **¼ teaspoon seasoned salt**
- **¼ teaspoon ground nutmeg**
- **1 cup chopped ham**

Pierce bottom and sides of pie shell. Bake at 375 degrees for 10 minutes. Sprinkle ¾ cup cheese and mushrooms in bottom of crust. Arrange asparagus in a spoke wheel design. Beat together eggs, half-and-half, zest, juice, salt, nutmeg and ham. Pour egg mixture over asparagus. Top with ¼ cup remaining cheese. Bake at 375 degrees for 45 minutes or until center is set and browned on top.

Serves 8

May substitute green onions for asparagus and bacon for ham.

Hospice

Hospice — what doubt and anxiety that word produced! I knew nothing about it, only that my adored and terminally ill sister needed in-hospice care. With trepidation we carried her to Whispering Pines. Her private room with a large picture window looking out on grass and trees eased our concerns somewhat. However, we were still troubled and unsure of the quality of care. What a wonderful experience was ahead for us! The care, kindness and love the staff showed each patient and their families were phenomenal! We expected a sad, dreary place, at best, and instead found it cheerful and compassionate. One of my fondest memories is the Halloween Party. Once again, we expected a generic, ho hum occasion. BIG surprise! The entire staff wore terrific costumes and "The Pines" was spectacularly decorated! The food was colorful, delicious and plentiful. The rollicking Dixieland Band was delightful and even a masseur was provided to give sore, aching muscles a welcome massage. We whipped around all afternoon enjoying one fun activity after another. Later, on the way back to her room, my sister smiled and said, "I've had the most wonderful day!" What a special memory! We were blessed in finding Hospice and left surrounded by God's love and grace through the kindness and care of the staff.

~Jimmie Haynes
Tupelo, MS

"If I can stop one heart from breaking,
I shall not live in vain;
If I can ease one life the aching,
Or cool one pain,
Or help one fainting robin
Unto his nest again,
I shall not live in vain."

~Emily Dickinson

Lemon Sunshine Bread

- 1½ cups sugar, divided
- ¼ cup butter, softened
- 2 eggs
- ½ cup milk
- 1½ cups all-purpose flour
- Dash of salt
- 1 teaspoon baking powder
- Zest of one lemon
- ½ cup chopped nuts
- Juice of one lemon

Cream together 1 cup sugar and butter. Beat in eggs and milk. Add flour, salt, baking powder, zest and nuts. Mix until well blended. Pour batter into a greased 9 x 5 x 3-inch loaf pan. Bake at 350 degrees for 50 minutes. Cool in pan for 5 minutes. Invert bread onto a plate. Whisk together ½ cup sugar and lemon juice until sugar dissolves. Drizzle glaze over bread.

Serves 12

Cheese Puff

- 8 slices bread, crust removed
- 1½ cups shredded Cheddar cheese, divided
- 2 eggs, beaten
- 2 cups milk, divided
- ½ teaspoon salt
- ½ teaspoon pepper
- Dry mustard to taste

Place 4 slices of bread in the bottom of a buttered 11 x 7 x 2-inch baking dish. Sprinkle with 1 cup cheese. In a bowl, combine eggs, 1½ cups milk, salt, pepper and mustard. Pour over cheese. Layer remaining slices of bread. Top with remaining ½ cup cheese and ½ cup milk. Refrigerate for 3 to 4 hours or overnight. Set baking dish in large roasting pan. Fill roasting pan half way with water. Bake at 350 degrees about 40 minutes until custard is set and bread is puffy. It will resemble a soufflé.

Serves 4-8

Blueberry Morning Muffins

- 2 cups sifted all-purpose flour
- ½ teaspoon salt
- 2½ teaspoons baking powder
- ½ cup sugar
- 1 egg
- ¾ cup milk
- ¼ cup vegetable oil
- 1 (15 ounce) can blueberries, rinsed and drained

Sift together flour, salt, baking powder and sugar. Make a well in the center of dry ingredients. Place egg, milk and oil into well. Stir just until blended. Add blueberries. Spoon batter into greased muffin cups. Bake at 400 degrees for 20 to 25 minutes.

Serves 12 muffins

Orange Slice Nut Bread

- 1 cup candied orange slices, finely chopped
- 1 tablespoon sugar
- ¼ cup butter, softened
- ½ cup sugar
- 1 egg
- ½ cup mashed banana
- 2½ cups sifted all-purpose flour
- 2 teaspoons baking powder
- ½ teaspoon baking soda
- ½ cup chopped nuts
- 1 cup milk

Sprinkle orange pieces with 1 tablespoon sugar to prevent sticking. Cream butter with sugar. Add egg and banana and mix well. In a separate bowl, sift together flour, baking powder and baking soda. Add nuts and orange pieces to flour mixture. Add flour mixture and milk, alternately, to creamed mixture. Pour batter into a greased and floured 8 x 4 x 3-inch loaf pan. Bake at 350 degrees for 65 minutes or until tester comes out clean. Let stand overnight before slicing.

Serves 1 loaf or 5 mini loaves

Don't throw out your bagels that are getting hard. Cut crosswise into 1/8 slices and arrange in a single layer on a cookie sheet. Toast in a 350° oven for 5 minutes on each side. Brush with olive oil and sprinkle with salt, herbs, or other toppings before toasting.

~from
The New Food
Lover's Tiptionary

Glazed Craisin Scones

- 3 cups all-purpose flour
- ⅓ cup plus 2 tablespoons sugar, divided
- 2½ teaspoons baking powder
- ½ teaspoon baking soda
- ¾ teaspoon salt
- ¾ cup butter, softened
- 1 cup buttermilk
- ¾ cup craisins
- 1 teaspoon orange zest
- 1 tablespoon heavy cream
- ¼ teaspoon cinnamon

Preheat oven to 425 degrees. Combine flour, ⅓ cup sugar, baking powder, baking soda and salt. Stir with a fork to aerate. Cut in butter with pastry blender until mixture resembles bread crumbs. Add buttermilk, craisins and zest. Mix until dry ingredients are moistened. Shape dough into a ball. Knead 12 times on a floured surface. Flatten dough to ½-inch thickness. In a small bowl, blend cream, cinnamon and 2 tablespoons sugar. Brush dough with glaze. Cut dough into 16 wedges. Place scones ½-inch apart on a baking sheet. Bake at 425 degrees for 12 minutes or until tops are browned. Serve hot.

Serves 16

I've long said that if I were about to be executed and were given a choice of my last meal, it would be bacon and eggs...nothing is quite as intoxicating as the smell of bacon frying in the morning, save perhaps the smell of coffee brewing.

~James Beard, American cookbook author.

~from The New Food Lover's Tiptionary

Whole Wheat Sausage Bread

1 (8 ounce) package spicy Italian pork sausage
⅓ cup shredded carrot
¼ cup chopped onion
1 (8 ounce) container cream cheese with chives and onions, softened
5 ounces frozen chopped spinach, thawed and well drained
⅓ cup chopped pecans, toasted
¼ cup fine dry bread crumbs
1 (16 ounce) loaf frozen whole wheat or white bread dough, thawed
Melted butter

Cook sausage, carrot and onion until browned. Drain well. Transfer to a bowl. Add cream cheese, spinach, pecans and bread crumbs and mix well. Roll out dough to a 12 x 9-inch rectangle. Evenly spread filling over dough to ½-inch of edges. Starting with long edge, roll up dough and place seam side down on baking sheet. Let rise for 30 minutes. Bake at 350 degrees for 30 minutes. Brush with melted butter.

Serves 10

Cream Cheese Breakfast Pastry

2 (8 ounce) packages cream cheese, softened
1¼ cups sugar, divided
1 teaspoon vanilla
2 (8 ounce) cans refrigerated crescent rolls
½ cup butter, melted
1 teaspoon cinnamon

Combine cream cheese, 1 cup sugar and vanilla. Unroll and lay one can of dough in bottom of 13 x 9 x 2-inch baking dish. Do not press seams together. Spread cream cheese mixture on top. Unroll and lay second can of dough on top. Pour butter over dough. Combine ¼ cup sugar and cinnamon. Sprinkle over butter. Bake at 350 degrees for 30 minutes. Cool slightly and cut into squares.

Serves 24-30

Corn Fritters

1 cup all-purpose flour
2 eggs, beaten
½ cup whole milk
¼ cup creamy Italian dressing
¼ cup heavy cream
1 (17 ounce) can whole kernel corn, drained
½ cup shredded Cheddar cheese
¾ cup chopped green onions
½ teaspoon Creole seasoning
¼ cup vegetable oil

Beat flour, eggs, milk, dressing and cream until smooth. Add corn, cheese, onion and seasoning and mix well. Heat oil in a skillet. Drop batter by tablespoons and flatten with spoon. Cook until browned. Turn and cook on other side. Drain on paper towels.

Serves 6

Chocolate Gravy

¾ cup sugar
3 tablespoons cocoa powder
3 tablespoons all-purpose flour
Dash of salt
2 cups milk
2 tablespoons butter
1 teaspoon vanilla

Sift together sugar, cocoa, flour and salt. Pour milk into a saucepan. Slowly add dry ingredients to milk. Cook over medium heat, stirring constantly, until mixture coats back of spoon and is smooth. Stir in butter and vanilla. Serve over hot biscuits.

Serves 8

Yummy Crummy Cake

2 (8½ ounce) packages pie crust mix
⅔ cup sugar
2 tablespoons cinnamon
2 tablespoons water
3 tablespoons butter, cubed
1 (18 ounce) package yellow cake mix, without pudding
Powdered sugar for garnish

Combine pie crust mix, sugar, cinnamon, and water in a bowl. Cut in butter until mixture resembles bread crumbs. Prepare cake according to package directions. Pour batter into a greased and floured 15 x 10 x 1-inch jelly-roll pan. Bake 350 degrees for 12 minutes. Remove from oven. Top with sugar crumbs mixture. Return to oven and bake an additional 15 minutes. Cool completely. Sprinkle with powdered sugar.

Serves 20

This is a great seller at bake sales. Prepare in two rectangle foil cake pans. May also cut cake and sell by the slice!

The egg is
to cuisine what
the article is
to speech.

~Anonymous

~from
The New Food
Lover's Tiptionary

Anne's Egg Casserole

- 6 hard-cooked eggs
- 2 teaspoons dry mustard
- 2 tablespoons sour cream
- Italian dressing to taste
- Dash of salt
- 1 medium bell pepper, chopped
- ½ cup onion
- 2 tablespoons butter
- Olive oil
- 2 tablespoons pimento
- 1 (8 ounce) container sour cream
- 1 (10¾ ounce) can cream of mushroom soup
- ½ cup shredded Cheddar cheese

Cut egg in half. Remove yolk from eggs and mix with mustard, sour cream, dressing and salt. Place yolk mixture back into white of egg. Set aside. Sauté bell pepper and onion in butter and oil. Add pimento, sour cream and mushroom soup and mix well. Spread sauce into 13 x 9 x 2-inch baking dish. Place eggs in sauce, yolk side up. Sprinkle with cheese. Bake at 350 degrees until sauce is bubbly.

Serves 12

Sweet Potato Cornbread

- 1 cup sifted all-purpose flour
- 1 cup yellow cornmeal
- 4 teaspoons baking powder
- 1 teaspoon salt
- ½ cup sugar
- 1 (15 ounce) can sweet potatoes, mashed
- 2 eggs
- 6 tablespoons milk
- 3 tablespoons vegetable oil

Combine flour, cornmeal, baking powder, salt and sugar. In another bowl, combine sweet potatoes, eggs, milk and oil. Stir dry ingredients into wet ingredients just until moistened. Spoon into mini-muffin cups. Bake at 425 degrees for 15 to 20 minutes.

Serves 24 mini-muffins

It takes a long time to grow an old friend.
Recognize, cherish and treasure that person.
We are not allowed very many.

~Reprinted from the book *Mama Said*
by Martha Houston Reed Hammond

Oh, Hospice Where Art Thou

In June of 1998 my husband of six years was diagnosed with small cell inoperable lung cancer. He was 51 years old. After two years of chemo/radiation treatment, he passed away on October 2, 2000. During the last month and a half of his life, he was hospitalized three different times; the last stay was for two weeks. The day before we were to bring him home and take care of him with home health care – he died. He was 53 years old. Those two weeks were the worst weeks of our lives and although the hospital took good care of him medically, they did not advise us that his death was imminent nor did they prepare us for his death. His last days were spent going through endless painful medical procedures that weren't needed and that he really did not want; there was no emotional support or help for our family to prepare for his approaching death. It was the most difficult experience of my life. I have known friends and families over the years that have faced the death of a family member with Hospice Care and they have nothing but praise for that experience.

After retiring in June of 2002, I relocated to Tupelo to be closer to family and friends and in the Fall I kept reading and hearing about Celebration Village! I shopped for three days with friends and family and spent way too much money! At Celebration Village I signed a list indicating interest in becoming involved with Sanctuary Hospice House, so here I am today serving as Co-Chairwoman of the Cook Book Committee! In memory of my husband, I feel a personal commitment to be involved with the Sanctuary Hospice House because anyone facing death deserves all the emotional support, medical management of pain, dignity and love that's available. The families and friends of the dying also need the loving care, compassion and support that hospice offers.

~Holly Temple
Tupelo, MS

Mama Mat's Oven Omelet

This is a recipe we used early in our marriage when funds ran low. It is great for breakfast as well as a light dinner meal served with a green salad. We still use it all the time, not out of necessity now, but because it is so good and easy.

~Virginia Mathews, Tupelo, MS

- 6 eggs
- Salt and pepper to taste
- 1 cup shredded Cheddar cheese
- 2 tablespoons butter
- Salsa, black olives or green onion for garnish

Beat eggs and season with salt and pepper. Set aside. Place cheese and butter in a 1½-quart casserole dish. Cover and bake at 350 degrees for about 10 minutes until cheese and butter melts. Stir eggs into cheese and bake, uncovered, an additional 25 minutes or until eggs come to a peak. Garnish with salsa, black olives or green onions.

Serves 2-3

Seasoned Tomato and Garlic Quiche

- 2 medium tomatoes, chopped
- 2 chicken or vegetable bouillon cubes
- 1 (16 ounce) container sour cream
- 3 large eggs
- ½ cup Parmesan cheese, divided
- 1 (9-inch) deep dish pie shell, unbaked
- ¼ cup seasoned bread crumbs
- 2 garlic cloves, finely chopped

Preheat oven to 350 degrees. Combine tomatoes and bouillon in a small saucepan. Cook over medium-high heat, stirring frequently, until bouillon is dissolved. Remove from heat. Combine sour cream, eggs and ¼ cup Parmesan cheese in a bowl. Pour egg mixture into pie shell. Combine bread crumbs, remaining ¼ cup Parmesan cheese and garlic. Sprinkle over egg mixture. Spoon tomato mixture over filling. Bake at 350 degrees for 50 to 60 minutes or until filling is set.

Serves 6-8

Soups, Salads and Sandwiches

Elvis Birthday Bash

Butter Bean Cakes with Creole Sauce, page 31

Grace's Sunday Roast, page 118

Spicy Squash Casserole, page 188

Mashed Potatoes

Whipped Cream Pound Cake, page 227

Laura's Banana Fritters with
Chocolate Hazelnut Sauce, page 200

Gazpacho

- 1 (11½ ounce) can tomato juice
- 1 (14½ ounce) can beef broth
- 3 tablespoons vegetable oil
- 2 tablespoons vinegar
- ½ teaspoon paprika, divided
- Salt and pepper to taste
- ½ cup butter
- ¼ teaspoon garlic salt or powder
- ¼ teaspoon dried thyme
- ¼ teaspoon dried rosemary
- ¼ teaspoon cayenne pepper
- ½ teaspoon dried parsley
- 15-18 slices sandwich bread
- 2 ripe tomatoes, finely chopped
- 1 cucumber, finely chopped
- 1 bell pepper, finely chopped
- 2 green onions, finely chopped
- 2 stalks celery, finely chopped

Combine tomato juice, broth, oil, vinegar, ¼ teaspoon paprika and season with salt and pepper and mix well. Refrigerate until cold. To make croutons, melt butter in saucepan. Add garlic salt, thyme, rosemary, ¼ teaspoon paprika, cayenne and parsley. Remove crusts from bread and cut bread slices into small cubes. Add to butter mixture and stir until butter is absorbed. Place bread cubes on baking sheet. Bake at 200-250 degrees for 45-60 minutes or to desired crispness. Cool completely. Serve cold gazpacho with chopped vegetables and croutons served on the side to be added according to individual tastes.

Serve 2-4

Duck N' Andouille Sausage Gumbo

- 6 duck breasts, cut into bite-size pieces
- ¾ cup vegetable oil
- ¾ cup all-purpose flour
- 6 slices bacon
- 2 cups chopped onion
- ½ cup chopped celery
- 1 green bell pepper, chopped
- 1 red bell pepper, chopped
- 3 carrots, peeled and thinly sliced
- ½ cup chopped garlic
- ½ cup snipped fresh parsley
- 4 quarts chicken broth
- ½ bottle red wine
- 8 bay leaves
- Salt, pepper and cayenne pepper to taste
- 1 pound andouille sausage, sliced
- 1 quart raw oysters
- Hot cooked rice
- Chopped green onions and filé for garnish

Brown duck in oil in a skillet but do not fully cook. Remove duck and reserve. Stir in flour to make a dark brown roux. Cook bacon in a large stockpot. Add brown roux to bacon and drippings and mix well. Add onion, celery, green bell pepper, red bell pepper, carrot, garlic and parsley. Cook until tender. Add broth, wine, bay leaves and season with salt, pepper and cayenne. Stir in reserved duck and andouille. Bring to boil. Reduce heat and simmer 1 to 2 hours or until duck is tender. Remove any excess oil from top of gumbo. Add oysters and cook 15 to 20 minutes or until oysters curl. Remove bay leaves. Serve gumbo over cooked rice. Garnish with green onion and filé.

Serves 1 gallon

Beef Stew

3 pounds beef chuck roast, cubed
¼ cup butter
3 stalks celery, chopped
1 (8 ounce) container sliced mushrooms
1 onion, cut into wedges
2 (10½ ounce) cans beef broth
½ cup red wine

Melt butter in a saucepan. Add beef and brown. Add celery, mushrooms, onion and cook for 20 minutes over low heat. Add broth and wine. Cover and simmer 1 hour.

Serves 6-8

Tomato-Basil Artichoke Soup

3 (10¾ ounce) cans tomato soup
2 (10¾ ounce) cans whole milk
¼ cup heavy cream
1 (14½ ounce) can diced tomatoes with juice
1 (14 ounce) jar artichokes, chopped
½ teaspoon chopped fresh basil
Salt and pepper to taste

Combine soup, milk, cream, tomatoes, artichokes and basil in stockpot. Season with salt and pepper. Heat soup thoroughly.

Serves 4-6

Mexican Corn Soup

4 cups fresh or frozen corn kernels
½ cup chopped onion
2 tablespoons butter
2 tablespoons all-purpose flour
Salt and pepper to taste
2 cups chicken broth
2 cups milk
1 cup shredded Cheddar cheese
1 (4 ounce) can chopped green chilies
Tortilla chips
½ cup cooked and crumbled bacon for garnish
Shredded mozzarella cheese for garnish

Sauté corn and onion in butter until tender. Stir in flour, salt and pepper and cook for 1 minute. Gradually stir in broth alternating with milk until thickened. Stir in cheese and chilies. Cook over low heat, stirring constantly, until cheese melts. Ladle into soup bowls. Crumble 4 to 5 tortilla chips in each bowl. Top with bacon and mozzarella cheese.

Serves 8

All In One Fiesta Soup

- 3 tablespoons all-purpose flour
- ½ teaspoon ground cumin
- ½ teaspoon chili powder
- ½ teaspoon garlic powder
- ¼ teaspoon cinnamon
- 1½ pounds lean beef chuck, cut into 1-inch cubes
- 2 tablespoons vegetable oil
- 1 cup beef broth
- ½ cup apple juice
- 1 medium bell pepper, cut into 2-inch pieces
- 1 medium sweet red pepper, cut into 2-inch pieces
- 1 medium sweet potato, peeled and quartered
- 6 small white potatoes, peeled and quartered
- 1 medium onion, slivered
- 1 (10 ounce) can tomatoes with green chilies
- 1 (8 ounce) can tomato sauce
- 2 tablespoons honey
- 2 Granny Smith apples, cut into 1-inch cubes
- 1 (15½ ounce) dark red kidney beans, drained
- 2 tablespoons chopped flat-leaf parsley
- Shredded Cheddar cheese and chopped black olives for garnish

Combine flour, cumin, chili powder, garlic powder and cinnamon in a large bowl. Add beef cubes and toss to coat. Heat oil in a large stockpot over medium-high heat. Brown beef cubes in batches. Return all beef to pot and add broth and juice. Cover and simmer about 1 hour or until meat is tender. Add peppers, potatoes, onion, tomatoes, tomato sauce and honey. Cover and simmer for 30 to 35 minutes until potatoes are tender. Stir in apples and beans. Cover and simmer for 15 minutes. Add parsley. Serve in shallow bowls and garnish with cheese and olives.

Serves 6

Tuscany Soup

- 2 teaspoons olive oil
- ½ cup chopped onion
- 2 (14½ ounce) cans chicken broth
- 1 (14½ ounce) can Italian-style stewed tomatoes
- 1 (16 ounce) package frozen potato pierogies
- 1 (15½ ounce) can red kidney beans, rinsed and drained
- 1 pound escarole or spinach, coarsely chopped
- 1 teaspoon Italian seasoning
- Parmesan cheese and crushed red pepper for garnish

Heat oil in a large saucepan over medium-high heat. Sauté onion for 3 minutes. Add broth and tomatoes. Bring to boil. Add pierogies and return to boil. Boil for 4 minutes. Add beans, escarole and seasoning. Return to boil. Reduce heat and simmer, covered, for 1 minute or until escarole is barely tender. Ladle into bowls and garnish with Parmesan cheese and pepper.

Serves 4-6

Tortellini may be substituted for pierogies.

Chicken Chili

1 teaspoon vegetable oil
1 pound ground chicken
1 tablespoon minced garlic
2 (14½ ounce) cans diced tomatoes
2 teaspoons ground cumin
2 teaspoons chili powder
1 (15½ ounce) can kidney beans, rinsed
1 (15 ounce) can black beans, rinsed
1 (15¼ ounce) can whole kernel corn
Reduced-fat sour cream, shredded jalapeño cheese, tortilla chips for garnish

Heat oil in a large nonstick skillet on medium high heat. Add chicken and cook 5 minutes until browned. Reduce to low heat and add garlic, tomatoes, cumin and chili powder. Cover and cook 5 minutes, stirring occasionally. Stir in kidney beans, black beans and corn. Cover and heat thoroughly. Serve with sour cream, cheese and tortilla chips.

Serves 6-8

Fresh Tomato Soup with Basil

2 tablespoons unsalted butter
2 leeks, well rinsed and chopped
4 tomatoes, peeled, seeded and chopped
4 cups chicken broth
Salt and pepper to taste
⅓ cup thinly sliced basil leaves

Melt butter in a stockpot. Cook leeks, stirring often, until softened. Add tomatoes and cook for 5 minutes. Pour in broth and simmer for 15 minutes. Season with salt and pepper. Add basil just before serving.

Serves 4-6

Missionary Bean Soup

1½ cups mixed dry beans
1 teaspoon salt
1 pound ham pieces
1 large onion, chopped
1 large garlic clove, chopped
1 (10 ounce) can diced tomatoes with green chilies
Juice of one lemon
Mexican cornbread

Rinse and soak beans overnight. Drain. Combine beans, 2 quarts water, salt and ham. Simmer for 3 hours. Add onion, garlic, tomatoes and juice. Simmer for 2 more hours. Serve with cornbread.

Serves 4-6

Tuscan Tomato Soup

- 2½ cups French bread cubes
- 1 teaspoon olive oil
- 4 garlic cloves, minced
- 2 (14 ounce) cans diced tomatoes
- 1 (14½ ounce) can chicken broth
- 1 tablespoon balsamic vinegar
- 1½ teaspoons dried parsley
- 1 teaspoon dried oregano
- ½ teaspoon pepper
- 5 teaspoons Parmesan cheese

Preheat oven to 400 degrees. To make croutons, arrange bread cubes in a single layer on a jelly-roll pan. Lightly coat bread with cooking spray. Bake at 400 degrees for 10 minutes or until dry and toasted. Set aside. Heat oil in a large saucepan over low-medium heat. Sauté garlic for 2 minutes. Add tomatoes, broth, vinegar, parsley, oregano and pepper. Bring to boil. Reduce heat and simmer for 10 minutes, stirring occasionally. Divide croutons among five bowls. Ladle 1 cup soup over croutons and sprinkle each with 1 teaspoon cheese.

Serves 5

Italian Mushroom Soup

- 1 tablespoon butter
- 1 tablespoon olive oil
- 1 medium onion, finely diced
- 1 tablespoon minced garlic
- 1 pound mushrooms, thinly sliced
- 3 tablespoons tomato paste
- 3 cups chicken broth
- 2 tablespoons red sweet Italian vermouth
- Salt and pepper to taste
- 1½ tablespoons dried parsley
- 2½ tablespoons Parmesan cheese
- ¾ cup cholesterol-free egg product or 4 egg yolks, beaten
- 1 tablespoon dry sherry
- Toasted bread slices

In a heavy stockpot, melt butter with oil. Sauté onion and garlic, stirring frequently, until translucent. Add mushrooms and sauté for 5 minutes. Stir in tomato paste and mix well. Add broth, vermouth and season with salt and pepper. Simmer for 15 minutes. In a bowl, whisk together parsley, Parmesan cheese and egg product. Add sherry and mix well. Whisk egg mixture into simmering soup. Serve as soon as egg mixture is incorporated. To serve, place a toasted bread slice in each bowl. Ladle soup over bread.

Serves 6

It is important that the soup not be boiling when the egg mixture is added because the egg may curdle. This will not ruin the soup but it detracts from the presentation.

Memories of Mom

My mom, Dora Helen McDonald Moree, was diagnosed with Multiple Myloma in April of 2001. She spent a year battling cancer. The first months were tough; however, the last three months were even tougher. Pain management and fragile bones became such an issue that she was recommended for twenty-four hour care at Whispering Pines Hospice in Ridgeland, Mississippi. Thanks to God, through my husband and my child's understanding, I was able to spend each weekend from February 2002 until May 4, 2002 taking care of her at the hospice hospital. During this time, I missed my husband, Mike, and my child, Jason, but I am so thankful for every second I was able to spend with my mom. I often wish I could have a conversation with mama, see her smile or listen for her humor. She was so fragile during her battle with cancer and I am sure her walk into the arms of God was much easier than her last few months.

My mom was buried at Carolina Presbyterian Church Cemetery, which is in the woods of Philadelphia, Mississippi. This area of Mississippi is a place my mom truly loved. She was so proud to have been a part of Carolina Presbyterian Church and was happiest when walking on the red dirt that is a part of Neshoba County. My mom is now safely in heaven. I realize good health, enjoying the little things in life, being close to family and having great friends are most important. These days my prayers seem to be strongest for those who suffer.

~Darlene Moree Oliver
Tupelo, MS

A new study shows that not getting enough potassium can raise your risk of stroke by 50%. Eat bananas, avocados, raisins, spinach, tomato juice, watermelon, orange juice and baked sweet potatoes.

~Reprinted from the book *Mama Said*
by Martha Houston Reed Hammond

Artichoke-Spinach Soup

- ½ cup chopped onion
- ⅓ cup chopped celery
- 2 garlic cloves, minced
- ¼ cup butter
- 4 cups chicken broth
- ¼ cup lemon juice
- 1 bay leaf
- Salt and pepper to taste
- 1 (10 ounce) package frozen chopped spinach, thawed and drained
- 1½ cups chopped artichoke hearts
- 2 egg yolks, slightly beaten
- 1 cup half-and-half

Sauté onion, celery and garlic in butter in a large saucepan until tender. Add broth, juice, bay leaf and season with salt and pepper. Simmer 15 minutes. Remove from heat. Remove bay leaf. Take 2 cups of onion mixture and puree with spinach in a blender. Pour into a separate saucepan. Take remaining onion mixture and puree with artichoke hearts. Add to saucepan containing spinach mixture. Stir in egg yolks and half-and-half. Cook over medium heat for 10 minutes. Check soup for seasoning. May store in refrigerator for 2 days.

Serves 6-8

Sweet Potato Chili

- 1 tablespoon olive oil
- 1 medium onion, chopped
- 2 tablespoons chili powder
- 1 teaspoon ground cumin
- 1 teaspoon ground coriander
- 2 garlic cloves, chopped
- 1 jalapeño pepper, seeded and chopped
- 2 (15 ounce) cans diced tomatoes
- ½ pound green beans, trimmed and cut in half
- 2 medium sweet potatoes, peeled and cut into ½-inch chunks
- 1 teaspoon salt
- 2 cups water
- 1 (15 ounce) can black beans, rinsed and drained

Heat oil in nonstick Dutch oven over medium heat until hot. Add onion and cook, stirring occasionally, for 10 minutes until tender. Add chili powder, cumin, coriander, garlic and jalapeño pepper and cook for 2 minutes. Add tomatoes, green beans, sweet potatoes, salt and water. Bring to boil over medium heat. Reduce heat, cover and simmer for 35 to 45 minutes until sweet potatoes and green beans are tender. Stir occasionally. Add black beans and heat thoroughly.

Serves 6

Vegetable Soup

- 4-5 pounds ground beef or stew meat
- 1 (10 ounce) package frozen vegetable blend (onions, bell pepper, celery), thawed
- Worcestershire sauce
- Garlic salt and garlic pepper
- Minced garlic to taste
- 1-2 (46 ounce) cans tomato juice
- 2 (14½ ounce) cans beef broth, double strength
- 2 soup cans of water
- 2 (14½ ounce) cans stewed tomatoes
- 3 beef bouillon cubes
- 1 (16 ounce) package frozen black-eyed peas
- 1 (16 ounce) package frozen butter beans
- 1 (16 ounce) package frozen green beans
- 1 (16 ounce) package frozen corn
- 1 (16 ounce) package frozen tomatoes
- 1 (16 ounce) package frozen onions
- 1 (16 ounce) package frozen carrots
- 3 potatoes, cut into 2-inch cubes or frozen
- 1 (16 ounce) package frozen okra, thawed

Brown meat with vegetable blend in a large stockpot. Season with Worcestershire sauce, garlic salt and garlic pepper. Add minced garlic. Stir in 1 can tomato juice, broth, water and tomatoes. Bring to boil. Add bouillon cubes. Continue to boil. Add black-eyed peas, butter beans, green beans, corn, tomatoes and onions. Stir in more tomato juice or water. Boil for 45 minutes. Add carrots, potatoes and okra. Return to boil for about 45 minutes until carrots are tender.

Serves 12-15

Black Bean Sausage Soup

- 8 ounces kielbasa sausage, sliced and quartered
- 1 onion, chopped
- 1 (14½ ounce) can stewed tomatoes, undrained
- 1 cup chunky salsa
- 1 (15 ounce) can black beans, undrained
- 1 (14½ ounce) can beef broth
- 2 garlic cloves, minced
- 1 teaspoon Tabasco sauce
- Salt and pepper to taste
- Chopped chives for garnish (optional)

Combine sausage, onion, tomatoes, salsa, black beans, broth, garlic, Tabasco, salt and pepper in a crock pot and cook on low for 4 hours or simmer on the stovetop for 1 hour. Garnish with chives.

Serves 8 (1-cup) servings

Corn and Black Bean Soup

- 1 quart chicken broth
- 2 cups water
- 1 onion, chopped
- 1 sweet red pepper, chopped
- 1 yellow pepper, chopped
- 2 Anaheim chilies, chopped
- 1 cup corn
- 3 (15 ounce) cans black beans, rinsed and drained
- 1 (12 ounce) bottle Corona beer
- 2 tablespoons ground cumin
- 1 tablespoon ground coriander
- Salt and pepper to taste
- 1 tablespoon lime juice
- 1 cup chopped fresh cilantro
- Sour cream and cilantro sprigs for garnish

Bring broth and water to boil. Add onion, red pepper and yellow pepper. Simmer for 15 minutes. Stir in chilies, corn, black beans, beer, cumin, coriander, salt, pepper, juice and cilantro. Simmer for an additional 10 minutes. Cool. Puree 2 cups of soup in a food processor. Return to pot and mix well. Serve hot garnished with a dollop of sour cream and sprig of cilantro.

Serves 6

Wild Rice and Mushroom Soup

- 1 cup finely chopped onion
- 1 teaspoon salt
- 1 teaspoon dried chervil
- 1 teaspoon curry powder
- ½ teaspoon dry mustard
- ½ teaspoon white pepper
- ¼ cup butter, melted
- 1 (8 ounce) package sliced mushrooms
- ½ cup finely sliced celery
- ½ cup all-purpose flour
- 6 cups chicken broth
- 2 cups cooked wild rice
- 2 cups half-and-half
- ⅔ cup dry sherry
- Chopped parsley and chopped chives for garnish

Combine onion, salt, chervil, curry, mustard, pepper with butter in a Dutch oven over medium heat. Cook, stirring constantly, until onion is tender. Add mushrooms and celery and cook until mushrooms are tender. Reduce heat to low. Stir in flour and cook 1 minute. Gradually add broth, stirring constantly, until thickened. Stir in rice, half-and-half and sherry. Cook until thoroughly heated. Ladle soup into individual soup bowls. Garnish with parsley and chives.

Serves 12 cups

Hearty Bean Soup

- 3 cups chopped parsnips or turnips
- 2 cups chopped carrots
- 1 cup chopped onion
- 1½ cups dry great Northern beans
- 5 cups water
- 1½ pounds smoked ham hocks or ham shanks
- 2 garlic cloves, minced
- 2 teaspoons salt
- ½ teaspoon pepper
- ⅛-¼ teaspoon Tabasco sauce

In a 5-quart slow cooker, place parsnips, carrot and onion. Top with beans. Add water, ham, garlic, salt, pepper and Tabasco. Cover and cook on high for 6 to 7 hours or until beans are tender. Remove meat and bones when cool enough to handle. Cut meat into bite-size pieces and return to slow cooker. Heat thoroughly.

Serves 6

Cheese Potato Soup

- 7 large red potatoes, peeled and diced
- 7 cups water
- 7 chicken bouillon cubes
- ½ onion, chopped
- 1 (8 ounce) package cream cheese, softened
- 1 (8 ounce) box processed cheese loaf (optional)

Combine potatoes, water, bouillon cubes and onion in a large stockpot. Cook until potatoes are fork tender. Add cream cheese and simmer for 30 minutes. Partially mash potatoes. Add cheese loaf and cook over low heat until cheese melts. This soup freezes well.

Serves 6

Baked Potato Soup

- ½ cup chopped onion
- ½ cup chopped celery
- 3 tablespoons butter, divided
- 4 cups half-and-half
- 1½ teaspoons salt
- 1½ teaspoons pepper
- 3 tablespoons all-purpose flour
- 2 large potatoes, baked, peeled, cut into ¾-inch cubes
- 1 cup shredded Cheddar cheese
- ½ cup bacon bits
- ½ cup sour cream
- Chopped fresh chives

Sauté onion and celery in 1 tablespoon butter in a large saucepan. Add half-and-half, salt and pepper. Bring to boil, stirring occasionally. Reduce to simmer. In a separate saucepan, melt 2 tablespoons butter. Whisk in flour and cook for 3 minutes. Whisk roux into cream soup until well blended. Stir in potatoes and heat thoroughly. Ladle soup into four bowls. Top each with cheese, bacon, sour cream and chives.

Serves 4

Broccoli Soup with White Beans

- ½ cup dry white beans
- 2 cups water
- 3 tablespoons olive oil
- ¼ cup plus 2 tablespoons butter
- 2 onions, diced
- 4 cups chicken broth, divided
- 2 bunches broccoli, cut into small pieces and steamed
- ½ cup small pasta, cooked al dente
- Parmesan cheese for garnish

Soak beans overnight. Drain. Cover with water. Bring to boil. Reduce heat and simmer for 30 minutes. Drain well. Toss with olive oil. Set aside.

Melt butter in large stockpot. Sauté onion until translucent. Add two cups broth and broccoli. Simmer 2 to 3 minutes. Add remaining broth. Heat thoroughly. To serve, ladle pasta, beans and broccoli mixture into individual soup bowls. Top with Parmesan cheese.

Serves 4-6

Delmarva Chicken Corn Chowder

- 3 slices bacons, diced
- ½ cup diced celery
- ½ cup diced onion
- ½ cup diced carrot
- 3 tablespoons all-purpose flour
- 4 cups chicken broth
- 2 cups chopped cooked chicken
- 2 cups peeled and chopped potatoes
- 1 (20 ounce) package frozen creamed corn, thawed
- 1 cup canned whole kernel corn or frozen
- ½ teaspoon poultry seasoning
- 1 cup heavy cream
- Salt and pepper to taste
- Cooked and crumbled bacon for garnish (optional)

Cook bacon in a Dutch oven until crisp. Remove bacon. Pour off drippings, reserving 1 tablespoon in pan. Sauté celery, onion and carrot until tender. Stir in flour, stirring constantly, for 3 minutes. Slowly whisk in broth, scraping sides of pan.

Add chicken, potatoes, creamed corn, whole corn and poultry seasoning. Cook for 10 minutes until potatoes are tender. Stir in reserved bacon and cream. Cook 3 minutes until heated through. Season with salt and pepper. Garnish with crumbled bacon. Serve with a congealed salad and corn sticks or muffins.

Serves 4-6

Pasta e Fagioli

- 8 slices salt pork
- 1½ onion, chopped
- 5 garlic cloves, chopped
- 4 tablespoons chopped parsley
- 2 tablespoons dried basil
- 3 bay leaves
- Salt, pepper and cayenne pepper to taste
- 1 (16 ounce) can whole tomatoes, broken apart with juice
- 4 (15 ounce) cans cannellini, undrained
- 2 (15 ounce) cans chickpeas, undrained
- 3 cans of water
- 5 tablespoons grated Romano cheese
- ¼ head escarole, rinsed and chopped into small pieces
- 1 potato, peeled
- Olive oil for sautéing
- 1 (16 ounce) package ditalini pasta or other small pasta, cooked al dente

Cook salt pork in a large stockpot. Remove pork leaving drippings in pot. In a separate saucepan, sauté onion, garlic, parsley, basil, bay leaves, salt, pepper and cayenne in olive oil. Transfer to pot with drippings.

Stir in tomatoes with juice, cannellini beans, chickpeas and water. Press some beans along side of pot. Add cheese and escarole. Bring to boil. Add potato. Reduce heat, partially cover and simmer 1 hour to 1 hour, 30 minutes. Stir every 20 minutes.

Remove potato and serve separately. Place hot pasta in a serving bowl. Pour bean mixture over pasta and mix thoroughly.

Serves 6-8

Oyster Stew

- 2 cups oyster liquor, divided
- 2 cups heavy cream
- ¼ cup butter
- Celery salt and pepper to taste
- 1 quart oysters, well drained

Bring 1 cup oyster liquor to boil in a large saucepan. Simmer 5 minutes. Skim off foamy top. Add cream, butter and season with celery salt and pepper. Cook oysters in remaining cup of liquor for 5 minutes until edges begin to curl. Strain and add to cream mixture. Serve immediately.

Serves 4

Bouillabaisse

Rouille (Make and reserve for Bouillabaisse)

- **1 head of garlic, cut crosswise in half**
- **Pinch of salt**
- **½ teaspoon plus ½ cup olive oil**
- **1 egg**
- **3 teaspoons fresh lemon juice**
- **1 tablespoon chopped parsley**
- **½ teaspoon salt**
- **¼ teaspoon cayenne pepper**

Preheat oven to 375 degrees. To make rouille, place garlic on a square of foil. Sprinkle with salt and drizzle with ½ teaspoon oil. Seal foil over garlic and roast 30 minutes or until soft. Press garlic from skin and place in food processor with egg. Blend 10 seconds. Add juice. With motor running, slowly add ½ cup oil. Mixture will be thick like mayonnaise. Add parsley, salt and cayenne. Pulse 3 to 4 times. Store up to 24 hours in a covered container in the refrigerator.

Bouillabaisse

- **1¼ pounds fish fillets (perch, bass, catfish, orange roughy, or trout)**
- **2 teaspoons salt, divided**
- **¼-½ teaspoon cayenne pepper, divided**
- **1½ cups chopped onions**
- **1 cup chopped bell peppers**
- **½ cup chopped celery**
- **1 tablespoon chopped garlic**
- **¼ cup butter**
- **2 cups chopped, peeled and seeded tomatoes or canned tomatoes**
- **3 bay leaves**
- **½ pound medium shrimp, peeled and deveined**
- **¼ cup dry white wine**
- **1 tablespoon chopped parsley**

Season fish with half the salt and cayenne. Combine onion, bell pepper, celery and garlic in a bowl. Season with remaining salt and cayenne. Melt butter in a large Dutch oven or stockpot. Add one-third vegetable mixture, tossing to coat in butter. Place one-third tomatoes and 1 bay leaf over vegetables. Top with one-third of fish. Repeat with two more layers of ingredients in same order. Scatter shrimp on top. Pour wine down the side of pot. Cover and simmer 1 hour without removing the lid. Remove the bay leaves. Serve in large soup bowls and garnish with parsley. Drizzle 1 tablespoon of the Rouille over the Bouillabaisse. Serve with French bread and green salad. May be served over rice.

Serves 5-6

Lagniappe Crawfish and Corn Chowder

For an over salted soup or stew, add a sliced, peeled raw potato and simmer for 10-15 minutes. Remove the potato before serving the soup.

~from The New Food Lover's Tiptionary

- **1 large onion, finely chopped**
- **½ cup celery, finely chopped**
- **¼ cup butter**
- **1 teaspoon minced garlic**
- **¼ cup all-purpose flour**
- **4 cups shoe peg corn**
- **4 cups chicken broth**
- **2 tablespoons Tabasco sauce**
- **1 bunch green onions, finely chopped, white and green parts**
- **¼ cup chopped fresh parsley**
- **Salt and pepper to taste**
- **1½ pounds cooked crawfish tails**
- **2 cups heavy cream**

Sauté onion and celery in butter until tender. Add garlic and whisk in flour. Stir until blended. Add corn and broth, stirring until thickened. Add Tabasco, green onions, parsley and season with salt and pepper. Simmer for 15 minutes. Add crawfish and cream. Do not boil. Simmer 5 minutes longer.

Serves 4-6

Shrimp Chowder

If you can make soups a day ahead and refrigerate overnight, do so to let the flavors meld and heighten.

~from The New Food Lover's Tiptionary

- **1 pound shrimp**
- **2 tablespoons butter**
- **6 green onions, chopped including tops**
- **2 (10¾ ounce) cans cream of potato soup**
- **2 cups milk**
- **½ cup shredded Cheddar cheese**
- **2 tablespoons dry sherry or vermouth**
- **Dash of white pepper**
- **Snipped parsley for garnish**

Cook shrimp in salted boiling water for 5 minutes until pink. Cool, peel and devein shrimp. In a 2-quart saucepan, melt butter and sauté green onion. Stir in soup and milk. Bring to boil over medium heat, stirring occasionally. Add cheese, sherry, pepper and shrimp. Cook for 5 minutes, stirring occasionally, but do not boil. Ladle into soup bowls and garnish with parsley.

Serves 4

Great reheated the next day!

Creole Gumbo

- ¼ cup vegetable oil
- 2 tablespoons all-purpose flour
- 1 cup chopped celery with leaves
- 1 large onion, chopped
- 1 bell pepper, chopped
- 1 (16 ounce) can whole tomatoes
- 3 cups chicken broth
- 1 bay leaf
- ¼ teaspoon ground thyme
- 2 cups sliced okra
- 2 tablespoons chopped fresh parsley
- Salt to taste
- ¼ teaspoon Tabasco sauce
- 3 cups coarsely cut cooked chicken
- 1 pound shrimp (raw or cooked)
- 1 pint oysters
- Hot cooked rice

Heat oil in a large saucepan. Whisk in flour until dark brown. Add celery, onion and pepper and cook until tender. Add tomatoes, broth, bay leaf, thyme, okra, parsley, salt and Tabasco. Cover and simmer for 45 minutes. Add chicken, shrimp and oysters. Taste seasonings and simmer 10 minutes longer. Remove bay leaf. Serve in large, shallow bowls over hot rice.

Serves 6-8

Don't pluck thyme leaves one by one. Instead, pinch the top of a sprig and run the thumb and forefinger of your other hand down the length of the stem. This also works for marjoram, and oregano.

~from The New Food Lover's Tiptionary

Seafood Bisque

- 2 (6 ounce) cans crabmeat, undrained
- 2 (6 ounce) cans shrimp, undrained
- 1 (10¾ ounce) can tomato soup
- 1 (10¾ ounce) can cream of shrimp soup
- 1 cup half-and-half
- Large dash sherry (not cooking sherry)

Combine crabmeat, shrimp, tomato soup, shrimp soup, half-and-half and sherry in a buttered crockpot. Cover and cook on low heat for 3 to 5 hours, stirring occasionally.

Serves 4-6

Bama's Catering

For as long as I can remember, I've been drawn to some form of cooking. I grew up in rural Pinedale, Mississippi, at a time when mealtime meant families sharing the day's events, laughing together, and most importantly growing closer. I love to think back to the day my mother taught me to bake a cake, or how my father taught me to fry fish so that it would be so tender and moist it would melt in our mouths! These are the memories that instilled in me a great passion for cooking – not because of the joy it brings me, but because of the joy that I am able to spread to people through the foods that I prepare.

This love of cooking and people led me to a career in the catering business that lasted twenty-five years. As I reflect on those wonderful days gone by, I still laugh out loud when I recall the time I prepared for an entire week for a wedding reception only to show up at the church to find that there was no one there! You can only imagine the shock and surprise I felt when I finally realized that yes, in fact, I was not only at the wrong church, but I was also in the wrong town! This is just one example of the effect a harried schedule along with raising three children had on this old cook's mind!

Good luck in your pursuit of the noble goals you have set for yourselves in providing compassionate care for our aging population. I hope that this small contribution aids in furthering those goals. Happy cooking and as always, God Bless.

~Bama Strawn
Tupelo, MS

Food has certainly become a big part of my life since marrying into the Malone family several years ago. The Malone family has been in the catfish restaurant business for twenty-six years. I have enjoyed learning a lot about cooking and serving large portions of food.

~Missy Malone, Saltillo, MS

Mae's Fruit Salad

- 2 (¼ ounce) envelopes unflavored gelatin
- ¼ cup cold water
- 1 cup hot fruit juice (from pineapple and cherry juice)
- 1 (20 ounce) can pineapple chunks, juice reserved
- 1 (16 ounce) can white cherries, juice reserved
- 1 (16 ounce) can grapefruit sections
- ¼ cup sugar
- ¼ teaspoon salt
- ¼ cup lemon juice

Dissolve gelatin in water. Combine gelatin with hot fruit juice, pineapple, cherries and grapefruit. Add sugar and salt and stir until dissolved. Pour in lemon juice. Mix thoroughly. Pour mixture into a 13 x 9 x 2-inch baking dish. Refrigerate until ready to serve.

Serves 12

Grape Salad

- 1 (8 ounce) package cream cheese, softened
- 1 (8 ounce) container sour cream
- ½ cup sugar
- 1 teaspoon vanilla
- 8 cups grapes, rinsed and dried
- ¼ cup packed brown sugar
- 1 cup pecans

Blend cream cheese, sour cream, sugar and vanilla. Add grapes and mix thoroughly to coat. Spoon mixture into a serving bowl. Sprinkle with brown sugar. Top with pecans. Refrigerate overnight before serving.

Serves 8

Congealed Buttermilk Salad

- 1 (20 ounce) can crushed pineapple with juice
- 1 (6 ounce) package orange or strawberry gelatin
- 2 cups buttermilk
- 1 (8 ounce) container frozen whipped topping, thawed
- 1 cup nuts

Heat pineapple with juice in a saucepan. Do not boil. Add gelatin and stir to dissolve. Pour in buttermilk. Remove from heat and cool. Fold in whipped topping and nuts. Spoon into a serving bowl. Refrigerate until set.

Serves 6-8

Spiced Peach Salad

Rather one bite of a peach than a basketful of apricots.

~Chinese proverb

~from The New Food Lover's Tiptionary

- **2 jars pickled peaches, drained reserving 1 cup juice and chopped**
- **2 (3 ounce) packages lemon flavored gelatin**
- **½ cup water**
- **½ cup orange juice**
- **Juice of one lemon**
- **Dash of salt**
- **1 cup chopped pecans**
- **Lettuce leaves**

Heat peach juice in a saucepan. Stir in gelatin until dissolved. Add water, orange juice, lemon juice, salt, pecans and chopped peaches. Mix well. Pour into a 6-cup ring mold or 11 x 7 x 2-inch baking dish. Refrigerate until set. Serve over lettuce leaves.

Serves 6-8

Pickled peaches (page 194) are difficult to find in the grocery store and small, fresh canning peaches are not always available. This is a good, tasty substitute.

Orange Spinach Salad

On the subject of spinach; divide into little piles. Rearrange again into new piles. After five or six maneuvers, sit back and say you are full.

~Delia Ephron, American author

~from The New Food Lover's Tiptionary

- **6 tablespoons sugar, divided**
- **¼ cup rice wine vinegar**
- **½ teaspoon Tabasco sauce**
- **½ teaspoon salt**
- **6 tablespoons vegetable oil**
- **½ cup pecans, halved**
- **6 cups baby spinach, rinsed**
- **1 cup halved seedless green grapes**
- **1 (11 ounce) can Mandarin oranges, drained**
- **1 medium Vidalia onion, thinly sliced**

To make dressing, combine 4 tablespoons sugar, vinegar, Tabasco, salt and oil in a saucepan. Cook, stirring constantly, until sugar is dissolved. Refrigerate until cold. In a separate saucepan, melt remaining 2 tablespoons sugar. Add pecans and cook until browned. Remove from pan and set aside to cool. In a large bowl, toss nuts, spinach, grapes, oranges and onion. Pour dressing over salad and toss to coat.

Serves 6

Pear Salad with Orange Whipped Cream

1 (8 ounce) package cream cheese, softened
2 tablespoons mayonnaise
18 gingersnap cookies, crushed
½ cup crushed pineapple
1 egg, beaten
½ cup sugar
½ cup orange juice
1 cup heavy cream, whipped
1 (29 ounce) can pear halves, drained

Blend cream cheese, mayonnaise, cookie crumbs and pineapple. Refrigerate. Combine egg, sugar and orange juice in the top of a double boiler. Cook, stirring constantly, until thick. Cool and fold in whipped cream. Place a pear half on individual salad plates. Spoon 1½ tablespoons cream cheese mixture into pear well. Top with a dollop of orange whipped cream.

Serves 6

When one has tasted watermelons one knows what angels eat. It was not a Southern watermelon that Eve took; we know it because she repented.

~Mark Twain

~from The New Food Lover's Tiptionary

Delta Frozen Salad

1 (12 ounce) can frozen orange juice concentrate, thawed
2 orange juice cans filled with water
1 cup sugar
1 (16 ounce) can apricots, drained and chopped
1 (20 ounce) can crushed pineapple, drained
6 medium bananas, cubed
1 (8 ounce) package chopped walnuts
1 (7 ounce) package sweetened coconut
36 foil muffin cup liners

Combine orange juice, water and sugar in a large bowl. Add apricots, pineapple, banana, walnuts and coconut and mix well. Divide mixture among 36 lined muffin cups (or pour into a 13 x 9 x 2-inch baking dish). Freeze overnight. Prior to serving, remove from muffin liner (or cut into squares) and place on a bed of leaf lettuce.

Serves 36

Store frozen salads in large plastic bags until ready to serve. This salad may be frozen for several weeks.

Apple Salad

- 1 (20 ounce) can crushed pineapple with juice
- ½ cup all-purpose flour
- ¾ cup sugar
- ¼ teaspoon salt
- ⅛ cup butter
- 4 medium Granny Smith apples, peeled and chopped
- 1 (8 ounce) container frozen whipped topping, thawed
- 1 (8 ounce) package cream cheese, softened
- Toasted chopped nuts for garnish

Combine pineapple with juice, flour, sugar and salt in a saucepan. Cook and stir over low heat until thickened. Remove from heat. Stir in butter and cool. Add apples and mix well. Pour into a serving bowl. Blend whipped topping and cream cheese until smooth. Spread over apples. Top with nuts.

Serves 6-8

Layered Fruits in Lemon-Pear Sauce with Toasted Almonds

- 1 (29 ounce) can pear halves in heavy syrup, drained, reserving 1 cup syrup
- 1 egg, beaten
- 2 tablespoons all-purpose flour
- 1 teaspoon butter
- 2 teaspoons lemon juice
- 1 cup heavy cream, whipped and sweetened with powdered sugar
- 2 tablespoons powdered sugar
- 1 (16 ounce) can pineapple chunks, drained
- 1 banana, sliced
- 1 pint strawberries, sliced
- 1 (11 ounce) can Mandarin oranges, drained
- 2 kiwi, refrigerated
- ¼ cup slivered almonds, toasted

Combine pear syrup, egg and flour in saucepan. Cook over medium heat, stirring often, until thickened. Stir in butter and juice. Cool completely. Fold in whipped cream. Cut 4 pear halves in half lengthwise and reserve. Dice remaining pears. Layer diced pears, pineapple, banana, strawberries and oranges in a large glass bowl. Spread cooled topping over all. Cover and refrigerate overnight. Just before serving, peel and slice kiwi. Decorate layered fruit with reserved pear slices, kiwi and almonds.

Serves 8-10

Baked Fruit

- 1 (16 ounce) can pears, reserving juice
- 1 (16 ounce) can peaches, reserving juice
- 1 (20 ounce) can pineapple chunks, reserving juice
- 1 (16 ounce) can white cherries, reserving juice
- ½ cup golden raisins
- 1½ oranges, sliced, do not peel
- 2 tablespoons all-purpose flour
- ¾ cup sugar
- ½ teaspoon salt
- ¾ cup mixed juice
- 3 tablespoons butter
- ½ cup sherry

Drain all fruit together. Reserve ¾ cup mixed juice for sauce. Cover raisins with boiling water. Let stand. Cover orange slices with water in a saucepan. Bring to boil. Simmer for 5 minutes. Drain raisins and oranges together. To make sauce, sift together flour, sugar and salt into a saucepan. Add mixed juice and butter. Cook and stir until thickened. Cool and stir in sherry.

Arrange fruit in the bottom of a 13 x 9 x 2-inch baking dish. Pour sauce over fruit. Cover and refrigerate overnight. Bake at 350 degrees for 1 hour.

Serves 8-10

Town and Country Salad

- ¼ onion, minced
- ½ cup sugar
- ½ cup vegetable oil, divided
- ⅓ cup apple cider vinegar, divided
- 1 teaspoon dry mustard
- 1½ teaspoons poppy seeds
- ½ cup slivered almonds
- ¼ cup sugar
- Romaine, Bibb or red leaf lettuce, torn
- Strawberries, sliced
- Brie cheese, cubed (do not use double-cream Brie)

Whisk together onion, sugar, half the oil and half the vinegar. Mix well. Slowly add the remaining oil and vinegar. Stir in mustard and poppy seeds. Refrigerate. Combine almonds and sugar in a skillet. Cook over medium heat, stirring constantly, until sugar melts and is browned. Spread onto foil to cool. Combine lettuce leaves, strawberries and cheese in a serving bowl. Pour in poppy seed dressing and toss to coat. Top with caramelized almonds.

Serves 8

Greek Potato Salad: Patatosalata

Keep potatoes for salad snowy-white by adding a teaspoon or two of lemon juice to the cooking water.

~from
The New Food Lover's Tiptionary

2 pounds red potatoes, boiled and quartered
1 medium red onion, halved and sliced into half moons
2 green onions, thinly chopped
24 kalamata olives, pitted and halved
1 tablespoon finely chopped dill
1 tablespoon finely chopped oregano
¼ cup olive oil
1 tablespoon red wine vinegar
Juice from one lemon
Kosher salt and ground pepper to taste

In a salad bowl, combine potatoes, onion, green onion, olives, dill and oregano. In a small bowl, whisk together oil, vinegar, lemon juice and season with salt and pepper. Pour dressing over salad and toss to coat. Refrigerate until ready to serve.

Serves 4-6

Bacon Blue Cheese Potato Salad

2½ pounds red potatoes, cut into eighths
½ cup mayonnaise
¼ cup sour cream
1 tablespoon red wine vinegar
½ teaspoon salt
¼ teaspoon pepper
6 slices bacon, cooked and crumbled
4-6 green onions, chopped
3 ounces crumbled blue cheese

In a large pot, combine potatoes with enough water to cover by 2 inches. Bring to boil. Cook for 20 minutes or until potatoes are tender. Drain and set aside. Whisk together mayonnaise, sour cream, vinegar, salt and pepper until smooth. Place potatoes, bacon, onion and blue cheese in a large bowl. Gently stir in mayonnaise mixture. Serve immediately or cover and refrigerate until ready to serve.

Serves 6-8

Jim's Broccoli Salad

- **¾ cup mayonnaise**
- **½ cup sugar**
- **2 tablespoons vinegar**
- **1 bunch broccoli, cut into florets**
- **½ red onion, sliced**
- **4 slices bacon, cooked and crumbled**
- **½ cup pecans**

Combine mayonnaise, sugar and vinegar in a small saucepan. Cook over low heat until sugar dissolves. Set aside. Place broccoli in a large bowl. Pour boiling water over broccoli. Refrigerate for 30 minutes. Drain water. Add onion, bacon and pecans. Toss dressing with salad. Refrigerate until ready to serve.

Serves 4

Feta, Green Bean and Walnut Salad

- **½ cup extra virgin olive oil**
- **¼ cup white wine vinegar**
- **1 tablespoon dill or ½ teaspoon dried**
- **1 garlic clove, minced**
- **Salt and pepper to taste**
- **1½ pounds green beans, fresh or frozen**
- **½ medium red onion, thinly sliced**
- **4 ounces crumbled feta cheese**
- **1 cup coarsely chopped walnuts, toasted**

Whisk together oil, vinegar, dill, garlic and season with salt and pepper. Refrigerate dressing at least 2 hours. Steam green beans until crisp-tender. Plunge beans into a bowl of ice water to stop cooking. Mix beans, onion, feta cheese and walnuts in a serving bowl. Pour dressing over salad at least 1 hour before serving. May serve cold or room temperature.

Serves 6

Betsey's Gazpacho Salad

- **Broken dry toast**
- **Sliced tomatoes**
- **Salt and pepper to taste**
- **Finely chopped garlic**
- **Sliced onions**
- **Chopped bell pepper**
- **Sliced cucumbers**
- **Mayonnaise**

Place a layer of broken toast in the bottom of a salad bowl. Layer sliced tomatoes and season with salt and pepper. Sprinkle with garlic. Layer sliced onions. Sprinkle with bell pepper. Layer sliced cucumbers. Spread a layer of mayonnaise. Repeat all layers in same order until bowl is full. Refrigerate at least 12 hours. Toss once or twice. Each layer is solid except garlic and bell pepper.

Serves 8-10

Crunchy Romaine Toss

- 1 cup vegetable oil
- 1 cup sugar
- ½ cup wine vinegar
- 1 tablespoon soy sauce
- Salt and pepper to taste
- 1 cup walnuts, chopped
- 1 package Ramen noodles, uncooked, broken, discard flavor packet
- ¼ cup unsalted butter
- 1 bunch broccoli, coarsely chopped
- 1 head romaine lettuce, rinsed and torn
- 4 green onions, chopped

Whisk together oil, sugar, vinegar, soy sauce, salt and pepper until sugar dissolves. Refrigerate sweet and sour dressing. Brown walnuts and noodles in butter. Remove to paper towels to cool. Combine walnuts, noodles, broccoli, romaine and green onions in a serving bowl. Just prior to serving, pour on sweet and sour dressing and toss to coat.

Serves 4

Vicksburg Tomato Aspic Salad

- 2 (3 ounce) packages cream cheese, softened
- 1 teaspoon minced onion
- 2 teaspoons pickle relish
- 2 tablespoons mayonnaise
- 2 teaspoons chili sauce
- Tabasco sauce to taste
- 5 tablespoons gelatin
- 1 (46 ounce) can tomato juice or tomato-vegetable juice cocktail
- 3 onions, quartered
- 3 stalks celery, chopped
- 3 tablespoons celery seed
- 3 tablespoons vinegar
- 1 tablespoon Worcestershire sauce
- Juice of two lemons
- 3 bay leaves
- 1 tablespoon sugar
- Salt, cayenne pepper and Tabasco sauce to taste
- Bibb lettuce, torn

Blend cream cheese, onion, relish, mayonnaise, chili sauce and Tabasco until smooth. Shape into balls. Set aside. Sprinkle gelatin over 1 cup cold water. Set aside to soften. Combine tomato juice, onion, celery, celery seed, vinegar, Worcestershire sauce, lemon juice, bay leaves, sugar, salt, cayenne and Tabasco in a large stockpot. Bring to boil. Remove from heat. Stir in gelatin. Strain mixture into salad molds. Cool to lukewarm. Drop a cheese ball into each mold. Refrigerate at least 6 hours. Unmold and serve on a bed of Bibb lettuce.

Serves 8-10

Sweet Potato Salad

- **3 pounds sweet potatoes, cooked, peeled and cubed**
- **½ cup finely chopped onion**
- **1 cup chopped bell pepper**
- **¼ teaspoon pepper**
- **1½ cups reduced-fat mayonnaise**
- **Dash of Tabasco sauce**

Combine potatoes, onion, bell pepper and pepper in a large bowl. Stir in mayonnaise and Tabasco. Mix well. Cover and refrigerate at least one hour before serving.

Serves 10

A surprisingly different taste from regular potato salad.

Hidden Treasure

- **2 cups mayonnaise**
- **½ cup horseradish, drained**
- **2 teaspoons dry mustard**
- **2 teaspoons lemon juice**
- **½ teaspoon salt**
- **1 pound medium shrimp, cooked and peeled**
- **1 pint cherry tomatoes, halved**
- **1 (6 ounce) can black olives, drained and pitted**
- **1 (8 ounce) can water chestnuts, drained**
- **1 (7 ounce) can whole mushrooms, drained**
- **½ head cauliflower, separated into small florets**

Combine mayonnaise, horseradish, mustard, juice and salt and mix well. Set aside. Combine shrimp, tomatoes, olives, water chestnuts, mushrooms and cauliflower in a serving bowl. Add mayonnaise mixture and toss to coat. Refrigerate until ready to serve.

Serves 6-8

Old Spain Caesar Salad

- **2 eggs**
- **2 tablespoons dry mustard**
- **1 tablespoon Worcestershire sauce**
- **½ cup apple cider vinegar**
- **1 teaspoon salt**
- **2 (2 ounce) cans anchovies**
- **2 large garlic cloves**
- **½ cup vegetable oil**
- **¼ cup lemon juice**
- **2 heads Romaine lettuce, cut into small strips**
- **1 cup croutons**
- **¼ cup Parmesan cheese**
- **Pepper to taste**

To make dressing, blend eggs, mustard, Worcestershire sauce, vinegar, salt, anchovies, garlic, oil and juice in a blender until smooth. Combine lettuce, croutons and cheese in a serving bowl. Season with pepper. Add dressing and toss to coat.

Serves 6-8

Red, White and Green Salad

- 2 cups mayonnaise
- 1 cup sour cream
- 2 tablespoons vinegar
- ¼ cup sugar
- 2 bunches broccoli, cut into florets, about 5 cups
- 1 head cauliflower, cut into florets, about 2½ cups
- 1 bunch green onions, chopped including tops
- 2 cups cherry tomatoes, halved
- 1 cucumber, sliced
- Salt and pepper to taste
- Leaf lettuce

Mix together mayonnaise, sour cream, vinegar and sugar. Combine broccoli, cauliflower, green onion, tomatoes and cucumber in a large bowl. Pour dressing over vegetables and toss to coat. Season with salt and pepper. Cover and refrigerate at least 24 hours. Drain vegetables when ready to serve. Arrange vegetables on leaf lettuce on individual salad plates. Store drained dressing in the refrigerator to use again.

Serves 6-8

Orzo Salad

- ¼ cup lemon juice
- Zest from one lemon
- 4-6 tablespoons olive oil
- ¼ cup chopped dill
- 2 garlic cloves, chopped
- Salt and pepper to taste
- 1 pound orzo pasta, cooked al dente
- 6 ounces crumbled feta cheese
- 1 yellow pepper, finely chopped
- 1 sweet red pepper, finely chopped
- ½ cup kalamata olives, pitted and quartered
- 2 green onions, finely sliced
- 1 tablespoon finely chopped oregano

For vinaigrette, whisk together juice, zest, oil, dill and garlic. Season with salt and pepper. In a large bowl, combine cooked pasta, feta cheese, yellow pepper, sweet red pepper, olives and green onion. Pour vinaigrette over pasta and mix well. Add oregano and season with salt and pepper.

Serves 6-8

Sometimes one little spark of kindness is all it takes to re-ignite the light of hope in a heart that's blinded by pain.

~Anonymous

Pasta Salad

- 1 (16 ounce) package small multi-colored egg noodles
- 1 bunch green onions, chopped
- 1 red onion, finely chopped
- 1 bell pepper, finely chopped
- 1 tomato, chopped
- 1 (16 ounce) bottle McCormick Salad Supreme
- 1 (16 ounce) bottle zesty Italian dressing

Cook noodles in a large pot of salted boiling water until tender. Drain. Combine noodles, green onion, red onion, pepper, tomato, salad dressing and Italian dressing and mix well. Refrigerate until ready to serve.

Serves 6-8

This recipe was contributed by State Representative Eloise Scott. Mrs. Scott taught home economics for many years in Lee County area schools. She is beloved by her students and the many people she has served.

Chicken Pasta Salad with Feta and Artichokes

- 2-4 boneless, skinless chicken breast halves, seasoned with salt and pepper
- Juice from one lemon
- Olive oil to cover
- 2-3 garlic cloves, minced
- 1 heaping tablespoon Dijon mustard
- Juice of one-half lemon
- ¼ cup white wine vinegar
- Dash of sugar (optional)
- ¼-½ cup extra virgin olive oil
- Kosher salt and pepper to taste
- 1 pound penne pasta, cooked al dente and drained
- 4-6 ounces crumbled feta cheese
- 1 small red onion, diced
- 1 sweet red pepper, sliced into thin strips
- 1 (14 ounce) jar artichoke hearts, drained and quartered
- ¼ cup chopped parsley

Marinate chicken in mixture of lemon juice, oil and garlic for 30 minutes or up to 4 hours. Grill chicken over medium-high heat for 5 to 6 minutes per side or until done. Set aside to cool. To make dressing, combine mustard, lemon juice, vinegar, sugar, oil, salt and pepper in a jar. Seal tightly and shake well. Refrigerate dressing. Combine pasta, feta cheese, onion, pepper strips and artichokes in a large bowl. Diagonally slice cooled chicken into strips and add to pasta. Add dressing and mix well. Refrigerate until ready to serve. Sprinkle with parsley prior to serving.

Serves 6-8

Ginna's Pasta with Feta and Spinach

Ginna Parsons is a food editor for the Northeast Mississippi Daily Journal. She has graciously supported our efforts to bring this cookbook together.

~Holly Temple, Tupelo, MS

6 cups penne pasta
3 tablespoons extra virgin olive oil
1 tablespoon balsamic vinegar
3 garlic cloves, minced
1 (2¼ ounce) can sliced black olives, drained
2 cups fresh spinach, rinsed and chopped
¾ cup crumbled feta cheese

Cook pasta according to package directions. In a large bowl, combine oil, vinegar, garlic, olives, spinach and feta cheese. When pasta is cooked, drain. Add hot pasta to bowl and allow spinach to wilt. Mix salad thoroughly. Serve warm or room temperature.

Serves 4-6

Marinated Shrimp Salad

2 (14 ounce) jars artichoke hearts, drained and quartered
3 (4 ounce) jars whole mushrooms, drained
1 medium Vidalia onion, chopped
15 cherry tomatoes, halved
½ cup extra virgin olive oil
¾ cup balsamic vinegar
4 garlic cloves, minced
1 (0.7 ounce) envelope Italian dressing mix
2 pounds medium shrimp, cooked, peeled and deveined
1 head Romaine lettuce, torn

Combine artichokes, mushrooms, onion and tomatoes in a bowl. Whisk together oil, vinegar, garlic and dressing mix until blended. Add shrimp to artichoke mixture and toss. Add dressing and toss to coat. Cover and marinate in refrigerator for 2 to 3 hours. Serve over Romaine lettuce.

Serves 8-10

May also serve with wheat crackers.

Rice Salad à la Nicole

- 1½ cups mayonnaise
- 1 tablespoon spicy brown mustard
- 2 teaspoons lemon juice
- Dash of Tabasco sauce or more to taste
- 2 cups cooked rice
- 1 (6 ounce) package frozen crabmeat, cooked
- 2 pounds lobster meat or scallops, cooked
- ¾ pound shrimp, cooked, peeled and deveined
- 1 cup cooked diced ham
- 1 (8 ounce) can black olives, sliced
- 4 stalks celery, chopped
- 1 large tomato, chopped
- 2 hard-cooked eggs, chopped
- Parsley sprigs for garnish

Whisk together mayonnaise, mustard, juice and Tabasco. Set aside. Combine rice, crabmeat, lobster, shrimp, ham, olives, celery, tomato and eggs in a large serving bowl. Add dressing and gently toss. Refrigerate until cold. Prior to serving, garnish with parsley.

Serves 8

Better to prepare salad a day in advance.

Fruit and Chicken Salad

- ½ cup fat free sour cream
- ½ cup fat free mayonnaise
- 1 tablespoon frozen orange juice concentrate
- ⅛ teaspoon ground ginger
- Dash of cayenne pepper
- 2 cups thinly sliced celery
- 1½ cups seedless grapes, sliced
- 1½ cups chopped cooked chicken
- ½ cup dried apricots, slivered
- Lettuce leaves
- Plum tomatoes, sliced
- 1 cucumber, sliced

Whisk together sour cream, mayonnaise, orange juice, ginger and cayenne. Combine celery, grapes, chicken and apricots in a bowl. Add sour cream dressing and mix well. Cover and refrigerate for 4 hours. To serve, arrange lettuce leaves on individual salad plates. Place a scoop of chicken salad in center of lettuce. Arrange tomatoes and cucumbers around chicken salad.

Serves 4

Baked Chicken Salad

- 3 cups cooked chicken, diced
- 1 tablespoon minced onion
- 1 cup diced celery
- 1 (8 ounce) can water chestnuts, drained and sliced
- 1 teaspoon salt
- 1 teaspoon pepper
- 2 tablespoons lemon juice
- 1 cup mayonnaise
- 1 (2 ounce) jar chopped pimentos
- ½ cup slivered almonds
- ½ can French fried onion rings, crumbled
- Shredded Cheddar cheese

Combine chicken, onion, celery, water chestnuts, salt, pepper, juice, mayonnaise, pimentos and almonds. Pour mixture into a greased 3-quart casserole dish. Top with cheese and onion rings. Cover and bake at 350 degrees for 30 minutes.

Serves 6-8

Dill Chicken Salad

- 1 (1 ounce) envelope dry ranch dressing mix
- 1 (16 ounce) container sour cream
- 1 cup mayonnaise
- 1 cup milk
- 3 tablespoons minced fresh dill or 1 tablespoon dried
- ½ teaspoon garlic salt
- 1 (16 ounce) package rotini pasta, cooked al dente
- 3 cups cubed cooked chicken
- 1 cup chopped celery
- ½ cup chopped onion
- 1 (10 ounce) package frozen green peas, thawed

Whisk together dressing mix, sour cream, mayonnaise, milk, dill and garlic salt until smooth. Set dressing aside. Combine pasta, chicken, celery, onion and peas in a serving bowl. Pour dressing over salad and toss to coat. Refrigerate at least 3 hours.

Serves 10-12

Holly's Chicken Salad

2 cups chopped cooked chicken
4 hard-cooked eggs, chopped
1 cup seedless grapes, halved
½ cup pecans, chopped
½ cup finely chopped celery
½ cup chopped sweet pickles
1 cup mayonnaise
1 teaspoon sugar
Salt and pepper to taste
Lettuce leaves

Combine chicken, eggs, grapes, pecans, celery, pickles, mayonnaise, sugar and season with salt and pepper and mix well. Arrange lettuce on salad plates and top with chicken salad.

Serves 4-6

Smoked Duck Salad

1 cup vegetable oil
1 cup sugar
½ cup red wine vinegar
3 teaspoons soy sauce
Focaccia bread
½-¾ cup crumbled goat cheese, room temperature, divided
4 duck breasts, smoked and thinly sliced
4-5 cups mixed salad greens
1 cup pine nuts, toasted in 2 tablespoons butter
1 caramelized onion, thinly sliced
1 (10 ounce) package dried cranberries

Whisk together oil, sugar, vinegar and soy sauce. Set dressing aside. Slice bread into 8 wedges, then cut each wedge in half. Warm bread and spread 1 tablespoon goat cheese on each bread slice. Combine remaining goat cheese, duck, salad greens, nuts, onion and cranberries. Toss with small amount of dressing. Serve with warm bread slices.

Serves 4

Vinaigrette

3 tablespoons olive oil
2 tablespoons balsamic vinegar
1 tablespoon minced garlic or shallot
1 teaspoon raspberry preserves
⅛ teaspoon cracked black pepper
¼ teaspoon kosher salt

Whisk together oil, vinegar, garlic, preserves, pepper and salt until well blended.

Serves ⅓ cup

After cleaning wooden salad bowls, rub them with a crumpled piece of wax paper to seal surface.

~from The New Food Lover's Tiptionary

Honey Dressing

- 2/3 cup sugar
- 1 teaspoon dry mustard
- 1 teaspoon paprika
- 1 teaspoon celery seed
- 1/4 teaspoon salt
- 1/3 cup honey
- 1/3 cup vinegar
- 1 tablespoon lemon juice
- 1 teaspoon minced onion
- 1 cup vegetable oil

Combine sugar, mustard, paprika, celery seed and salt in a bowl. Stir in honey, vinegar, juice and onion. With an electric mixer running, add oil in a steady stream and blend until emulsified. Serve over fruit salads.

Serves 2 cups

Orange-Cranberry Salad with Sweet and Sour Dressing

- 2/3 cup sugar
- 1 teaspoon dry mustard
- 1 teaspoon paprika
- 1/4 teaspoon salt
- 1/3 cup honey
- 1/3 cup white vinegar
- 1 tablespoon lemon juice
- 1 cup vegetable oil
- Red leaf lettuce
- Mandarin oranges
- Dried cranberries
- Toasted almond slivers
- Crumbled feta cheese (optional)
- Vidalia onion rings (optional)

Combine sugar, mustard, paprika and salt. Blend in honey, vinegar and lemon juice. With electric mixer running, add oil in a steady stream and blend until thickened. Combine lettuce, oranges, cranberries, almonds, cheese and onion in a serving bowl. Add dressing and toss to coat.

Serves 4, 2 cups dressing

The dressing is great to baste chicken or pork while grilling or baking. Also serve warm as a meat sauce.

Cornbread Salad

- 1 (1 ounce) envelope dry ranch dressing mix
- 1 cup sour cream
- 1 cup mayonnaise
- 1 (9-inch) pan prepared cornbread, crumbled
- 2 (16 ounce) cans pinto beans, drained and divided
- 3 ripe tomatoes, chopped
- 1 medium bell pepper, chopped
- ½ cup chopped green onions
- 1 (8 ounce) package shredded Cheddar cheese
- 10 slices bacon, cooked and crumbled
- 2 (17 ounce) cans whole kernel corn, drained

Whisk together dressing mix, sour cream and mayonnaise until blended. Set aside. Place half of cornbread in bottom of a large bowl. Top with half of beans. In a medium bowl, combine tomatoes, bell pepper and onion. Layer half of tomato mixture over beans. Layer half of the cheese, bacon, corn and dressing. Repeat layering starting with remaining cornbread and ending with dressing. Cover and refrigerate at least 2 to 3 hours.

Serves 6-8

Italian Bean Roll-Ups

- 1 loaf soft sandwich bread, crust removed
- 1 (16 ounce) bottle Italian dressing
- 1 tablespoon Durkee's mustard
- ½ cup mayonnaise
- 1 (14½ ounce) can green beans, drained

Roll bread slices to flatten. Combine dressing, Durkee's and mayonnaise. Spread a thin layer of sauce on each bread slice. Place some beans on edge of bread. Roll up bread and place seam side down on baking sheet. Bake at 350 degrees for 15 minutes or until lightly browned.

Serves 24

Hot Open-Faced Sandwiches

- Rye bread slices
- Dijon mustard
- Sliced tomatoes
- Shaved deli ham
- Sour cream
- Lemon pepper to taste
- Swiss cheese slices

Spread each bread slice with mustard, top with tomatoes and then ham. Spread sour cream over ham and season with lemon pepper. Top with cheese slices. Place open bread on a broiler pan. Broil until cheese melts. Serve immediately.

Serve 1

Memories of Grandmama and Mama

My earliest memories of Grandmama and Mama are in the kitchen! Grandmama watched my brother and I after school along with her own son, Bill. She cooked something sweet everyday or so. We loved to eat the raw cake batter from her cakes and especially her pound cakes. She would have all three of us little bowls of cake batter to eat when we got off the school bus. Between those "little bowls" and a big chunk of pound cake, we all grew up to become members of the Wellness Center! But, that's another story.

Mama cooked birthday cakes or pies for everyone at Eljer Plumbing Company where she worked. I remember going to bed at night listening to the mixer going for somebody's cake. She made cakes for the office and plant workers. I believe at least one half of the year was spent in the kitchen. People loved Mama's baking and remember her generosity in baking and giving. Grandmama made the famous "lunchroom rolls" with her own twist to the recipe. She gave away literally thousands of those rolls for everything from a "little happy" to taking food for a death in the family. Her rolls would be the kind that would melt in your mouth with a little butter!

Grandmama taught me how to make chicken and dressing when I was nineteen, before I moved away. She said, "There was no recipe." You just taste and put in the seasoning until you get it right." She gave me enough measurements of the basic ingredients to learn "how to taste." Grandmama's dressing went from Bermuda, Florida, Virginia and Maryland and then to Puerto Rico. I always had compliments and was asked for the recipe. I would say, "You know, you have to learn how to taste it!"

~Author Unknown

Be proud of your Southern heritage and don't apologize for your Southern accent – it's charming, usually, but be sure your grammar is correct. Our choice of words may be different from what Yankees would choose, but we mean the same thing. We say, "I'm fixin' supper." They say, "I'm making dinner." What's the big deal?????

~Reprinted from the book *Mama Said* by Martha Houston Reed Hammond by permission of author

Easy French Dip Sandwiches

3 pound beef brisket or roast
1 (1¼ ounce) envelope dry onion soup mix
1 (10½ ounce) can beef broth
8 mini baguettes or sandwich buns

Brown meat on all sides in oil in a skillet. Place in a crockpot. Combine soup mix and broth. Pour over meat. Cover and cook on low for 8 to 10 hours or until tender. Thinly slice meat and serve on sliced baguettes or buns.

Serves 8-10

Pimento and Cheese Spread

1 (16 ounce) package processed cheese loaf
⅓ cup milk
1 egg, well beaten
2 teaspoons vinegar
1 tablespoon sugar
2 (4 ounce) jars diced pimentos, drained
1-2 cups mayonnaise

Cook cheese and milk in the top of a double boiler over medium heat until cheese melts. Stir in egg, vinegar, sugar and pimentos. Cook and stir for 15 minutes or until thickened. Cool. Mix in 1 to 2 cups mayonnaise to reach desired spreading consistency.

Serves 4 cups

May store in the refrigerator for one month.

Date Sandwich Spread

1 (10 ounce) package pitted dates, chopped
1¾ cups sugar
⅔ cup milk
Dash of salt
2 tablespoons butter
1 cup walnuts or pecans, finely chopped
1 cup mayonnaise
1 loaf thin whole wheat sandwich bread

Combine dates, sugar, milk, salt and butter in a saucepan. Cook over low heat, stirring constantly, until dates melt and mixture thickens. Cool completely. Stir in nuts and mayonnaise. Spread on thin whole wheat bread.

Serves 15 sandwiches

Cucumber-Cream Cheese Tea Sandwiches

- 1 (8 ounce) package cream cheese, softened
- 1 teaspoon dried dill
- 1 teaspoon dried parsley
- 1 medium cucumber, peeled and thinly sliced
- 10 thin slices wheat or white sandwich bread
- Dash of pepper

Blend cream cheese, dill and parsley. Spread each bread slice lightly with cream cheese mixture. Top five bread slices with cucumber slices and sprinkle with pepper. Place remaining five bread slices over cucumbers, spread side down, to make a sandwich. Cut each sandwich into quarters.

Serves 20 finger sandwiches

Olive Spread

- 1 (8 ounce) package cream cheese, softened
- 1 (4¼ ounce) can chopped olives, drained, reserving liquid
- 2½ tablespoons olive liquid
- 1 cup finely chopped pecans
- ½ cup mayonnaise

Blend cream cheese, olives, olive liquid, pecans and mayonnaise with an electric mixer until smooth. Refrigerate for 24 hours before serving.

Serves 2½ cups

Great spread on whole wheat bread slices.

Baked Chicken Sandwich

- ½ cup mayonnaise
- 2 cups diced cooked chicken
- ¼ cups diced green onions, including tops
- ¼ cup ripe olives, sliced
- 1 cup sliced mushrooms, drained
- 2 hard-cooked eggs, chopped
- ½ teaspoon lemon pepper
- 16 slices thin sandwich bread, buttered on both sides
- 1 (10¾ ounce) can cream of chicken soup
- 1 cup sour cream
- Parmesan cheese and paprika for garnish

Combine mayonnaise, chicken, onion, olives, mushrooms, eggs and lemon pepper and mix well. Spread chicken mixture on one side of eight bread slices and top with remaining slices. Place sandwiches in a 13 x 9 x 2-inch baking dish. Cover and refrigerate for 24 hours. Mix together soup and sour cream. Pour over sandwiches. Sprinkle with Parmesan cheese and paprika. Bake at 350 degrees for 40 to 45 minutes.

Serves 8

Entrées

Meats, Seafood, Poultry and Pasta

Ladies That Lunch

Frozen Margaritas, page 50

Holly's Chicken Salad, page 107

Sweet Potato Cornbread, page 72

Fresh Tomato Slices

Cappuccino Pie, page 207

Southwestern Taco Pot Pie

- **1 pound lean ground beef**
- **1 (1¼ ounce) package taco seasoning mix**
- **⅓ cup water**
- **1 tablespoon vegetable oil**
- **1 (1 pound) package frozen bell, sweet red and yellow peppers and onion mix, thawed**
- **1 teaspoon garlic powder**
- **1 teaspoon onion powder**
- **¼ teaspoon salt**
- **⅛ teaspoon pepper**
- **1 (11 ounce) can whole kernel corn, drained**
- **½ cup salsa**
- **1 (15 ounce) package refrigerated pie crust, softened**
- **1 (8 ounce) package shredded Mexican blend cheese**
- **Sour cream and taco sauce for garnish**

Preheat oven to 400 degrees. Brown beef in skillet for 8 to 10 minutes. Drain well. Add taco seasoning and water. Mix well to coat meat. Set aside. Heat oil in a large saucepan. Add peppers and onion mix and cook 4 to 5 minutes or until tender. Remove from heat and drain excess liquid. Stir in garlic powder, onion powder, salt, pepper, corn and salsa. Prepare pie crusts as directed on package for 2-crust pie using a 9-inch glass pie pan. Add beef mixture to corn mixture and mix well. Sprinkle ½ cup cheese in bottom of pastry-lined pan. Spread half of beef mixture evenly over cheese, pat down. Repeat layers with ¾ cup cheese and remaining beef mixture, patting down. Top with remaining ¾ cup cheese. Top with remaining pastry and flute edges. Cut slits in several places. Bake at 400 degrees for 30 minutes or until crust is golden browned. Cover edge of crust with strips of foil or pie crust shield after 15 minutes of baking. Cool 5 minutes before serving. Serve with a dollop of sour cream and drizzle with taco sauce. Store in refrigerator.

Serves 6

To make with fresh vegetables, use 1½ cups chopped onion and 2½ cups chopped peppers. Increase stove top cooking time. May also garnish with guacamole, salsa and diced green chilies.

Mexican Meatloaf

- **1 pound ground turkey or beef**
- **½ cup minced onion**
- **1 (1¼ ounce) package taco seasoning mix**
- **3 taco shells, finely crushed**
- **½ cup picante sauce**

Combine meat, onion, seasoning mix, taco crumbs and picante sauce. Mix well. Shape mixture into a loaf and place in a nonstick 9 x 5-inch loaf pan. Bake at 400 degrees for 20 to 30 minutes.

Serves 6

Gourmet Burgers

- 1 cup wine vinegar
- ¼ cup vegetable oil
- 1 teaspoon Tabasco sauce
- 2 tablespoons black pepper
- 2 tablespoons Worcestershire sauce
- 2 garlic cloves, minced
- 2 tablespoons prepared yellow mustard
- Juice of two lemons
- 2 tablespoons salt
- 2 tablespoons packed brown sugar
- 1 tablespoon chili powder
- 1 tablespoon paprika
- ¾ cup ketchup
- 2 pounds ground beef

Combine vinegar, oil, Tabasco, pepper, Worcestershire sauce, garlic, mustard, lemon juice, salt, brown sugar, chili powder, paprika and ketchup in a saucepan. Bring to boil, stirring well. Reduce heat, cover and simmer for 15 minutes. Use ⅓ pound meat to form each burger patty. Line a baking sheet with foil. Spoon ¼ cup sauce onto foil and place patties on top. Pour more sauce over top of each patty. Cover and marinate in the refrigerator 6 to 8 hours. Bring to room temperature an hour before grilling. Grill to desired degree of doneness, basting frequently with sauce.

Serves 4-6

Lafayette Beef Burgundy

- 2 pounds boneless beef sirloin
- ¼ cup all-purpose flour
- 6 tablespoons butter
- 1 onion, sliced or 2 (4 ounce) jars pearl onions
- 3 stalks celery, diced
- 3 carrots, peeled and chopped
- 1 (10½ ounce) can beef consommé
- 1 cup red wine
- 1 (7 ounce) jar mushrooms, drained
- Salt, pepper and garlic powder to taste
- Hot cooked noodles or mashed potatoes

Dredge beef in flour. Melt butter in skillet and brown beef on all sides. Transfer beef to a 3-quart saucepan, reserving drippings in skillet. Add onion and sauté until tender. Add onions and drippings to saucepan with beef. Add celery, carrot, consommé, wine and mushrooms to saucepan. Season with salt, pepper and garlic powder. Simmer at least 2 hours. Serve over cooked noodles or mashed potatoes.

Serves 8-10

Indo-Flank Broil

- 2 tablespoons packed light brown sugar
- 2½ teaspoons ground coriander
- 2 garlic cloves, minced
- 2 tablespoons olive oil
- 1½ teaspoons chili powder
- ½ teaspoon pepper
- ½ teaspoon salt
- ½ teaspoon ground ginger
- 3 pounds beef flank steak

Preheat grill. Combine brown sugar, coriander, garlic, oil, chili powder, pepper, salt and ginger. Rub mixture into both sides of steak. Grill steak 8-inches from heat source for 15 minutes, turning once. Cut steak across the grain into ¼-inch slices.

Serves 6

Grilled Sirloin Steak with Asparagus Tapenade

- 1 pound asparagus, peeled and trimmed
- 2 garlic cloves, crushed
- ½ cup fresh basil leaves
- ¼ cup pine nuts
- 2 teaspoons kosher salt, divided
- 3 tablespoons olive oil, divided
- 2 tablespoons fresh thyme leaves
- ¼ teaspoon pepper
- 3 pounds sirloin steak, 1-inch thick

Cut asparagus spears in half and reserve the tops for another use. Cook stalk bottoms in lightly salted boiling water for 3 to 4 minutes or until crisp-tender. Drain and rinse under cold water to stop cooking. Coarsely chop stalks. Process asparagus stalks, garlic, basil, nuts and 1 teaspoon salt in food processor. With motor running, pour in 1 tablespoon olive oil and process until smooth. Set aside. In a small bowl, combine remaining teaspoon salt, 2 tablespoons oil, thyme and pepper. Rub mixture over steak. Grill or broil steak 4 to 5 minutes per side for medium. Divide steak into 6 portions and serve topped with dollops of Asparagus Tapenade.

Serves 6

Ten Minute Gourmet Sukiyaki

- 3 tablespoons vegetable oil
- 1 onion, sliced
- 4 large mushrooms, sliced
- ½ pound lean beef, sliced
- ¼ pound fresh spinach, torn
- 2 stalks celery, thinly sliced

Heat oil in a skillet. Add onion, mushrooms, beef, spinach and celery. Cook, stirring constantly, until beef is desired degree of doneness. Do not overcook. Serve over cooked rice and with a green salad.

Serves 4

Grace's Sunday Roast

- 3 pounds beef chuck or round roast
- 1 teaspoon salt
- 1 teaspoon ground ginger
- 1 cup vinegar
- 3 cups water
- 1 medium onion, chopped
- 2 tablespoons pickling spice
- 2 bay leaves
- ½ teaspoon pepper
- 4 whole cloves
- 3 tablespoons sugar

Rub meat with salt and ginger. Combine vinegar, water, onion, pickling spice, bay leaves, pepper, cloves and sugar in a large bowl. Place roast in marinade. Cover and refrigerate for 1 to 2 days. Remove meat from marinade. Bake at 300 degrees until thermometer reaches 165 degrees for well done. Cool completely and refrigerate. Slice and serve cold.

Serves 10-12

Marinated Eye of Round

- ¼ cup vegetable oil
- 2 tablespoons lemon pepper
- ½ cup wine vinegar
- ½ cup lemon juice
- ½ cup soy sauce
- ½ cup Worcestershire sauce
- 5 pounds eye of beef round roast
- Parsley sprigs and cherry tomatoes for garnish

Combine oil, lemon pepper, vinegar, juice, soy sauce and Worcestershire sauce. Pour marinade over roast and refrigerate for 1 to 3 days, turning at least once a day. Place roast and marinade in a Dutch oven. Roast at 250 degrees for 3 hours. Cool completely and refrigerate overnight. Cut roast into thin slices and serve with heated marinade. Garnish with parsley and cherry tomatoes.

Serves 10-15

This is delicious entrée for a buffet supper. Cooked meat freezes well also.

Stuffed Tenderloin

¼ cup butter
1 pound mushrooms, chopped
½ cup chopped celery
½ cup chopped green onion
¼ cup chopped bell pepper
1 teaspoon salt
⅛ teaspoon pepper
⅛ teaspoon ground thyme
2 tablespoons all-purpose flour
1 (4 pound) beef tenderloin
Salt and pepper to taste

Melt butter in skillet. Sauté mushrooms until browned. Add celery, onion, bell pepper, salt, pepper and thyme. Sauté until vegetables are tender. Blend in flour. Butterfly the tenderloin. Spoon vegetable mixture evenly into tenderloin center. Fasten open ends with skewers and close tenderloin. Using kitchen twine, tie up meat to secure opening. Season outside of meat with salt and pepper. Place tenderloin in a roasting pan. Roast at 325 degrees for 60 minutes for medium rare or 1 hour, 20 minutes for medium well.

Serves 8-10

The nearer the bone, the sweeter the meat.

~British Proverb

~from The New Food Lover's Tiptionary

Benton Barbecued Brisket

1 (5-6 pound) beef brisket
⅓ cup liquid smoke
Garlic salt, onion salt, and celery salt to taste
5 tablespoons Worcestershire sauce
Salt and pepper to taste
¾ cup barbecue sauce
2 tablespoon all-purpose flour
½ cup water

Place brisket in a greased 13 x 9 x 2-inch baking dish. Pour liquid smoke on meat. Season with garlic salt, onion salt and celery salt. Cover and refrigerate overnight. Prior to cooking, season with Worcestershire sauce, salt and pepper. Place foil loosely on top of dish. Cook at 250 degrees for 5 hours. Pour barbecue sauce over meat and cook, uncovered, for another hour. Transfer meat to a platter and cool before slicing. Pour remaining pan sauce into a saucepan. Skim off fat. Add flour and water. Cook, stirring constantly, until sauce thickens. Serve sauce hot with meat.

Serves 10

Prime Rib

- 1 (9-10 pound) rib roast or eye of rib roast
- Lemon pepper to taste
- Seasoning salt to taste
- Onion salt to taste
- Garlic salt to taste
- ¼ cup horseradish
- 2 tablespoons vinegar
- 1 teaspoon salt
- 1 (8 ounce) container sour cream

Season all sides and ends of roast with lemon pepper, seasoning salt, onion salt and garlic salt. Place meat in a roasting pan. Roast at 500 degrees for 1 hour. Turn off oven and leave meat in oven for a minimum of 8 hours. Do not open oven door. Meanwhile, whisk together horseradish, vinegar, salt and sour cream. Refrigerate until ready to serve. Prior to serving, turn oven to 350 degrees for 30 minutes. Slice roast with electric knife into steaks. Serve with horseradish sauce.

Serves 8-10

Pickapeppa Pork Tenderloin

- 2 pork tenderloins
- Olive oil
- Salt and pepper to taste
- Lemon pepper to taste
- Creole seasoning to taste
- Pickapeppa sauce
- Worcestershire sauce
- Soy sauce
- Honey
- White wine

No measuring necessary for this recipe. Rub tenderloins with oil, salt, pepper, lemon pepper and Creole seasoning. Place tenderloins on a rack in a roasting pan. Drizzle with Pickapeppa sauce, Worcestershire sauce, soy sauce and honey. Cover bottom of pan with wine. Roast at 350 degrees for 45 minutes.

Serves 6-8

Slow-Cooked Pork Barbeque

- 3 pounds boneless pork loin roast, trimmed
- ¾ cup water
- 1 (4 ounce) bottle liquid smoke
- 1 (18 ounce) bottle barbeque sauce
- ¼ cup packed brown sugar
- 2 tablespoons Worcestershire sauce
- 1 teaspoon Tabasco sauce
- 1 teaspoon salt
- 1 teaspoon pepper
- 1 teaspoon crushed garlic

Place roast in a crock pot. Add water and liquid smoke. Cook on high for 7 hours or until tender. Shred meat with a fork. Add barbeque sauce, brown sugar, Worcestershire sauce, Tabasco, salt, pepper and garlic. Reduce heat to low and cook, covered, for 1 hour.

Serves 20

Memories

These memories will be about my mother, Ann B. Godfrey and my grandmother, Shirley Benson. They were hospice patients in December 2003 – January 2004 and May – July 2000, respectively. We received excellent care that was seasoned with professionalism, sympathy and just plain old common sense. I will always remember the visits that Dottie Patterson made taking care of my grandmother's every need. The day that Jessica Rodgers came to help fill out the paper work for my mother was hard, but Jessica was so caring and sympathetic. The night that Grandmama died, the nurse on call came out after she had made all the necessary phone calls and asked us if she could say a word of prayer. It was the most touching thing she could have done. It showed us that she really cared. That is the way I will always remember Hospice as an organization. They saw our faces, wiped our tears, if needed, but most of all saw us as hurting people who needed their love and support. I cannot say enough good things about all of the professionals involved in hospice – from the people who set up the equipment, to the last nurse you see on the day of death, to the grief counselor. They cared for our family.

~Author Unknown

Next Day Pork Tenderloin

- **½ cup peanut oil**
- **⅓ cup soy sauce**
- **¼ cup red wine vinegar**
- **3 tablespoons lemon juice**
- **2 tablespoons Worcestershire sauce**
- **1 garlic clove, crushed**
- **1 tablespoon chopped fresh parsley**
- **1 tablespoon dry mustard**
- **1½ teaspoons pepper**
- **2 (¾-1 pound) pork tenderloins**

Combine oil, soy sauce, vinegar, juice, Worcestershire sauce, garlic, parsley, mustard and pepper in a large zip-top plastic bag. Add tenderloins and marinate at least 4 hours or overnight in the refrigerator. Remove tenderloins and discard marinade. Grill over medium heat for 15 to 20 minutes or until thermometer registers 160 degrees. Cool 10 minutes before slicing.

Serves 6-8

Jay's Cubbie Bare Bone Ribs

This recipe comes from a former Chicago Cub baseball player. He loves to cook and eat!

~Jason Boehlow (Jay), Webster Groves, MO

3 slabs of beef or pork ribs, cut into 3 to 4 rib sections
1 gallon apple cider or 6-pack cider beer
2 cups apple cider vinegar
1 onion, chopped
2 garlic cloves, chopped
Salt and pepper to taste
Favorite barbeque sauce

Combine ribs, cider and vinegar in a large bowl. Cover and marinate overnight in refrigerator. Transfer marinade and ribs to a large stockpot. Add onion, garlic and season with salt and pepper. Bring to boil. Reduce heat and simmer for 1 hour. Grill ribs over medium heat, basting with barbeque sauce as they cook. Basting the bones is very important for this recipe.

Serves 10

Crusted Pork Loin with Pepper Jelly Glaze

1 garlic clove, minced
½ teaspoon fresh rosemary, finely chopped
¼ teaspoon salt
¼ teaspoon pepper
1-1½ pounds boneless pork loin roast
1 tablespoon olive oil
2 tablespoons Dijon mustard
¼ cup bread crumbs
1 cup pepper jelly
1 cup apple cider or juice
1 cup cider vinegar

Combine garlic, rosemary, salt and pepper. Rub seasoning mixture into pork. Stir together oil and mustard and spread over pork. Roll pork in bread crumbs, coating evenly. Bake at 350 degrees for 1 hour, 15 minutes or until just done. Do not overbake. Heat jelly, apple cider and vinegar together in a saucepan. Pour over pork during last 30 minutes, basting every 10 minutes.

Serves 4-6

Sherried Apple Pork Chops

- 6 boneless pork chops, 1-1½-inch thick
- 3 medium Granny Smith apples, unpeeled, cored and sliced
- ¼ cup packed brown sugar
- ½ teaspoon cinnamon
- 2 tablespoons butter
- Salt and pepper to taste
- ½ cup sherry
- 2 tablespoons water

Preheat oven to 350 degrees. Brown chops on both sides in a skillet. Arrange chops in bottom of a greased 13 x 9 x 2-inch baking dish. Top with apple slices. Sprinkle with brown sugar and cinnamon, then dot with butter. Season with salt and pepper. Slowly pour in sherry and water. Cover tightly with foil and bake at 350 degrees for 1 hour, 30 minutes. Check every 20 to 30 minutes making sure chops are not drying out. Add 1 tablespoon water at a time if necessary.

Serves 6

Hams labeled "Cook before serving" must be heated to an internal temperature of 160°F.

~from The New Food Lover's Tiptionary

Baked Barbequed Baby Back Ribs

- 3 pounds baby-back pork ribs
- ¼ cup butter
- 2 medium onions
- Garlic powder to taste
- 2 tablespoons prepared mustard
- ¼ cup vinegar
- ¼ cup packed brown sugar
- 2 cups ketchup
- ¼ cup Worcestershire sauce
- 2 cups water

Bake ribs in a large roasting pan at 325 degrees, turning often, just until browned. Remove from oven and set aside. Melt butter in a saucepan. Sauté onion and garlic powder until tender. Add mustard, vinegar, brown sugar, ketchup, Worcestershire sauce and water. Cook over low heat for 15 minutes, stirring occasionally. Pour sauce over ribs. Cover tightly with foil. Bake at 325 degrees for at least 2 hours.

Serves 4-6

Boston Butt Roast

- 1 quart apple cider vinegar
- 1 quart white vinegar
- 1¾ cups sugar
- 1 tablespoon cayenne pepper
- ⅜ cup salt
- ¼ cup crushed red pepper
- ¾ teaspoon black pepper
- ¾ teaspoon paprika
- Garlic salt to taste
- 4 Boston butts

Whisk together cider vinegar, white vinegar, sugar, cayenne, salt, red pepper, black pepper and paprika. Simmer over low heat for 5 minutes. Set sauce aside. Sprinkle garlic salt on meats fatty side up. Grill meat indirectly off the coals for 8 to 9 hours, adding coals every couple of hours to keep the coals hot. May add hickory blocks also. Do not turn the meat. When cooked, remove the fat from top side. Finely chop the remaining meat. Spoon sauce over chopped meat and stir well.

Serves 15-20

A Place of Refuge

After deciding on the name, The Sanctuary, we added "A Place of Refuge". On one of our early trips to Washington, Nancy and I were excited about visiting the National Cathedral for church. We might even get to see the President. As we walked out of the hotel, we noticed a small church across the street half way down the block. For some unknown reason, we decided to go there instead. It was a small Presbyterian Church with about 50 people in attendance. The minister stood up, walked to the pulpit and said "Welcome to this sanctuary, a place of refuge". After the service, a gentleman came up and introduced himself as a former congressman from Alabama and Billy Crew's uncle. He became our mentor and on all subsequent Washington visits he showed us around, introduced us to key members of Congress and took us to eat in the House and Senate dining room.

~Carol Elliott,
Tupelo, MS

Gingered Ham Steak

- **1 fully cooked center-cut ham slice, 1-inch thick**
- **½ cup ginger ale**
- **½ cup orange juice**
- **¼ cup packed brown sugar**
- **1 tablespoon vegetable oil**
- **1½ teaspoons dry mustard**
- **1 teaspoon ginger or fresh ginger**
- **⅛ teaspoon ground cloves**

Slice fat edge of ham. Combine ginger ale, orange juice, brown sugar, oil, mustard, ginger and cloves. Pour marinade over ham, turning ham several times. Refrigerate overnight. Grill ham about 5 minutes per side.

Serves 2-4

Cucina Amore Meatballs

- **½ cup milk**
- **2 tablespoons finely chopped garlic**
- **¼ cup chopped fresh flat-leaf parsley**
- **½ cup soft bread crumbs**
- **2 eggs**
- **2 cups grated Pecorino Romano cheese**
- **2 tablespoons sugar**
- **1 teaspoon cinnamon**
- **1 teaspoon ground nutmeg**
- **½ teaspoon black pepper**
- **½ pound lean ground beef**
- **½ pound ground veal**
- **½ pound ground pork**
- **2 tablespoons olive oil**
- **6 cups spaghetti sauce**

Combine milk, garlic, parsley, bread crumbs, eggs, cheese, sugar, cinnamon, nutmeg and pepper in a large bowl. Mix well. Add ground meats and hand mix until completely incorporated. Shape 2 heaping tablespoons of mixture into meatballs. Mixture will make 32 to 34 meatballs. Cook as many as you need and freeze the rest.

Heat oil in a large skillet over high heat. Brown meatballs in several batches for 2 to 3 minutes on each side. Do not crowd the pan. Remove meatballs to drain on paper towels. Simmer your favorite spaghetti sauce. Place meatballs in sauce and simmer for 15 to 20 minutes.

Serves 6

The combination of meats adds a depth of flavor and the milk gives a tender texture. Simmering in sauce also adds zest to the meatballs.

Lay a slightly damp dish towel (or moist paper towel) underneath your cutting board to prevent skidding and to absorb any juices that run off from your food.

~from
The New Food Lover's Tiptionary

Stuffed Pillows

- **12 small thinly sliced veal cutlets**
- **12 small thin sliced prosciutto or ham**
- **¾ pound mozzarella cheese, thinly sliced**
- **½ cup plus 1 teaspoon butter, divided**
- **½ cup Marsala or sherry wine**
- **⅛ teaspoon salt**
- **⅛ teaspoon pepper**

Flatten veal cutlets with a mallet. Place one slice prosciutto and one slice of cheese on each cutlet. Fold together like an envelope, using toothpicks to hold it together. Melt 8 tablespoons butter in a skillet. Brown cutlets well on one side, then turn gently to brown other side. Cutlets cook in a very short time. Remove meat to a platter and pour in Marsala. Heat and stir to loosen browned bits from sides and bottom of skillet. Add 1 teaspoon butter, salt and pepper. Pour sauce over pillows on serving platter.

Serves 4

Veal Ratatouille

- **3 pounds lean veal, cut into 2-inch cubes**
- **Salt and pepper to taste**
- **½ cup corn oil**
- **2 cups pearl onions**
- **1 tablespoon minced garlic**
- **¼ cup all-purpose flour**
- **1 cup dry white wine**
- **2 cups chicken broth**
- **3 tablespoons tomato paste**
- **1 cup water**
- **1 teaspoon dried thyme**
- **1 large eggplant, cut into 2-inch cubes**
- **2 small zucchini, cut into 2-inch cubes**
- **2 bell peppers, cut into 1½-inch pieces**
- **2 large tomatoes, cut into 1-inch pieces**

Season veal with salt and pepper. Brown veal in oil in a large stockpot. Stir in onion and garlic. Add flour and stir well. Stir in wine, broth, tomato paste and water. Add thyme, eggplant, zucchini and bell pepper. Bring to boil. Reduce heat and simmer, covered, for 30 minutes. Add tomatoes and simmer an additional 15 minutes.

Serves 10-12

Fresh Herb Lamb Chops

½ cup extra virgin olive oil
1 teaspoon salt
1 teaspoon pepper
2 garlic cloves, crushed
1½ tablespoons chopped fresh rosemary or ¾ teaspoon dried
Salt and pepper to taste
1 rack of Frenched lamb rib chops
½ cup butter
Zest and juice of one lemon

Combine oil, salt, pepper, cloves and rosemary. Cook in microwave until bubbly. Cool slightly. Season chops with salt and pepper. Pour marinade over chops and refrigerate for 1 hour. Place chops in a roasting pan. Discard marinade. Melt butter in a saucepan and add lemon zest and juice. Pour over chops. Roast at 425 degrees for 12 to 15 minutes or until thermometer registers 135 degrees for medium rare.

Serves 3-4 chops per person

Rack of Lamb al Pesto

3 half racks of lamb, Frenched, reserving the trimmings
Salt and pepper to taste
3 tablespoons olive oil
1 cup pesto

Season lamb with salt and pepper. Sear lamb in hot oil. Discard oil and place lamb on a rack in a roasting pan. Roast at 400 degrees until lamb is cooked to 130 degrees for medium rare or desired degree of doneness. Remove from oven and spread pesto over meat portion. Allow to stand for 10 minutes. Return to oven and bake until pesto is lightly browned.

Serves 6-8

Smoked Sausage Jambalaya

1 cup instant rice
1 pound smoked sausage, cut into 1-inch pieces
1 medium onion, chopped
½ cup chopped bell pepper
½ cup sliced celery
1 (8 ounce) can tomatoes
4 drops Tabasco sauce
½ teaspoon pepper

Cook rice according to package directions. Heat a large greased skillet over medium heat. Sauté sausage, onion, bell pepper and celery until vegetables are tender. Stir in tomatoes, Tabasco and pepper. Drain cooked rice and stir into sausage mixture. Cook over low heat, stirring frequently, until thoroughly warmed.

Serves 4-6

Mexican Buffet

My sister, Jane Hawkins Talbert, was a senior at Blue Mountain College when she attended a party where this buffet was served. She brought the recipe home. It has been passed around to many people and served often. From children to adults, everyone likes a Mexican supper.

~Phyllis Harper
Tupelo, MS

Corn chips
Ground beef, cooked, drained and seasoned with salt, pepper and other desired spices
Shredded lettuce
Chopped tomatoes
Chopped onion
Shredded Cheddar cheese
Pinto beans, cooked and lightly seasoned
Salt, pepper and cayenne pepper to taste
Sour cream for garnish

Set a buffet table with separate serving dishes of corn chips, ground beef, lettuce, tomatoes, onion, cheese and beans. Guest may arrange layers on a dinner plate in order of dishes. Season to taste and top with sour cream.

Serves any number of guests

Great for serving any number of people. This informal buffet is one of my family's favorite meals. It is easy to prepare and serve. It can be dressed up with your best china and silver or serve in everyday cookware and dishes. Use chafing dishes to keep beef and beans warm.

Baked Ham with Bourbon Glaze

1 (6-8 pound) smoked ham half
1 cup honey
½ cup molasses
½ cup bourbon
¼ orange juice
1 tablespoon Dijon mustard

Trim excess fat from ham. Score ¼-inch thick into a diamond pattern. Place in a lightly greased 13 x 9 x 2-inch baking dish. Combine honey and molasses in a glass dish. Microwave on high for 1 minute. Whisk to blend. Whisk in bourbon, juice and mustard. Pour glaze evenly over ham. Place pan on lower oven rack. Bake at 350 degrees for 2 to 2 hours, 30 minutes or until thermometer reaches 140 degrees. Baste ham every 15 minutes with glaze. Remove ham from pan, reserving drippings. Cover ham and refrigerate, if desired. Refrigerate drippings in a saucepan. Remove and discard fat from drippings. Bring to boil. Serve warm with ham.

Serves 12-14

Mother's Way

The young bride was preparing to bake her first Easter ham. She sliced off the end of the ham before placing it in a baking pan. Her husband stood by waiting patiently for his Easter Feast and noticed the end of the ham was missing. The young bride explained that this was the way her mother prepared her ham. The next time mother visited, the bride asked her why she cut the ends off the ham. Mother replied that her mother had always done it that way, but she would ask grandmother. They called grandmother. Grandmother said, "Because my pan's too small!"

Oysters Randall

2 (12 ounce) jars oysters, undrained
1 cup chopped celery
1 cup chopped green onions
1 garlic clove, crushed
1 tablespoon chopped parsley
¼ cup chopped bell pepper
½ cup butter
2 (14 ounce) jars artichokes, drained
2 (8 ounce) cans sliced mushrooms, drained
1 (10¾ ounce) can cream of mushroom soup, undiluted
½ teaspoon salt
½ cup white wine
1 cup dry bread crumbs

Bring oysters to boil in own juice. Drain over a bowl and reserve oyster broth. Sauté celery, onion, garlic, parsley and bell pepper in butter. To vegetable mixture add oysters, artichokes, mushrooms and oyster broth. Stir in mushroom soup, salt and wine. Slowly stir in bread crumbs. Spoon mixture into 12 individual buttered shells or a buttered 13 x 9 x 2-inch baking dish. Bake at 350 degrees for 20 to 30 minutes.

Serves 12

Corn-Oyster Casserole

- 1 (14½ ounce) can cream-style corn
- 1 (8 ounce) can oysters, undrained
- ½ cup butter, melted
- 30 saltine crackers, crushed
- 1 cup milk
- Dash of lemon juice

Combine corn, oysters, butter, cracker crumbs, milk and juice. Pour into a buttered 2-quart casserole dish. Let stand for 1 hour. Bake at 350 degrees for 1 hour.

Serves 6-8

Scalloped Scallops

- 5 tablespoons butter, divided
- ½ cup soft bread crumbs (2 slices)
- 2 tablespoons Parmesan cheese
- 3 tablespoons chopped parsley
- 2 tablespoons chopped chives or ¾ teaspoon dried
- 3 tablespoons lemon juice
- 1 teaspoon Worcestershire sauce
- 1 pound fresh sea scallops (may use frozen)
- 1 (10¾ ounce) can cream of celery soup, undiluted

Melt 1 tablespoon butter in bowl in microwave. Add bread crumbs and cheese. Set aside. Melt remaining 4 tablespoons in a skillet. Add parsley, chives, juice and Worcestershire sauce. Add scallops, cover and simmer for 8 to 10 minutes. Divide cooked scallops among 4 buttered shells or baking dishes. Stir soup into juices in skillet. Bring to boil. Pour sauce over scallops. Top with cheese bread crumbs. Bake at 350 degrees for 15 to 20 minutes or until golden browned.

Serves 4

Grilled Shrimp

- 4 garlic cloves, crushed
- 1 cup olive oil
- ½ cup finely chopped fresh basil
- 2 tablespoons vinegar
- 1 tablespoon Worcestershire sauce
- ½ teaspoon Tabasco sauce
- 2 pounds large shrimp, peeled and deveined

Combine garlic, oil, basil, vinegar, Worcestershire sauce and Tabasco in a shallow dish. Mix well. Add shrimp and toss gently to coat. Cover and marinate 2 to 3 hours in the refrigerator, stirring occasionally.

Remove shrimp from marinade. Save marinade. Thread shrimp onto six 14-inch skewers. Grill over medium heat for 3 to 4 minutes per side. Baste frequently with marinade.

Serves 4

Shrimp Rémoulade

- 1½ cups vegetable oil
- ⅔ cup Creole mustard
- ⅓ cup apple cider vinegar
- 1 bunch green onions, finely chopped
- ½ teaspoon paprika
- 2 garlic cloves, finely minced
- Salt and Tabasco sauce to taste
- 1 pound shrimp in shells
- Shredded lettuce

Drizzle oil into mustard while constantly whisking. Slowly whisk in vinegar. Add onion, paprika, garlic, salt and Tabasco. Whisk until well blended. Set Rémoulade sauce aside. Cook shrimp in boiling water with shrimp boil seasoning. Drain and peel shrimp. Arrange lettuce on four salad plates. Top with shrimp and drizzle sauce over shrimp.

Serves 4

Having all of the wonderful recipes of my grandmothers, who was raised in New Orleans, has been a family institution. This is Grandmother Shubert's recipe.

~ Virginia Mathews, Tupelo, MS

Mississippi Marinated Shrimp

- ½ cup butter
- ⅓ cup Worcestershire sauce
- 1 teaspoon salt
- 1 teaspoon pepper
- 1 teaspoon cayenne pepper
- 2 teaspoons minced garlic
- 1 teaspoon ground thyme
- 2 teaspoons dried rosemary
- ½ teaspoon celery salt
- 1 teaspoon olive oil
- 50-60 medium shrimp, rinsed and unpeeled
- 1 loaf of French bread, sliced

Melt butter in a saucepan. Add Worcestershire sauce, salt, pepper, cayenne, garlic, thyme, rosemary, celery salt and oil. Cook, stirring constantly, over low heat for 10 to 15 minutes. Cool slightly and add shrimp. Pour shrimp and marinade into a 1½-quart glass dish. Marinate at least 2 to 3 hours or refrigerate overnight. Bake shrimp and marinade at 400 degrees for 18 to 20 minutes, stirring occasionally. After 12 minutes, taste shrimp to prevent over cooking. Cook further if necessary. Overcooked shrimp are hard to peel. Serve with French bread to dip in sauce.

Serves 4-6

This meal is messy, but worth it.

Cooked shrimp can be refrigerated airtight for up to 3 days.

~from The New Food Lover's Tiptionary

Shrimp in Beer Creole

- 2 pounds shrimp, peeled and deveined
- 7 tablespoons butter, divided
- 1/4 cup minced green onions
- 1 medium bell pepper, cut into strips
- 1 (8 ounce) container small mushrooms
- 1 tablespoon paprika
- Salt and pepper to taste
- 1 teaspoon tomato paste
- 1 cup beer
- 3/4 cup heavy cream
- 1/4 cup sour cream
- 1/2 cup sliced blanched almonds
- 1 tablespoon vegetable oil
- Hot cooked rice

In a saucepan, sauté shrimp in 4 tablespoons butter over medium heat until pink. Transfer shrimp and juices to a bowl and cover with waxed paper. Melt 2 tablespoons butter in same saucepan. Sauté onion and bell pepper until tender. Add mushrooms, paprika, salt and pepper. Cook mixture until mushrooms are tender. Stir in tomato paste, beer and reserved pan juices. Reduce to low heat and add heavy cream, sour cream and shrimp. Simmer just until hot. In a small skillet, sauté almonds in 1 tablespoon butter and oil until golden browned. Drain almonds on paper towels and sprinkle with salt. Serve shrimp over hot rice in a deep soup bowl. Garnish with almonds.

Serves 4

Shrimp Creole

- 1 medium yellow onion, chopped
- 1 1/2 cups chopped celery
- 1 garlic clove, minced
- 3 tablespoons vegetable oil
- 1 (14 1/2 ounce) can tomatoes, chopped
- 1 (8 ounce) can tomato sauce
- 1 teaspoon sugar
- 1 teaspoon chili powder
- 1 tablespoon cornstarch
- 1/2 cup chopped bell pepper
- 1 1/2 pounds shrimp, peeled and deveined
- Salt and Tabasco sauce to taste
- Hot cooked rice

Sauté onion, celery and garlic in oil in a stockpot until tender. Add tomatoes, tomato sauce, sugar and chili powder. Simmer, uncovered, for 45 minutes. Mix cornstarch with 2 teaspoons water. Add cornstarch and stir until thickened. Add bell pepper, cover and simmer for 30 minutes. Add shrimp, salt and Tabasco and cook for 15 minutes. Serve over cooked rice.

Serves 6

Creole Seafood Gumbo New Orleans Style

- 3½ pounds okra, cut or frozen
- All-purpose flour
- ¼ cup vegetable oil
- 3 medium onions, chopped
- 1 (28 ounce) can tomatoes
- 1 can water
- ⅔ cup chopped cooked ham
- 2 tablespoons minced fresh parsley
- ¼ teaspoon ground thyme
- 1 bay leaf
- 1 garlic clove, minced
- 3 pounds shrimp, peeled
- 1 pound crabmeat or 2 (6 ounce) cans
- Salt and pepper to taste
- Hot cooked rice

Lightly dust okra in flour. Brown okra in small batches in oil in an iron Dutch oven. Sauté onion in a large skillet. Add to okra. Stir in tomatoes, water, ham, parsley, thyme, bay leaf and garlic. Simmer, covered, for 1 hour to 1 hour, 30 minutes, stirring frequently. Gumbo may be frozen at this point. Add shrimp and crabmeat. Season with salt and pepper. Cook an additional 10 minutes. Serve over rice.

Serves 6-8

A Grandmother Shubert recipe dating back to the 1800's. The beauty of this recipe is that you do not have to make the time consuming roux. However, too much flour can make the gumbo too thick. This can be remedied by adding more liquid.

~ Virginia Mathews, Tupelo, MS

Lump Crabmeat and Shrimp

- ½ cup butter
- 1 tablespoon all-purpose flour
- 1 cup heavy cream
- ¼ cup sherry
- 2 tablespoons Worcestershire sauce
- Salt and cayenne pepper to taste
- ½ cup chopped celery
- ¼ cup chopped fresh parsley
- 1 cup mayonnaise
- 1 pound lump crabmeat
- ½ pound shrimp, cooked, peeled and deveined
- Crushed potato chips and shredded Cheddar cheese for garnish

Melt butter in a saucepan. Whisk in flour until smooth. Gradually stir in cream. Add sherry, Worcestershire sauce, salt, cayenne, celery and parsley. Cook and stir until sauce thickens. Cool slightly and add mayonnaise. Stir in crabmeat and shrimp. Spoon mixture into individual buttered shells or casserole dish. Sprinkle with potato chip crumbs and cheese. Bake at 325 degrees for 25 minutes.

Serves 6-8

This dish freezes well.

Shrimp Étouffée

- 3 pounds shrimp, rinsed, peeled and deveined
- Salt and pepper to taste
- ½ cup butter, divided
- 1½ cups chopped celery
- 2 large onions, chopped
- ½ cup less 1 tablespoon all-purpose flour
- 2-2½ cups chicken broth
- 1 (8 ounce) can tomato sauce
- 1 tablespoon Worcestershire sauce
- ¼ teaspoon cayenne pepper
- ½ teaspoon seasoned salt flavor enhancer (optional)
- 2 large bay leaves, broken in half
- ½ teaspoon dried thyme
- ¼ teaspoon Tabasco sauce
- ¼ cup sherry
- ½ cup fresh parsley, minced

Melt 1 teaspoon butter in a heavy stockpot with tight fitting lid. Add shrimp and season with salt and pepper. Cover and steam about 5 minutes, stirring occasionally, until shrimp turn pink. Drain shrimp over a bowl and reserve shrimp broth. Set shrimp aside. Melt 8 tablespoons butter in a 4-quart stockpot. Sauté celery and onion until translucent. Remove from heat and whisk in flour to make a smooth paste. If too dry, add more butter. Measure reserved shrimp broth and add enough chicken broth to equal three cups broth. Add 1 cup of broth and stir until sauce thickens. Add remaining 2 cups broth. Bring to boil, stirring constantly. Add tomato sauce, Worcestershire sauce, cayenne, seasoned salt, bay leaves and thyme. Reduce heat and simmer, stirring occasionally, for 15 minutes. Add cooked shrimp, Tabasco, sherry and parsley. Taste seasonings. Remove bay leaves. Heat thoroughly.

Serves 10-12

Seafood Quiche

- 1 (16 ounce) package frozen crabmeat, thawed and drained
- 1½ cups shrimp, cooked, deveined and chopped
- 1 (8 ounce) package shredded Swiss cheese
- ½ cup chopped celery
- ½ cup chopped green onions
- 2 (9-inch) pie shells, unbaked
- 1 cup mayonnaise
- 2 tablespoons all-purpose flour
- ½ cup dry white wine
- 4 eggs, slightly beaten

Combine crabmeat, shrimp, cheese, celery and onion. Divide mixture evenly among two pie shells. Mix together mayonnaise, flour, wine and eggs. Divide evenly and pour over seafood mixture. Bake at 350 degrees for 35 to 40 minutes.

Serves 8

Good served with a green salad and buttered garlic toast.

Baked Seafood Salad

- ¾ pound shrimp, cooked, peeled and deveined
- 1 cup crabmeat, drained and flaked
- 1 cup thinly sliced celery
- ½ cup chopped pecans
- ½ cup mayonnaise
- 3 tablespoons minced onion
- 1 tablespoon lemon juice
- 1 tablespoon Worcestershire sauce
- ½ teaspoon salt or Creole seasoning
- ⅛ teaspoon pepper
- 1 cup soft cubed bread crumbs

Refrigerate cooked shrimp until cold. Combine shrimp, crabmeat, celery, pecans, mayonnaise, onion, juice, Worcestershire sauce, salt and pepper and mix well. Spoon seafood mixture into an 8 x 8 x 2-inch baking dish or oven-proof baking shells. Sprinkle with bread crumbs. Bake at 350 degrees for 20 to 25 minutes.

Serves 6

Perdido Key BBQ Shrimp

- 5 pounds shrimp, rinsed and peeled
- ½ cup butter, melted
- 1 (16 ounce) bottle Italian dressing
- ½ cup Worcestershire sauce
- Juice of one lemon
- 3 teaspoons pepper

Layer shrimp in the bottom of a 13 x 9 x 2-inch baking dish. Combine butter, dressing, Worcestershire sauce, juice and pepper in a saucepan. Cook over medium heat until blended. Pour sauce over shrimp. Bake, uncovered, at 350 degrees for 20 to 25 minutes.

Serves 6

Maryland Crab Cakes

- 1 pound lump crabmeat, with shells removed
- ⅓ cup minced green onions
- ⅓ cup chopped fresh parsley
- 2 tablespoons lemon juice
- 1 tablespoon milk
- 1 teaspoon Tabasco sauce
- ½ teaspoon salt
- ¼ teaspoon pepper
- 4 large egg whites
- 1⅓ cups dry bread crumbs
- 2 tablespoons vegetable oil, divided
- Lemon wedges

Combine crabmeat, onion, parsley, juice, milk, Tabasco, salt, pepper and egg whites and mix well. Divide mixture into eight equal portions. Dredge crabmeat portions in bread crumbs while shaping into ½-inch patties. Heat 1 tablespoon oil in a non-stick skillet over medium-high heat. Add four patties and cook for 3 minutes. Carefully turn patties over and cook for 3 minutes more until golden browned. Repeat procedure with remaining 1 tablespoon oil and remaining patties. Serve with lemon wedges.

Serves 8

Stuffed Crabs

- 1 cup chopped onions
- ½ cup chopped celery
- 2 garlic cloves, minced
- ½ cup chopped bell pepper
- ½ cup butter or vegetable oil
- ½ teaspoon Worcestershire sauce
- 1 pound crabmeat
- Salt, pepper and cayenne pepper to taste
- ½ cup chopped green onion tops
- Chopped parsley to taste
- 1 cup evaporated milk
- 3 eggs
- 4 stale hamburger buns or 6 slices stale bread
- 12 artificial crab shells
- Bread crumbs

Sauté onion, celery, garlic and bell pepper in butter until tender. Add Worcestershire sauce, crabmeat and season with salt, pepper and cayenne. Cook, stirring constantly, over medium heat for 15 minutes. Add green onion and parsley. Whisk together milk and eggs in a bowl. Soak bread in milk mixture. Add to crabmeat mixture and mix well. Divide mixture and stuff into 12 artificial crab shells. Sprinkle with bread crumbs. Bake at 375 degrees for 10 minutes or until well browned.

Serves 12 stuffed crab shells

Shrimp/Scallop/Crabmeat Sauté

- 6 green onions, cut into 1-inch pieces
- 2 teaspoons minced garlic
- ½ cup butter, melted
- 1 pound shrimp
- ¾ pound scallops
- ½ pound lump crabmeat
- 1 (8 ounce) package sliced mushrooms
- 1 (8 ounce) can sliced water chestnuts, drained
- ½ cup finely chopped bell pepper
- 1 tablespoon plus ½ teaspoon salt-free herb/spice seasoning
- 1 tablespoon Worcestershire sauce
- 2 teaspoons chopped fresh parsley
- Hot cooked rice (optional)

Sauté green onion and garlic in butter in a heavy skillet for 1 minute. Add shrimp, scallops, crabmeat, mushrooms, water chestnuts, bell pepper, seasoning and Worcestershire sauce. Cook, stirring occasionally, for 6 to 8 minutes. Stir in parsley. Serve over hot rice.

Serves 6

Crab Au Gratin

- 6 tablespoons butter, divided
- ⅓ cup all-purpose flour
- ½ teaspoon lemon zest
- ½ teaspoon salt
- ¼ teaspoon dry mustard
- Dash of white pepper
- 1 egg, slightly beaten
- 2 cups half-and-half
- 1 pound lump crabmeat
- 3 tablespoons sliced green onions
- 1 cup soft bread crumbs (1½ slices)
- ½ cup shredded Swiss cheese
- ¼ cup thinly sliced almonds, toasted

In a saucepan, melt 4 tablespoons butter and blend in flour, zest, salt, mustard and pepper. Whisk together egg and half-and-half. Add to flour mixture. Cook and stir over medium heat until thickened. Do not boil. Stir in crabmeat and onion. Pour mixture into a buttered au gratin or shallow casserole dish. Bake at 350 degrees for 15 minutes. Melt remaining 2 tablespoons butter in microwave. Mix with bread crumbs, cheese and almonds. Sprinkle mixture around edges of dish. Bake an additional 5 minutes or until cheese melts.

Serves 6

They say, on the coast, that there is not a pound of anything that will serve as many people as a pound of crabmeat! Company fare that is.

~ Lucy Gaines, Tupelo, MS

Crawfish Grits

- 3 tablespoons olive oil
- 2 tablespoons chopped garlic
- 1½ cups chopped green onions, reserving chopped green tops
- Salt and cayenne pepper to taste
- 1 pound crawfish tails, rinsed and peeled
- 2 cups beef broth
- 2 cups half-and-half
- 1 cup heavy cream
- 1½ cups quick grits
- ¾ cup shredded Parmesan cheese

Heat oil in a saucepan. Sauté garlic for 1 minute. Add onion, salt and cayenne and sauté for 1 to 2 minutes until soft. Add crawfish and cook for 2 minutes. Pour in broth, half-and-half and cream. Bring to boil, reduce heat and simmer for 2 minutes. Add grits and cook, stirring constantly, for 8 to 12 minutes. Add cheese and stir until cheese melts. Stir in remaining green onion tops. Serve hot.

Serves 8

Crab and Mushroom Mornay

- **2 (6 ounce) cans mushrooms caps, drained or 2 pints fresh, stems removed**
- **1 (6 ounce) can crabmeat, flaked**
- **2 teaspoons lemon juice**
- **3 tablespoons butter**
- **3 tablespoons all-purpose flour**
- **1½ cups milk**
- **2 egg yolks, slightly beaten**
- **1½ cups shredded sharp Cheddar cheese, divided**
- **2 tablespoons sherry**
- **Toast points or thinly sliced toasted French bread**

Arrange mushrooms, hollow side up, in an 8 x 8 x 2-inch baking dish. Cover with crabmeat. Drizzle with juice. Melt butter in a saucepan. Whisk in flour. Add milk. Cook and stir until bubbly and thickened. Add a small amount of hot cream mixture to egg yolks. Return egg yolk mixture to creamed mixture. Cook 1 minute. Remove from heat. Add 1¼ cups cheese and sherry. Pour sauce over crabmeat. Sprinkle with remaining ¼ cup cheese. Bake at 350 degrees for 20 minutes or until very hot. Serve with toast points or French bread.

Serves 4-6

Catfish Court-Bouillon

- **½ cup vegetable oil**
- **½ cup all-purpose flour**
- **1 cup chopped onion**
- **1 cup chopped celery**
- **1 cup chopped bell pepper**
- **4 garlic cloves, minced**
- **6 cups chicken broth, fish broth or water**
- **1 (15 ounce) can tomato sauce**
- **1 (10 ounce) can diced tomatoes with chilies**
- **2 bay leaves**
- **3 pounds catfish fillets, cut into bite-size pieces**
- **Creole seasoning**
- **8 cups hot cooked rice**

In Dutch oven, cook oil and flour over medium heat until mixture boils, stirring constantly. Reduce heat and cook for 10 minutes until roux turns medium brown. Add onion, celery, pepper and garlic. Cook and stir until tender. Stir in broth. Add tomato sauce, tomatoes and bay leaves. Bring to boil. Reduce heat, cover and simmer for 30 minutes. Sprinkle catfish pieces with Creole seasoning. Add to tomato mixture. Cover and simmer an additional 25 minutes or until fish flakes easily. Season with more Creole seasoning. Remove bay leaves. Spoon 1 cup rice onto each serving plate. Spoon catfish mixture over rice.

Serves 8

Crawfish Pie

- 1 large onion, chopped
- ¼ cup minced green onions
- 2 garlic cloves, chopped
- ½ bell pepper, chopped
- 2 stalks celery, chopped
- ¼ cup butter
- 1 (10¾ ounce) can cream of celery soup
- ¼ cup tomato sauce
- 1 pound crawfish, rinsed and coarsely chopped
- ¼ cup minced parsley
- ½ cup seasoned dry bread crumbs
- 1 teaspoon salt
- ½ teaspoon cayenne pepper
- ½ teaspoon pepper
- 1 egg, beaten
- 1 cup milk
- Pastry for 10-inch double crust pie

Sauté onion, green onion, garlic, pepper and celery in butter until tender. Add soup, tomato sauce, crawfish and parsley. Cook over low heat for 10 minutes. Remove from heat and add bread crumbs, salt, cayenne, pepper and egg. Add milk and mix well. Press one pastry sheet into bottom of pie plate. Pour crawfish mixture into pastry-lined pie pan. Top with remaining pastry sheet and seal edges. Cut slits in top of pastry to allow steam to escape. Bake at 350 degrees for 35 to 40 minutes or until lightly browned.

Serves 8

The crawfish filling is best when made the day before to allow the flavors to blend. It is also good over cooked rice.

Crawfish Somethin'!

- ½ cup chopped bell pepper
- 1 cup chopped green onion
- 1 (10 ounce) can tomatoes with green chilies with juice
- 2 cups frozen crawfish tails, thawed
- 2 (10¾ ounce) cans cream of mushroom soup
- 2 (4 ounce) cans sliced mushrooms, drained
- ½-¾ cup mayonnaise
- 2 (6.9 ounce) packages long grain and wild rice, cook according to package directions

Combine pepper, onion, tomatoes with juice, crawfish, soup, mushrooms, mayonnaise and cooked rice. Mix well. Pour mixture into a 3-quart casserole dish. Bake at 350 degrees for 30 minutes.

Serves 6-8

Catfish Lucie

- 4 catfish fillets
- Salt and pepper to taste
- Juice of one lemon
- Garlic powder to taste or minced garlic
- 2 tablespoons white wine
- Worcestershire sauce to taste
- 4 slices bacon

Season fillets with salt and pepper. Place in a shallow baking dish. Sprinkle with juice and garlic powder. Pour wine and Worcestershire sauce over fillets. Place a slice of bacon on each fillet. Cover dish with foil. Bake at 350 degrees for 20 minutes. Uncover and bake 5 to 10 minutes more or until fish flakes easily.

Serves 4

Serve with a green salad and baked potato.

Catfish Étouffée

- 2 cups finely chopped onions
- ¼ cup finely chopped celery
- ¼ cup finely chopped bell pepper
- 12 tablespoons butter
- 3 pounds boneless catfish fillets, cut into 4-inch squares
- 1 teaspoon pepper
- 1 teaspoon cayenne pepper
- 1 teaspoon salt
- Hot cooked rice

Sauté onion, celery and bell pepper in butter over medium heat until translucent. Season fish with salt and pepper. Gently add fish to vegetables. Turn gently to avoid breaking fish. Do not stir. Reduce heat and simmer 20 to 25 minutes. Serve over cooked rice.

Serves 4-5

Pecan Catfish

- 2 tablespoons milk
- 3 tablespoons mustard
- 4 catfish fillets
- 1 cup ground pecans

Combine milk and mustard. Dip fillets in milk mixture and then dip in pecans, shaking off excess. Place on a greased baking sheet. Broil at 500 degrees for 10 to 12 minutes or until fish flakes easily.

Serves 4

Mustard and Dill Fish Fillets

- **1 pound fish fillets (sea bass, salmon, halibut or swordfish)**
- **¼ cup lemon juice**
- **¼ cup olive oil**
- **2 tablespoons chopped fresh dill or ¾ teaspoon dried**
- **1 tablespoon Dijon or grainy mustard**
- **1 garlic clove, minced**
- **Salt and pepper to taste**

Rinse fish and pat dry. Place fish in a shallow greased baking dish. Whisk together juice, oil, dill, mustard, garlic and season with salt and pepper. Pour mixture over fish and let stand for 1 hour. Bake at 375 degrees or grill over medium heat for 10 to 12 minutes or until fish flakes.

Serves 3-4

Foil Baked Fish

- **4 (6 ounce) white fish fillets**
- **½ cup sliced carrots**
- **½ cup diced bell peppers**
- **½ cup diced onion**
- **½ cup chopped celery**
- **1 cup fresh mushrooms**
- **1 tablespoon dried parsley**
- **½ teaspoon paprika**
- **½ teaspoon dried oregano**
- **4 teaspoons lemon juice**

Preheat oven to 450 degrees. Place fillets on foil. Combine carrots, bell pepper, onion, celery, mushrooms, parsley, paprika, oregano and juice. Mix well. Spread vegetable mixture over fish. Seal foil and bake at 450 degrees for 25 minutes.

Serves 4

Trout Rolls

- **1 cup cooked rice**
- **1 (10 ounce) package frozen chopped spinach, thawed and squeezed dry**
- **¼ cup diced onion**
- **¼ cup slivered almonds**
- **1 pound fresh or frozen trout fillets, thawed**
- **1 (10¾ ounce) can cream of mushroom soup**
- **Cajun seasoning to taste**

Combine rice, spinach, onion and almonds. Spread spinach mixture over fillets. Roll or wrap up fillets and secure with toothpicks. Place rolls in an 11 x 7 x 2-inch baking dish. Pour soup over trout rolls. Season with Cajun seasoning. Bake at 350 degrees for 1 hour. Remove toothpicks before serving. Prepare one roll per person.

Serves 3-4

Crunchy Catfish with Lemon Parsley Sauce

- 3 green onions, chopped
- 2 tablespoons lemon juice
- ½ cup plus 2 tablespoons butter, divided
- 1 tablespoon dried parsley
- ½ teaspoon salt
- ½ teaspoon pepper
- Dash of Tabasco sauce
- Worcestershire sauce to taste
- 2 large eggs, beaten
- 2 tablespoons water
- ½ cup round butter crackers, crushed
- ¼ cup Parmesan cheese
- 1 tablespoon Greek seasoning
- 4 large catfish fillets

Combine onion, juice, 8 tablespoons butter, parsley, salt, pepper, Tabasco and Worcestershire sauce in a saucepan. Keep sauce warm over low heat. Whisk together eggs and water. In a separate bowl, combine cracker crumbs, cheese and seasoning. Dip fillets in egg mixture and then in crumb mixture. Place in a 13 x 9 x 2-inch greased baking dish. Drizzle 2 tablespoons melted butter over fillets. Bake at 325 degrees for 30 minutes. Pour warm lemon parsley sauce over fish.

Serves 4

Spicy Low-Cal Baked Fish

- 1 teaspoon vegetable oil
- 1 medium onion, sliced
- ¼ teaspoon crushed red pepper
- 1 bell pepper, cut into ½-inch rounds
- ½ cup sliced carrots
- 1 bay leaf
- 1 (16 ounce) can Italian style tomatoes, drained and coarsely chopped
- ¼ teaspoon salt
- ¼ teaspoon pepper
- 1 (12 ounce) package frozen fish, thawed
- 2 tablespoons chopped fresh parsley
- Hot cooked rice

Preheat oven to 425 degrees. Heat oil on non-stick skillet. Sauté onion for 3 minutes until tender. Add red pepper, bell pepper and carrots. Cook until vegetables are lightly browned. Add bay leaf, tomatoes, salt and pepper. Cook, stirring occasionally, until liquid is reduced by half and thickened. Remove from heat and set aside. Arrange fish side by side in baking dish. Pour tomato sauce over fish. Bake at 425 degrees for 20 to 25 minutes. Remove from oven and remove bay leaf. Sprinkle with parsley and serve over cooked rice.

Serves 2 or more depending on number of fish fillets.

Baked Tilapia

1 tablespoon butter, melted
12 ounces frozen tilapia fillets, thawed (grouper, orange roughly or mahi-mahi)
¼ cup sour cream
¼ cup mayonnaise
½ teaspoon horseradish
Juice of one lemon
1 teaspoon dried dill
1 cup French fried onion rings

Drizzle butter over fish and bake at 375 degrees for 25 minutes or until fish flakes easily. Meanwhile, whisk together sour cream, mayonnaise, horseradish, juice and dill. Remove cooked fish from oven. Spread dill sauce evenly over fish and top with onion rings. Broil for 1 minute until onion rings are golden browned.

Serves 4

If using fresh fillets, may need to reduce baking time. Serve fish with steamed broccoli and boiled, seasoned new red potatoes.

Roast Salmon with Capers and Tarragon

3 tablespoons butter
⅓ cup dry bread crumbs
¼ cup loosely packed fresh parsley, minced
3 tablespoons capers, drained and minced
1 teaspoon dried tarragon, crushed
2 teaspoons lemon zest
¼ teaspoon salt
¼ teaspoon coarsely ground pepper
2 pounds whole salmon fillet
Lemon wedges and tarragon sprigs for garnish

Preheat oven to 450 degrees. Melt butter in a saucepan. Remove from heat. Stir in bread crumbs, parsley, capers, tarragon, zest, salt and pepper. Line a 15 x 10 x 1-inch jelly-roll pan with foil. Grease the foil. Place salmon, skin side down, on pan and pat crumb mixture on top. Roast at 450 degrees for 30 minutes or until salmon turns opaque throughout and topping is lightly browned. With two large spatulas, carefully transfer salmon to platter. Not to worry if skin sticks. Serve with lemon wedges and garnish with tarragon sprigs.

Serves 6

When serving food to seated guests, serve from the left; remove plates from the right.

~from The New Food Lover's Tiptionary

Salmon with Roasted Asparagus and Lemon-Caper Sauce

2 tablespoons fresh lemon juice
½ teaspoon lemon zest
2 tablespoons olive oil, divided
1 tablespoon capers, drained and chopped
1 teaspoon chopped fresh thyme
Salt and pepper to taste
1 pound asparagus, ends trimmed
4 salmon fillets, 1¼ to 1½-inches thick

Whisk together juice, zest, 1 tablespoon oil, capers and thyme in a small bowl. Season with salt and pepper. Set sauce aside. Preheat oven to 450 degrees. Arrange asparagus in an even layer in a rimmed baking sheet. Drizzle with remaining tablespoon oil and turn to coat. Season with salt and pepper. Place salmon atop asparagus. Sprinkle with salt and pepper. Bake at 450 degrees for 20 minutes until center is opaque. Transfer asparagus and salmon to serving platter. Spoon lemon-caper sauce over salmon.

Serves 4

Red Snapper En Papillote with Basil Butter

1 cup loosely packed basil leaves, chopped
¼ cup lemon juice
1 cup butter, softened
3 pounds red snapper fillets, skinned and cut into 6 pieces
Salt and pepper to taste
1 cup orange segments, fresh or Mandarin
2 bunches asparagus, sliced lengthwise

Cream together basil, juice and butter until smooth. Season fillets with salt and pepper. Place each fillet in a piece of greased parchment paper. Top with orange segments, asparagus and a spoonful of basil butter. Fold long sides of paper over fish and roll outer edges to seal. Place fillets on a baking sheet. Bake at 450 degrees for 10 minutes. Serve parchment packets to each guest, allowing each to open their own packet and get the full effect of the steamed fish, butter and vegetables.

Serves 6

Salmon with Onions and Capers

- 2 teaspoons olive oil, divided
- 4 salmon fillets, skinned
- ¼ teaspoon salt
- ⅛ teaspoon pepper
- 1 medium onion, sliced
- ¼ cup capers, drained
- 1 teaspoon sugar
- 1 tablespoon balsamic vinegar

Heat 1 teaspoon oil in a skillet. Over high heat cook salmon, rounded side down, for 2 minutes until lightly browned. Transfer salmon to a 13 x 9 x 2-inch baking dish. Sprinkle with salt and pepper. In a small skillet, heat remaining teaspoon oil. Sauté onion for 5 minutes or until tender. Add capers, sugar and vinegar and cook 2 minutes, stirring often. Spoon mixture over salmon. Cover with foil and bake at 350 degrees for 12 to 15 minutes or until fish flakes easily.

Serves 4

Orange Roughy with Dill

- 3 tablespoons butter, divided
- ½ cup soft bread crumbs
- ½ pound orange roughy fillets
- ¼ teaspoon dried dill or more to taste
- Salt and pepper to taste

Place 2 tablespoons butter in a microwave safe dish. Microwave on high for 25 to 30 seconds or until butter is melted. Stir in bread crumbs and cook 2 minutes, stirring after 1 minute. Remove crumbs from dish and set aside. Place 1 remaining tablespoon butter in dish and cook 10 to 15 seconds. Add fish, turning to coat in butter. Season with dill, salt and pepper. Cook 2 minutes. Let rest, covered, for 5 minutes. Drain any juices. Sprinkle bread crumbs over fish and cook, uncovered, for 30 to 45 seconds.

Serves 4

Asian Salmon Fillets

- 3 tablespoons soy sauce
- 3 tablespoons lemon juice
- 1 tablespoon honey
- ½ teaspoon chopped garlic
- 2-4 salmon fillets

Combine soy sauce, juice, honey and garlic in a jar. Cover and shake well. Place salmon fillets in a 13 x 9 x 2-inch glass baking dish. Spoon marinade over fillets. Refrigerate at least 30 minutes or more. Broil for 10 minutes per inch thickness of fish, turning once and basting. Broil until desired degree of doneness.

Serves 2-4

Smoked Salmon Tartare

- ¼ cup olive oil
- ⅓ cup lemon juice
- ¼ cup chopped green onion
- ¼ cup chopped fresh parsley
- Chopped fresh basil to taste
- ½ teaspoon Tabasco sauce
- 2 tablespoons capers
- 1 teaspoon pepper
- 1½ pounds smoked salmon, trimmed and coarsely chopped
- Pumpernickel rounds

Combine oil, juice, onion, parsley, basil, Tabasco, capers and pepper in a bowl. Add salmon and toss to coat. Taste seasonings. Refrigerate in marinade for several hours. Serve on pumpernickel rounds.

Serves 12-15

Bourbon-Glazed Salmon

- ¾ cup packed brown sugar
- 6 tablespoons bourbon or 4 tablespoons molasses
- ¼ cup soy sauce
- 2 tablespoons fresh lime juice
- 2 teaspoons grated fresh ginger
- ½ teaspoon salt
- ¼ teaspoon freshly ground black pepper
- 2 garlic cloves, crushed
- 8 (6 ounce) salmon fillets, 1-inch thick
- 4 teaspoons sesame seeds
- ½ cup thinly sliced green onions

Combine brown sugar, bourbon, soy sauce, juice, ginger, salt, pepper and garlic in a large zip-top plastic bag. Add salmon and marinate in refrigerator for 30 minutes, turning bag once. Remove fillets and discard marinade. Preheat broiler. Place fillets on greased broiler pan. Broil for 11 minutes or until fish flakes easily with a fork. Sprinkle each fillet with ½ teaspoon sesame seeds and 1 tablespoon green onion. Serve immediately.

Serves 8

Cocktail Sauce

- ¾ cup ketchup
- ¼ cup chili sauce
- 2 tablespoons fresh lemon juice
- 2-6 tablespoons horseradish
- 1 tablespoon Worcestershire sauce
- 2-4 dashes Tabasco sauce

Combine ketchup, chili sauce, juice, horseradish, Worcestershire sauce and Tabasco and mix well. Refrigerate until ready to use. Serve with oysters, shrimp or any seafood.

Serves 1½ cups sauce

Seafarer's Salmon Pie

- 1½ cups all-purpose flour
- ½ cup Parmesan cheese
- ¾ cup vegetable shortening
- 3-4 teaspoons water
- 1 (14¾ ounce) can Red Salmon, flaked
- 1 large onion, diced
- Garlic to taste
- 2 tablespoons butter, melted
- 1 (16 ounce) container sour cream
- 4 eggs, beaten
- 1½ cups shredded sharp Cheddar cheese
- ¼ teaspoon salt

To make Parmesan crust, combine flour and cheese. Cut in shortening until mixture resembles small peas. Sprinkle with 2 teaspoons water and shape into a ball. Add more water if necessary to reach desired consistency. Press into the bottom and up the sides of a 9-inch pie plate. Bake at 375 degrees for 10 minutes. For the filling, combine salmon, onion, garlic, butter, sour cream, eggs, cheese and salt. Pour mixture into crust. Bake at 375 degrees for 65 to 70 minutes. Cool 15 minutes in pan. (If using a glass pie plate, reduce cook time to 50 minutes.)

Serves 6

Rémoulade Sauce

- 1 garlic clove, crushed
- 2 cups mayonnaise
- 2 tablespoons Creole mustard
- 1 tablespoon horseradish
- ¼ cup lemon juice
- 2 tablespoons Worcestershire sauce
- Dash of Tabasco sauce
- Lemon pepper to taste
- ½ inch anchovy paste
- 3 tablespoons chopped parsley
- 2 tablespoons minced onion

Combine garlic, mayonnaise, Creole mustard, horseradish, juice, Worcestershire sauce, Tabasco, lemon pepper, anchovy paste, parsley and onion and mix well. Taste seasonings.

Serves 2 cups sauce

I was in the kitchen with my mother from the age of three or four. My German mother was an excellent cook but she had advanced rheumatoid arthritis – therefore cooking was my regular duty.

~Romaine Dickson, Belden, MS

Great Cooks

I grew up around some great cooks, including my mom, Aunt Judy, Great Aunt Willie Lee and though I had two terrific grandmothers, only one of them could really cook. Southern cooking meant more than good food; it was a way of life for us. Most of our gatherings were around a homemade meal fit for any southern king or queen along with the discussion of how much flour to add to the drippings for thick or thin gravy. So...when I was about twelve years old, our 4-H office held a cooking contest during Dairy Month. If you are a 4-H-er you know that June is Dairy Month. The contest was opened to the community. I encouraged my grandmother Davenport to enter knowing she had a real good chance of winning. Not to be partial, I mentioned the contest to my other grandmother, Willie Arnesen, the one that could not cook well.

Grandmother Arnesen had one dish that she could throw together that we would all ooh and aah over. It was a banana pudding with pineapple in it. To my surprise, she entered this dish in the contest. My grandmother Davenport entered a homemade pastry with fruit on the inside. A recipe that involved a lot of steps and a lot of time.

I felt embarrassed then, as I still feel, when I tell this story of the day I pitted my dear grandmothers against each other in a cooking contest. By now you have probably guessed the ending. Grandmother Arnesen won first place. Grandmother Davenport didn't even get in the top three. It just goes to show that southern beauty is not the only thing that is judged in the eye of the beholder!

Unsigned

As the wife of a pastor, I have discovered that "table fellowship" closely resembles the fellowship that believers will have in heaven. Some of our closest, most intimate times have been around our table with just family or friends.

~Anna Fortner, Tupelo, MS

Chicken Parmigiana

- **½ cup bread crumbs**
- **½ cup grated Parmesan cheese**
- **4 boneless, skinless chicken breast halves, pounded flat**
- **1 egg, beaten**
- **3 tablespoons olive oil**
- **1 (26 ounce) jar red pasta sauce**
- **½ cup shredded mozzarella cheese**
- **Hot cooked spaghetti or angel hair pasta**

Combine bread crumbs and Parmesan cheese. Dip chicken in egg and dredge in crumb mixture. Brown chicken in oil on both sides. Place chicken in a greased 11 x 7 x 2-inch baking dish. Pour sauce over chicken and top with cheese. Bake at 375 degrees for 20 minutes. Serve with spaghetti or angel hair pasta.

Serves 4-6

Chicken Enchiladas

- **2 cups chopped cooked chicken or turkey**
- **1 cup chopped bell pepper**
- **1 (8 ounce) package cream cheese, cubed**
- **1 (8 ounce) jar salsa, divided**
- **8 (6-inch) flour tortillas**
- **12 ounces processed cheese loaf, cubed**
- **¼ cup milk**

Combine chicken, pepper, cream cheese and ½ cup salsa in a saucepan. Cook and stir until cheese melts. Spoon ⅓ cup chicken mixture down the center of each tortilla. Roll up. Place seam-side down in a lightly greased 12 x 8 x 2-inch baking dish. Combine cheese loaf cubes and milk in a separate saucepan. Cook and stir until cheese melts. Pour cheese sauce over tortillas. Cover with foil. Bake at 350 degrees for 20 minutes or until heated. Pour remaining salsa over hot tortillas.

Serves 6-8

Curry Chicken Divan

- **½ cup honey**
- **½ cup Dijon mustard**
- **1 teaspoon curry powder**
- **2 tablespoons soy sauce**
- **4 boneless, skinless chicken breast halves**
- **Hot cooked rice**

Combine honey, mustard, curry and soy sauce. Mix well. Pour over chicken and marinate overnight in the refrigerator. Bake at 350 degrees for 1 hour. Serve over a bed of rice.

Serves 4

Chicken with Artichoke Hearts

- 8 boneless, skinless chicken breast halves
- ⅛ teaspoon salt
- ½ teaspoon pepper
- ½ teaspoon paprika
- 2 tablespoons butter
- 1 (15½ ounce) can artichoke hearts, drained
- 2 teaspoons olive oil
- 2 tablespoons all-purpose flour
- ¼ cup chopped onions
- 1 (6 ounce) jar sliced mushrooms
- ⅔ cup low-fat, low-salt chicken broth
- ¼ cup dry white wine
- ¼ cup dry sherry
- 1 teaspoon chopped fresh rosemary

Season chicken with salt, pepper and paprika. In a skillet, brown chicken on all sides in butter. Layer chicken in bottom of a 3-quart covered casserole dish. Arrange artichokes among chicken. Heat oil over medium heat in same skillet. Stir in flour. Sauté onion and mushrooms until tender. Add some broth if vegetables stick while cooking. Add all broth, wine, sherry and rosemary. Cook, stirring constantly, until thickened. Pour over chicken in dish. Cover and bake at 375 degrees for 1 hour or until chicken is tender.

Serves 8

Bali Chicken

- 4 boneless, skinless chicken breast halves
- Prepared mustard
- Gingersnap cookies, finely crushed
- 1 garlic clove, minced
- ½ cup finely chopped onion
- 2 tablespoons peanut oil
- ¼ cup rice wine vinegar
- 1 tablespoon crushed red pepper
- 2 teaspoons ground allspice
- 2 teaspoons packed brown sugar
- ¼ cup diced sweet bell pepper
- 2 teaspoons chopped fresh basil
- Hot cooked yellow rice or couscous

Flatten chicken with a mallet between sheets of waxed paper. Brush generously with mustard. Dredge chicken in cookie crumbs. Place in a 13 x 9 x 2-inch baking dish. Cover with foil and cut slit in top. Bake at 350 degrees for 20 minutes. Meanwhile make sauce by sautéing garlic and onion in oil until tender. Add vinegar, red pepper, allspice and brown sugar. Mix until blended. Transfer sauce to a food processor. Blend until mixed but not runny. Add bell pepper and basil. Serve chicken with sauce on the side and rice or couscous.

Serves 4

Sesame-Ginger Chicken

- 1 tablespoon sesame seeds, toasted
- 2 teaspoons grated fresh ginger
- 2 tablespoons honey
- 2 tablespoons low-salt soy sauce
- 4 boneless, skinless chicken breast halves
- Thin green onion strips for garnish

Combine sesame seeds, ginger, honey and soy sauce and mix well. Set aside. Use a mallet to flatten chicken between 2 sheets of heavy duty plastic wrap to ¼-inch thickness. Heat grill to medium heat. Grill chicken for 4 minutes on each side, basting frequently with soy sauce mixture. Transfer chicken to serving platter and garnish with green onion strips.

Serves 4

To peel fresh ginger, scrape the skin with the edge of a spoon.

~from
The New Food Lover's Tiptionary

Southwest Chicken Bundles

- 8 boneless, skinless chicken breast halves
- Salt and pepper to taste
- 1 cup shredded pepper Jack cheese
- 1 cup cream cheese, softened
- 8 thin slices bacon
- ½ cup ranch salad dressing, room temperature
- ½ cup mild picante sauce, room temperature
- Tomato wedges and jalapeño peppers for garnish

Flatten chicken with a mallet between two sheets of plastic wrap to ¼-inch thickness. Season with salt and pepper. Combine Jack cheese and cream cheese and divide into 8 equal portions. Roll into balls. Place 1 cheese ball in the middle of each chicken breast. Fold chicken around cheese to form a bundle. Wrap a piece of bacon around each bundle and fasten with a toothpick. Place bundles in a 13 x 9 x 2-inch baking dish. Bake, uncovered, at 350 degrees for 30 minutes or until tender. Broil chicken for 3 to 5 minutes until bacon is browned. Remove toothpicks. Combine dressing and picante sauce and serve over chicken bundles. Garnish with tomato wedges and jalapeño peppers.

Serves 8

Marinated Baked Chicken

- 2 cups sour cream
- ¼ cup lemon juice
- 2 teaspoons paprika
- 1 tablespoon salt
- 2 teaspoons celery salt
- 4 teaspoons Worcestershire sauce
- ½ teaspoon garlic salt
- 1 teaspoon pepper
- 12 boneless, skinless chicken breast halves
- 1½ cups crushed round butter crackers
- 1½ cups crushed saltine crackers
- 1 cup butter, melted

Combine sour cream, juice, paprika, salt, celery salt, Worcestershire sauce, garlic salt and pepper. Add chicken to marinade and refrigerate overnight. Mix together butter cracker crumbs and saltine cracker crumbs. Remove chicken from marinade and dredge in cracker crumbs. Place in a shallow dish. Spoon half of melted butter over chicken. Bake at 300 degrees for 1 hour. Spoon remaining butter over chicken and bake an additional 45 minutes.

Serves 12

Cold New Orleans Chicken

- 6 tablespoons wine vinegar
- ½ cup olive oil
- 1 teaspoon salt
- 1 teaspoon sugar
- 1 teaspoon paprika
- Tabasco sauce to taste
- ¼ teaspoon garlic powder
- 7 ounces vermicelli, cooked al dente
- 1 small whole chicken
- 4 stalks celery, divided
- Bell pepper, onion, salt and pepper to taste
- 1 cup mayonnaise
- Juice of one lemon

Combine vinegar, oil, salt, sugar, paprika, Tabasco, and garlic powder in a jar. Seal tightly and shake well. Season vermicelli with seasoned salt and add dressing. Marinate overnight. Cook chicken in a stockpot with 1 stalk celery, bell pepper, onion, salt and pepper. Cool completely. Cut up cooled chicken and mix with 3 stalks chopped celery. Add mayonnaise and mix well. Add vermicelli and mix well. Just before serving, sprinkle with lemon juice and stir. Serve cold.

Serves 8

Chicken and Asparagus Casserole

- 1 (14½ ounce) can asparagus, drained
- 2½ cups chopped, cooked chicken
- 1 (2 ounce) jar pimento, drained
- 3 hard-cooked eggs, sliced
- ½-1 cup shredded Cheddar cheese plus more for topping
- 1 cup crushed saltine crackers plus more for topping
- 1 (10¾ ounce) can cream of chicken soup
- ½ soup can milk or water
- 6 tablespoons butter, cut in slices

Layer half of asparagus, chicken, pimento, eggs, cheese and crackers crumbs in a greased 11 x 7 x 2-inch baking dish. Repeat layers in same order. Whisk together soup and milk. Pour over chicken mixture. Sprinkle with additional cheese and cracker crumbs. Dot with butter slices. Bake at 375 degrees for 30 minutes.

Serves 6

...like bread, potatoes and rice, chicken may be eaten constantly without becoming nauseating.

~Andre Simon, French gastronome

~from The New Food Lover's Tiptionary

Chicken and Rice Casserole

- 1 (10¾ ounce) can cream chicken soup
- ½ cup milk
- ¼ teaspoon pepper
- ½ teaspoon salt
- ⅓ cup mayonnaise
- 2 cups chopped, cooked chicken
- ½ cup chopped onions
- 1 cup frozen green peas, thawed
- ¼ cup chopped bell pepper
- 2 cups cooked white rice
- 1 cup shredded Cheddar cheese, divided

Blend together soup, milk, pepper, salt and mayonnaise. In a large bowl, combine chicken, onion, peas, pepper and rice. Stir in soup mixture and ½ cup cheese. Pour chicken mixture into a greased 11 x 7 x 2-inch baking dish. Top with remaining ½ cup cheese. Bake at 350 degrees for 25 minutes.

Serves 10

Chicken Salad Tart

- 2 (9-inch) frozen deep dish pie crusts
- 2 large boneless, skinless chicken breast halves, cooked and chopped
- 3 hard-cooked eggs, chopped
- 1 cup chopped celery
- ½ (8 ounce) can water chestnuts, diced
- ½ cup mayonnaise
- 1 (10¾ ounce) can cream chicken soup
- Juice of one-half lemon
- Salt and pepper to taste
- 1 cup shredded Cheddar cheese
- 1 (5½ ounce) bag potato chips, crushed
- Sweet pickles for garnish

Bake pie crust according to package directions. Set aside. Combine chicken, eggs, celery, water chestnuts, mayonnaise, soup and juice and mix well. Divide chicken mixture evenly between two crusts. Cover each with cheese and top with potato chip crumbs. Bake at 350 degrees for 30 minutes. Garnish with sweet pickles.

Serves 8-12

Chicken Olé Casserole

- ¼ cup butter
- 1 medium bell pepper, chopped
- 1 medium onion, chopped
- 1 (10¾ ounce) can cream mushroom soup
- 1 (10¾ ounce) can cream chicken soup
- 2 (10 ounce) cans diced tomatoes with green chiles
- 4 cups cubed cooked chicken
- 12 corn tortillas, torn into bite-size pieces
- 1 (8 ounce) package shredded Cheddar cheese

Preheat oven to 325 degrees. Melt butter in a large saucepan. Sauté pepper and onion for 5 minutes or until tender. Add soups, tomatoes and chicken and stir well. Layer tortillas, chicken mixture and cheese in a 13 x 9 x 2-inch baking dish. Bake at 325 degrees for 40 minutes or until cheese is bubbly.

Serves 8

Walnut Baked Chicken Supreme

- All-purpose flour
- Salt, pepper and paprika to taste
- 4 boneless, skinless chicken breast halves
- ½ cup unsalted butter
- 1 cup heavy cream
- ½ cup walnuts
- Hot cooked brown rice

Season flour with salt, pepper and paprika. Dredge chicken in flour mixture. Brown chicken in melted butter in skillet. Transfer chicken to an 11 x 7 x 2-inch baking dish. Pour melted butter from skillet over chicken. Pour in cream and top with walnuts. Bake at 350 degrees for 1 hour. Serve over brown rice with a green vegetable.

Serves 4

Magnolia Chicken Piccata

- 4 boneless, skinless chicken breast halves
- All-purpose flour
- Salt to taste
- 3 tablespoons butter
- 1 tablespoon lemon juice
- ½ cup water
- 1 chicken bouillon cube
- Lemon slices for garnish

Lightly flour chicken and season with salt. Brown chicken in melted butter in a skillet. Remove chicken to a plate. Add lemon juice, water and bouillon cube to skillet. Cook and stir until cube is dissolved. Return chicken to skillet and simmer for 15 to 20 minutes. Garnish with lemon slices.

Serves 4

Slow-Roasted Garlic and Lemon Chicken

- 1 whole chicken, cut up
- 1 garlic head, cloves separated and unpeeled
- 2 lemons, cut into eight wedges
- Fresh thyme to taste and for garnish
- 3 tablespoons olive oil
- ½ cup white wine
- Pepper to taste

Preheat oven to 300 degrees. Place chicken pieces into a roasting pan. Add garlic cloves and lemon wedges. Season with thyme. Add oil and mix to cover chicken. Chicken should be skin-side up. Pour in wine and season with pepper. Cover tightly with foil and bake at 300 degrees for 2 hours. Remove foil and turn oven to 400 degrees. Roast for an additional 30 to 40 minutes. Garnish with more thyme.

Serves 4-6

Roast Rock Cornish Game Hens

4 (1 pound) Cornish game hens
Salt and pepper to taste
Prepared bread stuffing (optional)
1/3 cup butter, melted
1/4 cup consommé
1/4 cup light corn syrup
Cooked brown or mushroom wild rice

Remove giblet from hens. Rinse hens with cold water and pat dry. Season inside and out with salt and pepper. If desired, stuff each hen with 1/4 cup stuffing. May roast without stuffing. Place breast side up on a rack in a shallow roasting pan. Brush with butter. Roast, uncovered, at 400 degrees for 45 minutes. Mix together consommé and corn syrup. During last 15 minutes, baste several times with sauce mixture. Serve with brown or mushroom wild rice.

Serves 4

Chicken Breast with Brown Butter Caper Sauce

6 boneless, skinless chicken breast halves
All-purpose flour
Salt and pepper to taste
6 tablespoons vegetable oil
2 cups butter
1 1/4 cups low-salt chicken broth
1/4 cup sherry vinegar, warmed and divided
1 (2 ounce) jar capers, drained
Chives for garnish

Using a mallet, pound chicken until flat. Lightly flour and season with salt and pepper. Brown in oil in a skillet. Keep warm. Cook butter, stirring constantly, over low heat until brown in color. Cool slightly. In a saucepan, boil broth until reduced by one-third. Cool slightly. Pour broth and half of vinegar into a blender. Process on low speed. Slowly add browned butter and blend until thickened. If needed, add 2 tablespoons of cold butter to reach desired consistency. Add remaining vinegar and capers. Pour sauce over chicken in skillet. Simmer for 2 minutes.

Serves 6

May substitute veal or fish for chicken.

Calhoun Chicken Cobbler

- 3 tablespoons olive oil, divided
- 1 onion, chopped
- 1 sweet red pepper, diced
- 1 jalapeño pepper, seeded and minced
- 1 garlic clove, minced
- ¾ cup all-purpose flour, divided
- 1 (14½ ounce) can chicken broth
- ¼ cup lime juice
- ½ teaspoon ground cumin
- ½ teaspoon lime zest
- 2 cups diced, cooked chicken
- ½ cup whole kernel corn
- ½ cup black beans
- 2 tablespoons chopped cilantro
- ½ cup cornmeal
- ¼ cup shredded Cheddar cheese
- ½ teaspoon chili powder
- 2 tablespoons sliced black olives
- 1 egg, beaten
- ½ cup milk

Heat 2 tablespoons oil in a large skillet. Sauté onion, red pepper, jalapeño pepper and garlic for 1 minute. Sprinkle ¼ cup flour and stir for 2 minutes. Add broth, juice, cumin and zest. Cook and stir for 8 minutes. Add chicken, corn, beans and cilantro and mix well. Pour chicken mixture into an 11 x 7 x 2-inch baking dish. Combine ½ cup flour, cornmeal, cheese, chili powder and olives in a bowl. In a separate bowl, whisk together egg, 1 tablespoon olive oil and milk. Slowly stir into flour mixture. Drop spoonfuls of batter over chicken mixture. Bake at 400 degrees for 30 to 35 minutes.

Serves 6-8

Stuffed Cornish Hens

- 1 cup wild rice
- ½ cup chopped onion
- 3 tablespoons butter
- ½ cup toasted almonds
- 1 teaspoon salt
- 1 teaspoon ground thyme
- ½ teaspoon ground marjoram
- 8 (1 pound) Cornish game hens
- Salt and pepper to taste
- 8 slices bacon

Cook and drain rice. Sauté onion in butter. Combine rice, onion, almonds, salt, thyme and marjoram and mix well. Season hens with salt and pepper. Stuff each hen with rice mixture. Wrap a slice of bacon around each hen. Roast, uncovered, at 325 degrees for 1 hour, 30 minutes to 2 hours. Baste occasionally with drippings.

Serves 8

Ginger Chicken

- ¼ cup soy sauce
- 1 cup water
- 2 tablespoons grated gingerroot
- 3 tablespoons butter
- 1 cup packed dark brown sugar
- 4 boneless, skinless chicken breast halves
- Steamed rice

Combine soy sauce and water in a large skillet. Stir in ginger, butter and brown sugar. Heat to a simmer, stirring until sugar dissolves. Add chicken and simmer for 30 to 45 minutes, turning chicken and basting with sauce. Serve over steamed rice.

Serves 4

Cajun Chicken Cordon Bleu

- 4-6 boneless, skinless chicken breast halves
- 2 tablespoons Cajun seasoning
- 2 tablespoons butter
- 1 cup half-and-half
- ½ cup cubed ham
- ¼ cup chopped green onion
- 1 tablespoon pepper
- ½ cup Parmesan cheese
- 1 cup cooked rice

Flatten chicken to ¼-inch thickness. Season with Cajun seasoning. Melt butter in cast iron skillet. Blacken chicken in hot skillet for 3 minutes on each side. Place skillet with chicken in a 350 degree oven for 15 minutes. In a saucepan, heat half-and-half, ham, onion and pepper until hot. Do not boil. Add cheese and keep warm on low heat. To serve, place chicken over a bed of rice. Pour sauce over chicken.

Serves 4-6

Chicken Italiano

- 2 (8 ounce) boneless, skinless chicken breast halves
- ½ cup all-purpose flour
- 2 tablespoons butter
- Salt and pepper to taste
- 2 slices prosciutto ham
- 2 slices fontina cheese
- ½ cup dry vermouth
- ½ cup tomato sauce
- 3 tablespoons heavy cream
- Cooked rice or pasta

Coat chicken in flour. Sauté chicken in butter for 4 minutes on each side. Season with salt and pepper. Cover chicken with ham and cheese. Pour in vermouth and cook until vermouth evaporates. Add tomato sauce and bring to boil. Blend in cream. Serve over rice pilaf or pasta

Serves 2

Bayou Chicken

- ½ cup plus 3 tablespoons all-purpose flour
- ½ cup plus 3 tablespoons vegetable oil
- 1 medium onion, chopped
- 1 medium bell pepper, chopped
- 2 garlic cloves, minced
- 1 (14½ ounce) can chicken broth
- 1 (15 ounce) can tomato sauce
- 3 bay leaves
- White wine to thin sauce
- 1 teaspoon garlic powder
- 1 teaspoon cayenne pepper
- 2 teaspoons dried oregano
- 1 teaspoon pepper
- 1 teaspoon chopped fresh basil
- ½ teaspoon ground thyme
- Chopped chives for garnish
- 2 pounds boneless, skinless chicken breast halves, cut into bite-size pieces

Blend ½ cup flour and ½ cup oil in a skillet over low heat. Sauté onion, bell pepper and garlic for 4 minutes. Add broth, tomato sauce and bay leaves. Simmer sauce, covered, for 20 minutes. Remove bay leaves. Add wine if necessary. In a bowl, combine 3 tablespoons flour, garlic powder, cayenne, oregano, pepper, basil and thyme. Coat chicken pieces with flour mixture. Heat 3 tablespoons oil in a separate skillet. Brown chicken on all sides in hot oil. Drain on paper towels. Add to tomato sauce. Cover and simmer on low heat for an additional 10 minutes.

Serves 4-6

Great served as a brunch dish over garlic grits.

Cashew Chicken

- 1½ cups diced cooked chicken
- 1 cup cream of mushroom soup
- ¼ cup water
- 1 (3 ounce) can chow mein noodles, divided
- ½ cup cashew halves
- 1 cup sliced celery

Combine chicken, soup, water, half of noodles, cashews and celery in a 2-quart casserole dish. Top with remaining noodles. Bake at 375 degrees for 15 minutes.

Serves 4

Hospitality
(hos pi tal' i ti)

The act of receiving and entertaining guests – either friends or strangers – generously and kindly. The practice of hospitality to a degree that seems extreme to us was quite common in biblical times.

~from
The New Food Lover's Tiptionary

Chicken Pontalba

- ½ cup butter
- 1 cup chopped onion
- 1½ cups thinly sliced green onion
- 1 tablespoon finely minced garlic
- 1¼ cups diced potatoes
- 1 cup diced lean ham
- 1¼ cups sliced fresh mushrooms
- ½ cup dry white wine
- 1 tablespoon minced fresh parsley
- 1 cup all-purpose flour
- 1 teaspoon salt
- ½ teaspoon pepper
- ⅛ teaspoon cayenne pepper
- 2 pounds chicken, deboned and cut into 1-inch pieces
- 1 cup vegetable oil
- 2 cups Béarnaise Sauce (recipe below)

Melt butter in a 10-inch heavy skillet. Sauté onion, green onion, garlic and potatoes for 15 minutes until browned. Add ham, mushrooms, wine and parsley and cook for 8 minutes. Using a slotted spoon, remove vegetables and ham and place in a large au gratin dish. Reserve butter in skillet. Place dish in 200 degree oven. Combine flour, salt, pepper and cayenne. Dredge chicken in flour mixture. Add oil to butter in skillet and heat. Brown chicken and drain on paper towels. Layer chicken over vegetables in au gratin dish. Return dish to oven and prepare Béarnaise Sauce. To serve, spoon sauce evenly over chicken and vegetables.

Serves 6-8

Béarnaise Sauce

- 2 tablespoons white wine
- 2 tablespoons tarragon vinegar
- 2 teaspoons dried tarragon
- 3 egg yolks
- 2 tablespoons lemon juice
- ¼ teaspoon salt
- ¼ teaspoon pepper
- Cayenne pepper to taste
- ½ cup butter, melted

Heat wine, vinegar and tarragon in a small saucepan until liquid is reduced. Set aside. Process egg yolks, juice, salt, pepper and cayenne in the blender. Add melted butter in batches and blend. Add wine mixture and pulse 1 to 2 times to blend. Pour over chicken and vegetables in au gratin dish and heat thoroughly.

Serves 2 cups

Roasted Scottish Pheasants with Apricots and Dates

- **½ cup apricots**
- **½ cup dry white wine**
- **½ cup Grand Marnier**
- **½ cup fresh lime juice**
- **2 tablespoons sugar**
- **2 (2½-3 pound) pheasants**
- **Salt and pepper to taste**
- **2 teaspoons dried thyme, crumbled and divided**
- **2 bay leaves, divided**
- **Vegetable oil**
- **½ cup pitted dates, chopped**
- **Thyme sprigs for garnish**

In a small heatproof bowl, cover apricots with boiling water and soak for 10 minutes. Drain apricots and cut into quarters. In a saucepan, simmer wine, liqueur, juice and sugar for 5 minutes. Set aside. Preheat oven to 375 degrees. Cut legs from pheasants. Season inside and out with salt and pepper. Place 1 teaspoon thyme and 1 bay leaf in each pheasant cavity. Close and secure with skewers or toothpicks. Brush pheasants with oil and place breast side down on a rack in a roasting pan. Roast at 375 degrees for 20 minutes. Discard any fat dripping. Turn pheasants over and add apricots, wine mixture and dates to pan. Roast an additional 25 minutes or until thermometer registers 160 degrees. Add ½ cup water if liquid evaporates. Let pheasants stand 10 minutes. Cut each in half and serve with apricot date sauce and garnish with thyme sprigs.

Serves 4

Chicken Spinach Casserole

- **6 boneless, skinless chicken breast halves**
- **Garlic powder, salt and pepper to taste**
- **½-1 cup white wine**
- **¼ cup butter, divided**
- **1 (8 ounce) package cream cheese, softened**
- **2 tablespoons Parmesan cheese**
- **3 (10 ounce) packages frozen chopped spinach, thawed and squeezed dry**
- **2 (10¾ ounce) cans cream mushroom soup**
- **Bread crumbs**

Season chicken with garlic powder, salt and pepper. Place chicken in a 13 x 9 x 2-inch baking dish. Pour in wine and 2 tablespoons melted butter. Cover and bake at 350 degrees for 1 hour. Remove and dice chicken. Reserve pan juice. Blend cream cheese and butter. Stir in Parmesan cheese and spinach. Press spinach mixture into the bottom of a grease 13 x 9 x 2-inch baking dish. Top with diced chicken. Mix soup contents with 2 measured cans of reserved pan juices. Pour over spinach and chicken. Top with bread crumbs. Bake at 350 degrees for 35 to 45 minutes.

Serves 8

Good-Easy Chicken Casserole

- **4 boneless, skinless chicken breast halves**
- **1 (8 ounce) package sliced Swiss cheese**
- **1 (10¾ ounce) can cream of chicken soup**
- **½ cup white wine**
- **1 cup butter, melted**
- **1 (8 ounce) package stuffing mix**

Arrange chicken in a greased 13 x 9 x 2-inch baking dish. Layer cheese slices over chicken. Whisk together soup and wine. Pour over cheese. Combine butter and stuffing mix, tossing lightly to coat. Spread stuffing over cheese. Bake at 325 degrees for 1 hour, 30 minutes.

Serves 8

Duck Sauce

- **1 (16 ounce) can Bing cherries**
- **1 cup sugar**
- **2 tablespoons mustard**
- **2 tablespoons Tabasco sauce**
- **2 tablespoons Worcestershire sauce**
- **1 (14 ounce) bottle ketchup**

Combine cherries and sugar in a saucepan. Bring to boil, stirring constantly, until sugar dissolves. Stir in mustard, Tabasco, Worcestershire sauce and ketchup. Serve with cooked duck or other game birds.

Serves 2½ cups sauce

Chicken Marbella

- **10-12 boneless, skinless chicken breast halves**
- **3-4 garlic cloves, finely chopped**
- **¼ cup dried oregano**
- **Freshly ground pepper**
- **½ cup red wine vinegar**
- **½ cup olive oil**
- **1 cup pitted prunes**
- **½ cup pitted Spanish olives**
- **½ cup capers with some juice**
- **6 bay leaves**
- **1 cup packed brown sugar**
- **1 cup white wine**
- **½ cup finely chopped parsley**

Combine chicken, garlic, oregano, pepper, vinegar, oil, prunes, olives, capers with juice and bay leaves. Cover and marinate overnight in the refrigerator. Arrange chicken in a single layer in a shallow pan. Spoon marinade over chicken. Sprinkle with brown sugar and pour wine around chicken. Bake at 350 degrees for 50 minutes. Using a slotted spoon, transfer chicken, prunes, olives and capers to a serving platter. Baste with pan juices. Sprinkle generously with parsley. Remove bay leaves and serve with pan juices.

Serves 10-12

Smitty's Sumptuous Feast

Carlyle "Smitty" Harris was a prisoner of war in North Vietnam for almost eight years. As an early shootdown, Smitty introduced the "Tap Code" (a 5 x 5 matrix of the alphabet) into the prison camp.

On Thanksgiving Day each of the POW's were in solitary with their hands bound behind their backs. Smitty backed up to the wall and tapped to Ron Storz (in the next cell) the description of a sumptuous feast. It took a lot of time and at the end Smitty tapped, "Ron, why don't you join me for this feast?" Ron never missed a beat and tapped right back, "Smitty, I'd love to join you but I'm all tied up today."

~Louise Harris (Mrs. Carlyle Harris)
Carlyle Harris is Building Chairman
Sanctuary Hospice House

Fancy Seasoned Turkey Breast

3 tablespoons lemon pepper
3 tablespoons garlic salt
1 tablespoon onion powder
1 teaspoon dried thyme
1 (4-6 pound) turkey breast
Cooking spray and large brown paper bag

Combine pepper, garlic salt, onion powder and thyme. Remove skin from turkey. Rinse and pat dry. Generously coat turkey with cooking spray. Sprinkle seasoning mixture over turkey, coating thoroughly. Spray the inside of a large brown paper bag. Place turkey inside bag. Fold ends and place on a broiler pan coated with cooking spray. Roast at 300 degrees for 22 minutes per pound or about 1 hour, 30 minutes to 2 hours, 20 minutes.

Serves 6-8

All good cooks learn something new every day.

~Julia Child

~from The New Food Lover's Tiptionary

Chicken Breasts Pierre

- 1/4 cup all-purpose flour
- 1 1/2 teaspoons salt
- Dash of pepper
- 6 boneless, skinless chicken breast halves
- 3 tablespoons butter
- 1 (14 1/2 ounce) can stewed tomatoes
- 1/2 cup water
- 2 tablespoons Worcestershire sauce
- 2 tablespoons packed brown sugar
- 2 tablespoons white vinegar
- 2 teaspoons chili powder
- 1 teaspoon dry mustard
- 1/2 teaspoon celery seed
- 1 garlic clove, minced

Combine flour, 1/2 teaspoon salt and pepper. Coat chicken in flour mixture. Melt butter in a large skillet. Brown chicken on all sides. Remove and drain on paper towels. In same skillet, add tomatoes, water, Worcestershire sauce, brown sugar, vinegar, 1 teaspoon salt, chili powder, mustard, celery seed and garlic. Bring to boil. Reduce heat and add chicken. Cover and simmer for 30 to 40 minutes or until chicken is tender.

Serves 6

Elegant Chicken and Artichoke Pasta

- 8 boneless, skinless chicken breast halves, cut in chunks
- 1/2 cup butter
- 1/2 stalk celery, chopped
- 1 medium onion, chopped
- 1 garlic clove, chopped
- 2 (14 ounce) cans artichoke hearts, drained, chopped
- 1/2 cup white wine
- Celery salt and pepper to taste
- 1 (10 3/4 ounce) can cream mushroom soup, undiluted
- 2 cups water
- 1 (8 ounce) package shredded mozzarella cheese
- 1 pound penne pasta, cooked al dente

Brown chicken in a greased skillet until golden browned. Remove chicken. Add butter to skillet. Sauté celery, onion and garlic until translucent. Add artichokes and wine. Cook on low heat for 20 minutes. Season with celery salt and pepper. Add reserved chicken, soup and water. Cook and stir until bubbly. Remove from heat. Add cheese. Cover skillet until cheese melts. Toss chicken sauce with penne. Serve with green salad and warm French bread.

Serves 8-10

Penne alla Boscaiola

1 (2½ ounce) package pine nuts, toasted
⅓ cup butter
3 tablespoons olive oil
2 garlic cloves, crushed
½-1 red onion, thinly sliced
2 cups shiitake mushrooms, thinly sliced
2 (1 pint) containers grape or cherry tomatoes, halved
Chopped fresh basil
⅓ cup chicken broth
2 (10 ounce) packages spinach leaves
1½ cups shredded Asiago cheese
12 ounces penne pasta, cooked al dente
Salt and pepper to taste

Heat butter and oil in a skillet. Sauté garlic and onion. Stir in mushrooms, tomatoes and basil. Add broth and cook over medium heat until hot. Add spinach and toss until wilted. Remove from heat. Top with cheese. Serve over pasta and top with pine nuts. Season with salt and pepper.

Serves 6-8

May add shrimp or chicken.

Penne with Tomatoes, Olives and Two Cheeses

6 tablespoons olive oil, divided
1½ cups chopped onion
1 teaspoon minced garlic
3 (28 ounce) cans Italian plum tomatoes, drained
2 teaspoons dried basil
1½ teaspoons crushed red pepper
2 cups low-salt chicken broth
Salt and pepper to taste
1 pound penne or rigatoni
2½ cups packed Havarti cheese
⅓ cup sliced kalamata olives
⅓ cup Parmesan cheese
¼ cup finely chopped fresh basil

Heat 3 tablespoons oil in heavy Dutch oven over medium heat. Sauté onion and garlic for 5 minutes until translucent. Add tomatoes, basil and red pepper. Pour in broth and bring to boil. Reduce heat to medium and simmer for 1 hour, 10 minutes or until mixture thickens to a chunky sauce and is reduced to 6 cups. Season with salt and pepper. (May be made 2 days in advance. Cover and refrigerate. Reheat over low heat before continuing.) Preheat oven to 375 degrees. Cook pasta al dente. Drain and return to same pot. Toss with remaining 3 tablespoons oil. Pour in tomato sauce and mix well. Stir in Havarti cheese. Pour pasta mixture into a 13 x 9 x 2-inch baking dish. Top with olives and Parmesan cheese. Bake at 375 degrees for 30 minutes. Sprinkle with fresh basil.

Serves 4

Delta Lasagna

- ¼ cup vegetable oil
- 1 medium onion, diced
- 2 garlic cloves, diced
- 1 pound lean ground beef, crumbled
- 1 pound pork sausage, crumbled
- ¼ cup dried parsley
- 2 teaspoons dried basil
- 1 teaspoon salt
- 1 teaspoon pepper
- 1 (14 ounce) can diced tomatoes
- 1 (6 ounce) can tomato paste
- 8 lasagna noodles, cooked al dente
- 3 (12 ounce) packages shredded mozzarella cheese
- 1 quart container cottage cheese
- Parmesan cheese or grated Cheddar cheese

Heat oil in large skillet. Sauté onion and garlic until tender. Add beef and pork and cook until browned. Add parsley, basil, salt, pepper, tomatoes and tomato paste. Cover and simmer 30 to 40 minutes. Preheat oven to 350 degrees. In a 13 x 9 x 2-inch baking dish, arrange alternating layers of meat sauce, mozzarella cheese, cottage cheese and lasagna noodles. Repeat all layers. End with meat sauce layer. Sprinkle with Parmesan cheese. Bake at 350 degrees for 20 minutes. Let stand 10 to 15 minutes before serving.

Serves 6-8

This pasta dish freezes well!

Penne in Cream Sauce with Sausage

- 1 tablespoon butter
- 1 tablespoon olive oil
- 1 medium onion, thinly sliced
- 3 garlic cloves, minced
- 1 pound sweet Italian sausage, skinned
- ⅔ cup dry white wine
- 1 (14½ ounce) can diced, peeled tomatoes with juice
- 1 cup heavy cream
- 6 tablespoons chopped Italian parsley, divided
- Salt and pepper to taste
- 1 pound penne pasta, cooked al dente
- 1 cup Parmesan cheese, divided

Melt butter with oil in a large heavy skillet over medium-high heat. Sauté onion and garlic for 7 minutes or until tender. Add sausage and cook for 7 minutes, breaking up meat into small pieces. Drain excess drippings from skillet. Stir in wine and bring to boil. Cook for 2 minutes or until most all liquid evaporates. Reduce heat and add tomatoes with juice and simmer for 3 minutes. Stir in cream and cook for 5 minutes until sauce thickens. Stir in 4 tablespoons parsley. Season with salt and pepper. Remove from heat. Mix together sauce and cooked pasta. Add ¾ cup cheese and toss to coat. Top with remaining ¼ cup cheese and 2 tablespoons parsley.

Serves 6-8

Chicken Florentine with Pasta

- 3 boneless, skinless chicken breast halves
- 1 cup sliced mushrooms
- 2 tablespoons butter
- 1 (10¾ ounce) can cream of mushroom soup, undiluted
- 1 (10 ounce) package frozen chopped spinach, thawed and well drained
- 1 cup shredded sharp Cheddar cheese
- 1 cup sour cream
- 1 teaspoon Creole seasoning
- 4 cups dry linguine or fettuccine, cooked al dente
- 1 cup grated Parmesan cheese

Sauté chicken and mushrooms in butter until chicken is tender. Stir in soup. Add spinach, Cheddar cheese, sour cream and Creole seasoning. Cook and stir until heated thoroughly. Serve chicken over pasta and top with Parmesan cheese.

***Serves* 6**

Everything you see I owe to spaghetti.

~Sophia Loren

~from The New Food Lover's Tiptionary

Italian Baked Spaghetti

- 1 (16 ounce) can diced tomatoes
- 2 (8 ounce) cans tomato sauce
- ⅓ cup tomato paste
- 1 cup water
- 2 garlic cloves, chopped
- ½ cup diced onion
- 1½ teaspoons Italian seasoning
- ½ teaspoon sugar
- ¼ cup chopped parsley
- 2 small bay leaves
- 1 pound ground beef
- 1 cup minced hot Italian sausage, skinned
- 8 ounces angel hair pasta, cooked al dente
- 1 (8 ounce) package cream cheese, softened and sliced
- 4 slices Swiss cheese
- 1 (8 ounce) package shredded Cheddar Jack cheese

Combine tomatoes, tomato sauce, tomato paste, water, garlic, onion, seasoning, sugar, parsley and bay leaves in a large stockpot. Bring to boil. Reduce to low heat and simmer, covered, for 1 hour. In a skillet, cook beef and sausage and drain. Add meat to tomato sauce. Simmer 20 minutes longer. Remove bay leaves. Spread one-third of sauce in the bottom of a 13 x 9 x 2-inch baking dish. Layer one-half of each of the pasta, cream cheese slices, Swiss and Cheddar cheeses. Repeat layers with remaining ingredients ending with sauce layer. Bake at 350 degrees for 30 minutes. Cut into squares.

***Serves* 12**

Al Dente (al-DEN-tay)

An Italian phrase meaning "to the tooth" used to describe pasta or other food that is cooked only until it offers a slight resistance when bitten into, but which is not soft or over done.

~from The New Food Lover's Tiptionary

Spaghetti with Egg and Bacon Sauce

- ¼ cup butter, softened
- 2 whole eggs
- 2 egg yolks
- 1 cup Parmesan cheese, divided
- 6-8 quarts water
- 1 teaspoon salt
- 1 pound spaghetti, vermicelli or linguine
- 8 slices bacon, cut crosswise into ¼-inch strips
- 1 teaspoon crushed red pepper
- ½ cup heavy cream
- Freshly ground pepper to taste

Cream butter until light and fluffy. Set aside. In a separate bowl, whisk eggs and egg yolks until well blended. Stir in ½ cup cheese. Set aside. Warm an ovenproof serving bowl or casserole dish in a 200 degree oven. Bring salted water to boil. Cook pasta for 7 to 12 minutes or until tender. Meanwhile, cook bacon in a skillet until crisp. Pour off half of bacon drippings. To reserved drippings, stir in red pepper and cream. Keep warm over low heat. When pasta is cooked, drain well and transfer to heated serving bowl. Add butter and toss pasta until well coated. Add hot bacon cream sauce and egg mixture. Mix thoroughly. Season with pepper. Serve with remaining ½ cup Parmesan cheese.

Serves 4

May substitute chopped ham for bacon.

Pasta Primavera with Shrimp and Basil

- 12 ounces linguine
- 1 cup fresh small broccoli florets
- ¼ pound fresh green beans, cut in half
- ¼ pound fresh asparagus, cut into 1-inch pieces
- ¼ pound fresh sugar snap peas
- ¼ cup olive oil
- 1 small sweet red pepper, quartered lengthwise and cut into strips
- 1 small yellow pepper, quartered lengthwise and cut into strips
- 1 small orange bell pepper, quartered lengthwise and cut into strips
- 2 teaspoons minced garlic
- 12 ounces shrimp, peeled and deveined
- Salt and pepper to taste
- 1 pint grape tomatoes, halved
- 2 cups fresh basil leaves, minced
- ⅓ cup Parmesan cheese
- 2 teaspoons lemon zest

Bring a large pot of water to boil. Cook pasta and add broccoli, beans, asparagus and snap peas 1 minute before pasta is done. Drain and keep warm. Heat oil in a large skillet. Sauté all pepper strips. Add garlic and shrimp and cook until shrimp turn pink. Season with salt and pepper. Add shrimp mixture to pasta. Stir in tomatoes, basil, cheese and zest. Toss to mix and serve immediately.

Serves 4-6

Royal Seafood Pasta

- **3 pounds shrimp, peeled and deveined**
- **1¼ cups unsalted butter, divided**
- **1½ bunches green onion, chopped**
- **1 cup fresh parsley, chopped**
- **1 onion, chopped**
- **6 tablespoons all-purpose flour**
- **1 pint heavy cream**
- **3 (8 ounce) jars oysters, with juice**
- **1½ cups white wine**
- **1 pound vermicelli, cooked al dente**

Sauté shrimp in ¾ cup butter in a large skillet until pink. Add green onion, parsley and onion. Cook and stir vegetables until tender. Add flour, ½ cup butter and cream. Cook and stir until thickened. Add oysters with juice and wine. Cook until oysters are heated thoroughly. Spoon mixture over hot pasta.

***Serves* 6**

Be sure to drain cooked pasta thoroughly. The cooking water dilutes the sauce.

~from The New Food Lover's Tiptionary

Fettuccine with Lobster

- **¾ cup butter, divided**
- **2 tablespoons chopped shallots**
- **2 cups cubed lobster meat**
- **1 tablespoon all-purpose flour**
- **3 tablespoons lemon juice**
- **½ cup dry white wine**
- **1 cup fish or chicken broth**
- **1 cup cooked white corn**
- **3 tablespoons chopped fresh tarragon**
- **3 tablespoons chopped fresh chives**
- **Salt and pepper to taste**
- **12 ounces fettuccine, cooked al dente**

Melt ½ cup butter in a skillet. Sauté shallots until tender. Add lobster and cook for 2 minutes. Combine flour and juice in a small bowl. Add flour mixture to skillet. Cook and stir until bubbly. Add wine and simmer 1 to 2 minutes. Add remaining ¼ cup butter and broth. Cook for 1 minute. Add corn, tarragon, chives and season with salt and pepper. Spoon mixture over fettuccine and garnish with fresh herbs.

***Serves* 6**

Shrimp and Spinach Pasta

When cooking pasta to be used in dishes requiring further cooking–casserole or soups–reduce the cooking time by a third. Cooking will continue when put in the final dish.

~from The New Food Lover's Tiptionary

- ½ **cup butter**
- 1½ **cups sliced mushrooms**
- ¼ **cup sun-dried tomatoes, finely diced**
- 2 **teaspoons salt-free Cavender's seasoning**
- ½ **teaspoon white pepper**
- 1 **tablespoon minced garlic**
- ⅛ **teaspoon salt-free herb and spice seasoning**
- ¾ **cup heavy cream**
- ⅓ **cup pine nuts**
- ½-¾ **cup dry white wine**
- 28-32 **shrimp, peeled and deveined**
- 2-3 **cups spinach leaves, rinsed and stemmed**
- 1 **(12 ounce) package angel hair pasta, cooked al dente**

Melt butter in a large skillet. Sauté mushrooms and tomatoes. Add Cavender's, pepper, garlic and spice seasoning. Cook for 5 minutes. Add cream, pine nuts, wine and shrimp. Cook for 3 to 5 minutes until shrimp turn pink. Arrange spinach leaves on four serving plates. Place pasta in the center. Top with shrimp mixture. Serve with crisp French bread.

Serves 4

White Clam Sauce

- 2 **garlic cloves, minced**
- ⅔ **cup olive oil**
- 1 **(8 ounce) bottle clam juice**
- ¼ **teaspoon salt**
- ¼ **teaspoon pepper**
- 2 **(6½ ounce) cans clams, undrained and minced**
- ½ **cup minced green onion tops**
- ½ **cup chopped fresh parsley**
- 1 **pound vermicelli, cooked al dente**
- **Parmesan cheese for garnish**

Sauté garlic in oil until tender. Add clam juice, salt and pepper. Simmer for 5 minutes. Add clams with juice. Cook for 8 to 10 minutes. Add green onion and parsley. Toss half of clam sauce with vermicelli. Top with remaining sauce and Parmesan cheese.

Serves 6

Feta Shrimp Pasta

6 tablespoons olive oil, divided
1½ pounds shrimp, peeled and deveined
2 tablespoons lemon juice
1 teaspoon white wine vinegar
¼ teaspoon lemon zest
1 tablespoon chopped fresh oregano
6 ounces feta cheese
3 tomatoes, chopped
1 cup thinly sliced celery
1 cup sliced black olives
3-4 ounces vermicelli, broken in half and cooked al dente
Fresh parsley and Parmesan cheese to garnish

Heat 2 tablespoons oil until slightly smoking. Sauté shrimp for 2 minutes until pink. Transfer to a large bowl and cool. In a small bowl, whisk together 4 remaining tablespoons oil with juice, vinegar, zest and oregano. Pour over shrimp. Add feta cheese, tomatoes, celery and olives to shrimp. Toss to coat. Prepare one day in advance to this point. Prior to serving, cook pasta and drain well. Toss shrimp mixture with pasta and garnish with parsley and Parmesan cheese.

Serves 8-10

Crawfish Fettuccine

2 onions, chopped
2 stalks celery, chopped
1 bell pepper, chopped
2 garlic cloves, chopped
1 cup butter
¼ cup all-purpose flour
3 tablespoons dried parsley
1 pound crawfish tails
1 pint half-and-half
1 (8 ounce) package processed cheese loaf, cubed
2 finely chopped jalapeño peppers
10 ounces fettuccine, cooked al dente
1 (3 ounce) package fresh Parmesan cheese

Sauté onion, celery, pepper and garlic in butter. Add flour and cook, stirring frequently, for 10 minutes. Add parsley and crawfish and cook 5 minute more. Slowly stir in half-and-half. Add cheese loaf cubes and jalapeño peppers. Cook and stir over low heat until cheese melts. Combine crawfish mixture with fettuccine. Pour pasta mixture into a greased 11 x 7 x 2-inch baking dish. Sprinkle with Parmesan cheese. Bake at 350 degrees for 20 minutes.

Serves 4-6

Mexican Chicken Pasta Salad

- ½ cup red wine vinegar
- 2 teaspoons sugar
- 2 tablespoons tomato paste
- 1½ tablespoons chili powder
- 4 garlic cloves, chopped
- Salt to taste
- 2 pounds boneless, skinless chicken breast halves, boiled and shredded
- ¾ cup chopped green onions
- 1 (16 ounce) can kidney beans, drained
- 8 ounces rotini or cavatappi, cooked al dente
- 6 cups salad greens
- 1 (8 ounce) package shredded Cheddar cheese
- ½ cup sliced black olives
- 1 (8 ounce) bottle zesty Italian dressing

Whisk together vinegar, sugar, tomato paste, chili powder, garlic and salt. Combine chicken, green onion, beans and pasta in a bowl. Pour in marinade and toss to coat. Cover and refrigerate overnight. Prior to serving, toss chicken mixture with greens, cheese and olives. Add enough Italian dressing to moisten salad. Serve immediately.

Serves 6-8

Never buy less than 2 pounds of green beans. It's not worth cooking fewer than that. Leftovers will keep a week in the fridge and are often better warmed up. The same goes for turnip greens…a good mess of green is at least two big bunches, and you can mix in one bunch of collards or mustard greens, too. Always cook beans and greens in a cast iron pot with lid. They cook better and taste better and are better. (Don't forget fat back, streak of lean or bacon drippings for flavor.)

~Reprinted from the book *Mama Said* by Martha Houston Reed Hammond by permission of author

Sides

Souper Sunday Football

Spinach Casserole

- 2 (10 ounce) packages frozen chopped spinach
- ¼ cup butter
- ¼ cup all-purpose flour
- 4 eggs, beaten
- 2 (8 ounce) containers cottage cheese
- 1 (8 ounce) package shredded Cheddar cheese

Cook spinach according to package directions. Drain and cool. Melt butter in a saucepan. Whisk in flour until bubbly. Cool slightly. Add spinach, eggs, cottage cheese and Cheddar cheese and mix well. Pour spinach mixture into a greased 13 x 9 x 2-inch baking dish. Bake at 350 degrees for 1 hour.

Serves 8

Yorkshire Pudding

- 2 cups all-purpose flour
- 1 teaspoon salt
- 2 cups milk, room temperature
- 4 eggs, room temperature
- ¼ cup vegetable oil or beef drippings

Sift together flour and salt. Beat in milk with an electric mixer. Add eggs, one at a time, beating well after each addition. Beat until large bubbles appear and batter is the consistency of heavy cream. Spoon ¼ cup oil or drippings into two 9-inch pie pans. Warm pans in a 450 degree oven. Evenly divide batter into hot pie pans. Bake at 450 degrees for 15 minutes. Reduce temperature to 350 degrees and bake for 15 minutes more. Serve around roasted meat.

Serves 8-12

Pudding may be cooked in roasting pan after drippings have been drained. May also prepare 1 to 2 hours in advance and store in refrigerator.

My Southern heritage instilled in me that just about any problem could be eased if not completely fixed with food. In our house, we ate country food: garden vegetables, fried chicken, bologna sandwiches and tomatoes. But on occasion, Mother would prepare one of the family's favorite recipes for our Southern table. It was about as ethnic and exotic to us as anything we had ever eaten. As an exchange student to England, Mother lived in many different homes and often food was rationed. If enough coupons were saved, the family would serve Mother their best, which was roast beef and Yorkshire pudding. The pudding is not a dessert. It is a bread complement to the roast, made with beef fat drippings. You bake it in a cake pan and serve along side of roast. Serve it hot, and it will melt in your mouth as you capture all the rich flavors of the roast. Mother perfected her Yorkshire pudding while still in England but it was years before she would make it for her family. Once she started cooking it for us, we wanted it for every meal.

~Eva Ann Beasley Dorris, Pontotoc, MS

Cranberry-Apple Casserole

- **3 cups unpeeled chopped apples**
- **2 (16 ounce) cans whole berry cranberry sauce**
- **½ cup packed brown sugar**
- **⅓ cup all-purpose flour**
- **⅓ cup chopped pecans**
- **⅓ cup butter**

Combine apples and cranberry sauce. Pour mixture into a greased 2-quart casserole dish. Combine brown sugar, flour and pecans. Cut in butter until crumbs form. Spoon mixture over fruit. Bake at 350 degrees for 50 minutes.

Serves 8

May be served hot but is preferred to prepare a day in advance and served cold!

Rummed Apples

- **4 large tart apples, peeled, cored and cut in half**
- **¼ cup peach or apricot preserves**
- **Juice and zest of one orange**
- **½ cup sugar**
- **½ cup water**
- **2 tablespoons rum**
- **Whipped cream topping**

Place cut side of apples up in a buttered 11 x 7 x 2-inch baking dish. Combine preserves, juice, zest, sugar and water in a saucepan. Cook over low heat until sugar is dissolved and sauce thickens. Remove from heat and stir in rum. Pour over apples. Cover with foil and bake, basting occasionally, at 350 degrees for 45 minutes to 1 hour or until tender. Serve at room temperature or cold with whipped cream.

Serves 4-8

Baked Apricots

- **3 (16 ounce) cans apricots, drained and divided**
- **⅔ cup packed light brown sugar, divided**
- **¾ cup crushed butter round cracker crumbs, divided**
- **½ cup butter, melted**

Arrange half of apricots, cup side up, in an 11 x 7 x 2-inch baking dish. Sprinkle half each of brown sugar and crumbs over apricots. Repeat layers. Drizzle with melted butter. Bake at 325 degrees for 30 minutes.

Serves 8

This is an excellent dish served with pork tenderloin, ham or turkey.

Pineapple Soufflé

4 cups torn croissants
1 (20 ounce) can crushed pineapple, drained
3 large eggs, beaten
2 cups sugar
1 cup butter, melted
1 teaspoon vanilla

Combine bread and pineapple. Place in a greased 2-quart casserole dish. Whisk together eggs, sugar, butter and vanilla. Pour over pineapple mixture. Bake at 350 degrees for 30 minutes.

Serves 8

Oak Ridge Hot Fruit Bake

1 (12 ounce) package pitted prunes
½ (11 ounce) package dried apricots
1 (13 ounce) can pineapple chunks, undrained
1 (20 ounce) can cherry pie filling
1½ cups water
¼ cup dry sherry
½ cup slivered almonds, toasted

Arrange prunes, apricots and pineapple in a 3-quart casserole dish. Combine pie filling, water and sherry. Pour over fruit and mix well. Stir in almonds. Cover and bake at 350 degrees for 1 hour, 30 minutes.

Serves 8

This dish freezes well and can be re-frozen.

Curried Fruit

1 (10 ounce) can pineapple chunks, well drained
1 (10 ounce) can peaches, well drained
1 (10 ounce) can pears, well drained
1 (14½ ounce) can cherries, well drained
1 cup packed brown sugar
2-4 teaspoons curry powder
¾ cup butter, sliced

Arrange fruit in a casserole dish. Combine sugar and curry. Sprinkle over fruit. Dot with butter slices on top. Bake, uncovered, at 350 degrees for 30 to 35 minutes.

Serves 8

Asparagus Caesar

- 1 bunch asparagus, parboiled or 2 (12 ounce) cans
- ¼ cup butter, melted
- 3 tablespoons lemon juice
- ½ cup Parmesan cheese
- Paprika for garnish

Place asparagus in a casserole dish. Combine butter and juice. Pour over asparagus. Top with cheese and sprinkle with paprika. Bake at 425 degrees for 20 minutes.

Serves 4

Chilled Asparagus with Parmesan and Balsamic Vinegar

- 3 pounds fresh asparagus, ends trimmed
- ¼ cup olive oil
- ½ cup balsamic vinegar
- Salt and pepper to taste
- ½ pound Parmesan cheese

Cook asparagus until crisp-tender. Drain and plunge into ice water to stop cooking. Drain well. Arrange asparagus on a serving platter. Drizzle with oil and vinegar. Season with salt and pepper. Shave paper thin slices of cheese over asparagus until it is covered. Serve immediately.

Serves 8

Baked Carrot Casserole

- 3 (13½ ounce) cans sliced carrots, drained
- 2 tablespoons horseradish
- ½ teaspoon salt
- ¼ teaspoon pepper
- ⅓ cup mayonnaise
- 2 tablespoons minced onion
- ¼ cup bread crumbs
- 1 tablespoon butter, melted
- Paprika for garnish

Combine carrots, horseradish, salt, pepper, mayonnaise and onion in a bowl. Pour mixture into a greased 2-quart casserole dish. Cover with bread crumbs and butter. Sprinkle with paprika. Bake at 375 degrees for 20 to 30 minutes.

Serves 8

Sweet-Sour Carrots

- 5 cups sliced carrots
- 1 (10¾ ounce) can tomato soup, undiluted
- ½ cup vegetable oil
- 1 cup sugar
- ¾ cup vinegar
- 1 tablespoon prepared mustard
- 1 medium onion, chopped
- 1 medium bell pepper, chopped
- Dash of Worcestershire sauce

Cook carrots in salted water until tender. Drain and set aside. Combine soup, oil, sugar, vinegar, mustard, onion, pepper and Worcestershire sauce in a saucepan. Cook, stirring often, over medium heat until vegetables are tender. Add carrots. Pour mixture into a covered dish or jar. Refrigerate overnight.

Serves 10

Cauliflower Shrimp Bake

- 1 medium head cauliflower, cut into florets
- Salt and pepper to taste
- ½ cup sour cream
- 1 (10¾ ounce) can cream of shrimp soup
- ½ cup shredded sharp Cheddar cheese

Steam cauliflower in salted boiling water until crisp-tender. Drain well. Place cauliflower in 1-quart casserole dish. Season with salt and pepper. Combine sour cream and soup. Pour over cauliflower. Sprinkle with cheese. Bake at 350 degrees for 10 minutes.

Serves 6

Terri's Southwest Corn

- 2 (1 pound) packages frozen whole kernel corn, thawed
- ¼ cup butter
- 1 (8 ounce) package cream cheese, softened
- 1 (7 ounce) can chopped green chilies, drained
- 1 cup shredded sharp Cheddar cheese
- Salt and pepper to taste

Combine corn, butter, cream cheese and chilies in a saucepan. Cook over medium heat, stirring constantly, for 5 minutes until well blended. Season with salt and pepper. Pour corn mixture into a 13 x 9 x 2-inch baking dish. Top with Cheddar cheese. Bake at 350 degrees until bubbly and browned on top.

Serves 8

If you've ruined a dish by over salting it, try stirring in 1 teaspoon each of sugar and vinegar; cook for a few minutes and taste.

~from The New Food Lover's Tiptionary

Muriel's Corn Casserole

- **1 egg**
- **Salt and pepper to taste**
- **1 cup cream-style corn**
- **1 cup whole kernel corn, including 3 tablespoons corn liquid**
- **2 tablespoons butter, sliced plus more for topping**
- **⅓ cup half-and-half**
- **24-30 saltine crackers, crushed, reserve some for topping**

Beat egg with a fork until frothy. Season with salt and pepper. Add cream-style and whole corn with liquid, 2 tablespoons butter slices, half-and-half and cracker crumbs. Mix well. Pour into a buttered 1-quart casserole. Top with reserved crumbs. Dot generously with butter slices. Bake at 350 degrees for 30 minutes.

Serves 4

This is Mrs. Hubert Humphrey's recipe. We have prepared this for Thanksgiving for many years.

Crusty Corn Casserole

- **1 (15 ounce) can cream style corn**
- **1 (15 ounce) can whole kernel corn**
- **1 (9 ounce) package cornbread mix**
- **1 onion, chopped**
- **1 (8 ounce) container sour cream**
- **½ cup butter, melted**
- **1 cup shredded sharp Cheddar cheese**

Combine cream style corn, kernel corn, cornbread mix, onion, sour cream, butter and cheese. Mix well. Pour into a 2-quart casserole dish. Bake, uncovered, at 325 degrees for 45 minutes.

Serves 6-8

Layered Vegetable Soufflé

- 1 (10 ounce) package frozen green peas, thawed
- 1 (10 ounce) package frozen French-style green beans, thawed
- 1 (10 ounce) package frozen baby lima beans, thawed
- 1 bell pepper, cut into julienne strips
- 2 cups mayonnaise
- ⅓ cup Parmesan cheese
- Salt and pepper to taste
- 1 pint heavy cream, whipped

Cook each vegetable separately with equal amounts of pepper strips. Do not cook completely. Drain and layer vegetables in a 9 x 9 x 2-inch buttered baking dish. Combine mayonnaise, Parmesan cheese and season with salt and pepper. Fold in whipped cream. Pour topping over vegetables. Bake at 350 degrees for 30 minutes or until top is golden brown.

Serves 6-8

Spinach and Artichoke Bake

- 2 (10 ounce) packages frozen chopped spinach, thawed
- ½ cup green onions, chopped including tops
- ½ cup butter
- 1 (10 ounce) can artichoke hearts, drained
- 1 cup sour cream
- 1 cup Parmesan cheese, divided
- Garlic salt and pepper to taste

Prepare spinach according to package direction. Drain well. Sauté onions in butter. Add cooked spinach, artichokes, sour cream and ½ cup Parmesan cheese. Season with garlic salt and pepper and mix well. Pour mixture into a 2-quart casserole dish. Sprinkle with remaining ½ cup Parmesan cheese. Bake at 350 degrees for 30 minutes.

Serves 6-8

Sweet Sour Green Beans

- ¾ cup butter
- 1 cup packed light brown sugar
- 1 (12 ounce) can limeade concentrate, thawed and undiluted
- 3 (14½ ounce) cans cut green beans, drained

Combine butter, brown sugar and limeade in a saucepan. Bring to boil, stirring constantly. Pour over beans. Cover and refrigerate overnight. Heat beans until hot before serving.

Serves 10-12

May be made several days in advance. Use sliced or cut green beans and may double recipe for buffets.

Tomato Pie

- 1 (9-inch) pie shell, baked
- 3 large tomatoes, chopped and drained
- 1 cup mayonnaise
- 2 tablespoons chopped onion
- 2 tablespoons chopped bell pepper
- 1 cup shredded Cheddar cheese
- ½ teaspoon salt
- ½ teaspoon pepper
- ½ teaspoon dried oregano

Arrange tomatoes in baked pie shell. Combine mayonnaise, onion, pepper, cheese, salt, pepper and oregano. Spoon mixture over tomatoes. Bake at 350 degrees for 25 to 30 minutes.

Serves 6

Great for a ladies luncheon.

Marigold Tomatoes

- 2 (16 ounce) cans diced tomatoes
- ½ cup chopped onions
- ¼ cup chopped bell pepper
- 1 cup cornbread stuffing
- 1 cup packed light brown sugar
- 1 tablespoon Worcestershire sauce
- ¾ teaspoon Creole or Cajun seasoning
- 1 cup shredded sharp Cheddar cheese (optional)

Combine tomatoes, onion, pepper, stuffing, brown sugar, Worcestershire sauce and seasoning. Mix well. Pour mixture into a 13 x 9 x 2-inch baking dish. Top with cheese. Bake at 350 degrees for 30 minutes or until bubbly.

Serves 12

Broccoli with Olive Butter

- 2 garlic cloves, crushed
- ⅔ cup butter
- 4 teaspoons fresh lemon juice
- Dash of pepper
- 12 large stuffed olives, sliced
- 4 (10 ounce) packages frozen broccoli spears, steamed and drained
- Seasoned salt

Sauté garlic in butter in a saucepan for 15 minutes. Add juice, pepper and olives. Heat thoroughly, but do not boil. Arrange broccoli in a heated serving dish. Sprinkle with seasoned salt. Pour sauce over broccoli. Serve immediately.

Serves 12-14

Tomato Relish

- **2 gallons tomatoes, peeled and chopped**
- **2 teaspoons ground pickling spice**
- **6 large onions, finely chopped**
- **5 cups sugar**
- **5 jalapeño peppers, finely chopped**

Combine tomatoes, pickling spice, onion, sugar and jalapeño pepper in a saucepan. Bring to boil. Reduce heat and simmer for several hours until thickened, stirring often. Pour mixture into sterilized jars. Seal jars tightly and process in water bath for 10 minutes. Serve with meats, green beans, black-eyed peas, and mustard or turnip greens.

Serves 2 gallons plus

My husband and I enjoy being in the kitchen together. We relax and talk about our day at work while we prepare dinner together. My mother, Peggy Comer, was a fabulous cook and her tomato relish was the best topping on mustard greens. She loved to make it for us. Before she passed away in 1999, she taught us how to cook her tomato relish.

~Linda Caldwell, Tupelo, MS

Stuffed Tomato Surprise

- **3 slices bacon**
- **¼ cup chopped onion**
- **½ pound fresh spinach, chopped**
- **½ cup sour cream**
- **Dash of Tabasco sauce**
- **4 medium tomatoes**
- **Salt to taste**
- **½ cup shredded mozzarella cheese**

Cook bacon until crisp. Drain, reserving 2 tablespoons drippings. Crumble bacon and set aside. Sauté onion in drippings until tender. Stir in spinach. Cover and cook 3 to 5 minutes until tender. Remove from heat. Stir in sour cream, reserved bacon and Tabasco.

Cut tops from tomatoes. Scoop out pulp, leaving shells intact. Chop pulp and add spinach mixture. Drain tomato shells and sprinkle with salt. Fill shells with spinach mixture. Place stuffed tomatoes in an 8 x 8 x 2-inch square baking dish. Bake at 375 degrees for 20 to 25 minutes. Top each tomato with cheese and bake an additional 3 minutes or until cheese melts.

Serves 4

Marinated Green Beans and Artichokes

- 1½ cups sugar
- 2 cups vegetable oil
- 1 cup apple cider vinegar
- 2 garlic cloves, minced
- 1 tablespoon salt
- 4 (14½ ounce) cans whole green beans, drained and rinsed
- 2 (14 ounce) cans artichoke hearts, drained

Whisk together sugar, oil, vinegar, garlic and salt. Pour over beans and artichokes in bowl. Cover and refrigerate overnight. Warm in a saucepan before serving.

Serves 12

Orange Sauce for Hot Vegetables

In a saucepan, combine 2 tablespoons thawed orange juice concentrate and 2 tablespoons butter. Cook and stir over low heat until warm. Serve over hot cooked green beans or carrots.

Serves 3-4

Bell Pepper Frittata

- 3 garlic cloves, minced
- 1 large red onion, sliced
- 2 sweet red peppers, cut into thin strips
- 1 yellow pepper, cut into thin strips
- 3 tablespoons olive oil, divided
- 2 yellow squash, thinly sliced
- 2 zucchini, thinly sliced
- 1 (8 ounce) package mushrooms, sliced
- 6 large eggs
- ¼ cup heavy cream
- 2½-3 teaspoons salt
- 2 teaspoons pepper
- 8 slices white sandwich bread, cubed and divided
- 1 (8 ounce) package cream cheese, cubed
- 1 (8 ounce) package shredded Swiss cheese

Sauté garlic, onion, red pepper and yellow pepper in 1 tablespoon oil in a large skillet until tender. Drain, pat dry and set aside. Sauté squash and zucchini in 1 tablespoon oil until tender. Drain, pat dry and set aside. Sauté mushrooms in remaining 1 tablespoon oil until tender. Drain, pat dry and set aside. Whisk together eggs, cream, salt and pepper in a large bowl. Stir in vegetables, half of bread cubes, cream cheese cubes and Swiss cheese. Press remaining bread cubes in the bottom of lightly greased 10-inch springform pan and place on baking sheet. Pour vegetable mixture into pan. Bake at 350 degrees for 1 hour. Cover with foil after 45 minutes of baking to prevent excessive browning.

Serves 8

Cooking mushrooms in an aluminum pan will cause them to darken.

~from The New Food Lover's Tiptionary

Barbequed Green Beans

1 (16 ounce) can whole green beans, drained
3 slices bacon, cooked crisp and crumbled
½ onion, chopped and sautéed
⅓ cup packed brown sugar
⅓ cup ketchup

Combine green beans, bacon, onion, brown sugar and ketchup. Pour into a 1-quart casserole. Cover and bake at 350 degrees for 30 minutes.

Serves 2

Recipe may be double or tripled.

Bacon grease adds wonderful flavor to many foods. Cooks, particularly in the South, use it in cornbreads, to fry foods like hush puppies and catfish, as a flavoring for vegetables, and so on.

~from
The New Food Lover's Tiptionary

Patio Beans

4-5 slices bacon
1 medium onion, chopped
1 (16 ounce) can white lima beans, drained
1 (16 ounce) can red kidney beans, drained
1 (16 ounce) can pork and beans
½ cup packed brown sugar
2 teaspoons Worcestershire sauce
½ cup ketchup
1 (8 ounce) package block Cheddar cheese, cut into cubes
Parmesan cheese for topping

Cook bacon until crisp. Remove bacon and crumble. Drain drippings, reserving 1 tablespoon. Sauté onion in 1 tablespoon bacon drippings until tender. Combine onions with lima beans, kidney beans and pork and beans, brown sugar, Worcestershire sauce, ketchup and Cheddar cheese. Mix thoroughly. Pour mixture into a greased 2-quart casserole dish. Top with crumbled bacon and Parmesan cheese. Bake at 350 degrees until bubbly.

Serves 6-8

"What is there more kindly than the feeling between host and guest?"

~Aeschylus

Beans and Bacon

As newlyweds in the late '60s, my wife Sandi and I moved into an upstairs apartment only a few miles from Oakland, California, and the school where we both taught. Sandi, a native Californian, relished introducing me to Western cooking, and tried out new recipes passed on by her many wish-us-happiness friends. During my bachelor years, my daily sustenance was mostly Spam, Vienna sausage, and peanut butter and mayonnaise sandwiches. The vast array of new foods was exciting, and I never ceased praising Sandi's cooking.

She decided she wanted to cook the sorts of food I grew up on in Mississippi, and asked me what I liked. I named several things my mother served. I particularly remembered a delicious vegetable dish, which was a staple in our diet. "Green beans would be nice," I said. The next night Sandi served green beans. As soon as I put the first forkful into my mouth, I knew something was wrong. These green beans didn't taste anything like my mother's. They were flat and bland. "Like them?" she asked with a smile. "Wonderful," I said. After several more evenings of green beans, I realized the something missing in Sandi's green beans, I said, "You know, my mother's green beans had bacon in it." Always eager to please her Southern husband, Sandi proudly brought in the bowl of green beans the following evening and set them on the table. There, artfully sprinkled across the top of the green beans were small fragments of crispy fried bacon!

John Armistead
Tupelo, MS

Company Pecan Broccoli

- **1 bunch broccoli, cut into florets or (10 ounce) frozen package**
- **½ cup butter, melted**
- **1 (1¼ ounce) package dry onion soup mix**
- **½-1 cup chopped pecans**

Steam broccoli until crisp-tender. Drain well. Arrange broccoli in 11 x 7 x 2-inch baking dish. Combine butter, soup mix and pecans. Pour over broccoli. Bake at 350 degrees for 20 to 30 minutes or until bubbly.

Serves 8

Broccoli Two Cheese Casserole

- 4 (10 ounce) packages frozen chopped broccoli, thawed
- ¼ cup all-purpose flour
- ¼ cup butter, melted
- 2 cups milk
- 1 teaspoon seasoned salt
- Pepper to taste
- 1 teaspoon sugar
- 2 teaspoons Worcestershire sauce
- 2 tablespoons ketchup
- 2 tablespoons crumbled bleu cheese
- 2 (3 ounce) packages cream cheese, cubed
- 2 cups soft buttered bread crumbs

Cook broccoli according to package directions, reducing cooking time by 3 minutes. Drain well. Spread evenly in two greased 1½-quart casserole dishes. In a large skillet, add flour to butter, stirring constantly until smooth. Add milk, salt, pepper, sugar, Worcestershire sauce, ketchup, bleu cheese and cream cheese. Cook and stir until smooth. Pour cheese mixture over broccoli. Layer bread crumbs over top. Bake at 350 degrees for 25 minutes or until sauce is bubbly and crumbs are browned.

Serves 12

Zucchini and Tomatoes in Basil Cream Sauce

- 3 tablespoons butter
- 2 tablespoons all-purpose flour
- 1 cup half-and-half
- ¼ cup chopped fresh basil
- 1 bouillon cube
- Dash of Tabasco sauce
- Salt to taste
- 3 medium zucchini, thinly sliced
- 8 small tomatoes, peeled and thinly sliced
- 1 large onion, thinly sliced
- Salt and pepper to taste
- ½ cup Parmesan cheese, divided

Melt butter in a skillet. Whisk in flour until bubbly. Add half-and-half, stirring constantly. Add basil, bouillon cube, Tabasco and salt. Stir sauce until thickened. Preheat oven to 350 degrees. Layer half each of zucchini, tomato and onion in a greased 13 x 9 x 2-inch baking dish. Season each layer with salt and pepper. Sprinkle with ¼ cup cheese. Repeat layers except for cheese. Cover and bake at 350 degrees for 25 minutes. Remove from oven and drain off excess juice. Pour cream sauce over vegetables and top with remaining ¼ cup cheese. Bake, uncovered, for 20 minutes longer or until bubbly and browned.

Serves 4-6

Acorn Squash with Apple Stuffing

2 medium acorn squash
2 red delicious apples, chopped
½ cup chopped pecans
½ cup golden raisins
5 tablespoons packed brown sugar
3 tablespoons butter, melted

Cut squash in half. Remove and discard seeds. Place squash in baking dish, hollowed side up. Bake at 350 degrees for 30 minutes. Combine apples, nuts, raisins and brown sugar and mix well. Spoon apple mixture into squash shells. Drizzle with butter. Bake an additional 25 to 30 minutes.

Serves 4-6

Spicy Squash Casserole

2 (10 ounce) packages frozen yellow squash, thawed or 3 cups chopped fresh
½ medium bell pepper, chopped
1 medium onion, chopped
1 (4 ounce) jar processed cheese
½ (10 ounce) can diced tomatoes with chilies
Tortilla chips, broken

Cook squash, pepper and onion until tender. Drain well and mash. Stir in cheese and tomatoes. Pour mixture into a buttered 2-quart casserole dish. Sprinkle with broken tortilla chips. Bake at 350 degrees for 25 minutes or until bubbly.

Serves 6

Squash Dressing

2 cups cooked yellow squash
2 cups cornbread crumbs
1 bell pepper, chopped
1 medium onion, chopped
Salt and pepper to taste
1 tablespoon sugar
½ cup butter, melted
1 (10¾ ounce) can cream chicken soup
1 (5 ounce) can evaporated milk

Combine squash, cornbread crumbs, bell pepper, onion, salt, pepper, sugar, butter, soup and milk. Mix thoroughly. Pour into a 2-quart casserole dish. Bake at 350 degrees for 30 minutes.

Serves 6-8

Swiss Vegetable Custard

1½ cups yellow squash, sliced
1½ cups fresh or frozen broccoli, cut into 1-inch pieces
¼ cup butter
1 egg, beaten
¼ cup milk
¼ teaspoon dry mustard
½ cup shredded Swiss cheese
1 teaspoon salt
Dash of cayenne pepper
¼ cup Parmesan cheese

Sauté squash and broccoli in butter until crisp-tender. Place vegetables in a 1-quart casserole dish. Combine egg, milk, mustard, Swiss cheese, salt and cayenne. Pour milk mixture over vegetables. Sprinkle with Parmesan cheese. Bake at 375 degrees for 15 to 20 minutes or until custard is firm and cheese is lightly browned.

Serves 4-6

Roasted Vegetables with Fresh Sage

6 small zucchini, about 2 pounds
1 large sweet red pepper, cut into ½-inch strips
20 shallots
6 garlic cloves
3 tablespoons olive oil
½ teaspoon salt
½ teaspoon pepper
¼ chopped fresh sage

Cut each zucchini lengthwise into quarters. Cut quarters in half crosswise. Arrange zucchini, red pepper, shallots and garlic in a greased shallow foil-lined roasting pan. Drizzle with oil. Roast at 500 degrees for 25 minutes. Sprinkle with salt, pepper and sage. Serve immediately.

Serves 6

Baked Spicy Rice

1 tablespoon vegetable oil
½ cup long-grain rice
1 (10 ounce) can diced tomatoes with chilies
½ cup water
½ teaspoon salt
⅓ cup sliced pimento-stuffed olives
¼ cup chopped onion
½ cup shredded Monterey Jack cheese

Preheat oven to 350 degrees. Heat oil in a large skillet. Brown rice. Transfer to a 1-quart baking dish. Stir in tomatoes, water, salt, olives, onion and cheese and mix well. Cover and bake at 350 degrees for 45 minutes. Uncover and stir rice mixture. Bake an additional 15 minutes.

Serves 2-4

Picnic Rice with Cranberries

1½ cups brown rice
½ cup wild rice
4 cups water
⅓ cup dried cranberries
⅓ cup pine nuts, toasted
½ yellow pepper, chopped
½ large red onion, chopped
3 tablespoons fresh chopped parsley
¼ cup balsamic vinegar
⅓ cup walnut oil
Salt and pepper to taste

Combine brown rice, wild rice and water in a saucepan. Bring to boil. Reduce heat and simmer, covered, for 25 to 30 minutes or until rice is tender. Add cranberries, nuts, yellow pepper, onion, parsley, vinegar, oil and season with salt and pepper. Toss gently.

***Serves* 8**

Walnut oil may be found at health food stores.

Parisian Rice

1 (8 ounce) can sliced water chestnuts, drained and reserve liquid
1 (8 ounce) can mushrooms, drained and reserve liquid
½ cup butter
1 (10¾ ounce) can French onion soup
1 cup regular white rice

Combine reserved liquid from chestnuts and mushrooms. Add enough water to equal 1 cup. Sauté water chestnuts and mushrooms in butter until tender. Add soup, 1 cup of liquid and rice. Mix well. Pour rice mixture into a greased 2-quart casserole dish. Bake, covered, at 350 degrees for 1 hour.

***Serves* 6-8**

Rosemary New Potatoes

4 sprigs fresh rosemary, 4 inches each
4 cups new potatoes, cut into quarters
¼ cup butter, melted
¼ cup olive oil
Salt and pepper to taste
½ teaspoon curry powder (optional)

Remove rosemary leaves from woody stem. Toss rosemary with potatoes, butter, oil, salt, pepper and curry. Place potato mixture in a 13 x 9 x 2-inch baking dish. Bake, stirring occasionally, at 350 degrees for 45 minutes or until potatoes are tender.

***Serves* 6**

Hedgehog Potatoes

6 Yukon gold potatoes
Olive oil
Salt and pepper to taste

Preheat oven to 425 degrees. Cut potatoes lengthwise and lay flat on a baking sheet. On top of potatoes, cut out three to four diamond shapes to look like a hedgehog. Drizzle oil over potatoes. Generously season with salt and pepper. Bake potatoes at 425 degrees for 30 minutes or until fork tender.

Serves 6

This is a very popular English dish. Sweet potatoes are a great alternative.

Mash potatoes only until they're light. Overworking makes them sticky and starchy.

~from
The New Food Lover's Tiptionary

Flutters (Potato Mounds)

- **2 pounds red potatoes, peeled and diced**
- **2 tablespoons all-purpose flour**
- **½ teaspoon salt**
- **¼ teaspoon pepper**
- **2 tablespoons minced parsley**
- **1 garlic clove, minced**
- **2 eggs, beaten**
- **Paprika for garnish**

Cook potatoes in salted boiling water until tender. Drain and mash. Stir in flour, salt, pepper, parsley, garlic and eggs until smooth. Shape potato mixture into balls and place in a buttered shallow baking dish. Sprinkle with paprika. Bake at 350 degrees for 25 minutes until puffy and lightly browned.

Serves 6-8

My mother is an excellent cook and is well known among family and friends for her cooking talents. My husband will tell you the "worst" meal at my parents' home is better than the "best" meal anywhere else! We had three home cooked meals a day growing up, unlike the experience my boys have now. Now our family visits revolve around my mother's kitchen table.

~Carol Kloac
Guntown, MS

Brandied Sweet Potatoes

- 6 large sweet potatoes, cooked and cut into ½-inch slices
- ½ cup sugar
- 1 tablespoon cornstarch
- ½ teaspoon ground nutmeg
- 1 cup water
- ⅓ cup brandy
- 1 tablespoon lemon juice
- ½ cup chopped pecans
- 1½ cups miniature marshmallows (optional)

Arrange sweet potato slices in a greased 13 x 9 x 2-inch baking dish. Combine sugar, cornstarch and nutmeg in a saucepan. Gradually add water. Cook, stirring constantly, over medium heat until mixture comes to a boil. Boil for 1 minute. Stir in brandy and juice. Pour sauce over potatoes. Sprinkle with pecans. Bake at 375 degrees for 25 minutes. Top with marshmallows and bake 5 minutes more.

Serves 8-10

Nutty Buddy

- 3 large sweet potatoes, peeled
- 2 cups milk
- ½ cup butter, softened and divided
- 2 eggs
- 1½ cups sugar, divided
- 1½ teaspoons cinnamon, divided
- ¼ teaspoon ground allspice
- ¼ teaspoon ground nutmeg
- ½ cup all-purpose flour
- 1 cup chopped nuts

Cook potatoes in boiling water. Drain well. Add milk and beat with an electric mixer. Add 4 tablespoons butter, eggs, 1 cup sugar, 1 teaspoon cinnamon, allspice and nutmeg. Beat until smooth. Spread potato mixture into a 13 x 9 x 2-inch baking dish. Combine flour, ½ cup sugar, ½ teaspoon cinnamon and nuts. Sprinkle over potatoes. Dot with remaining 4 tablespoons butter, cut into slivers. Bake at 375 degrees for 35 to 40 minutes.

Serves 6

Pushcart Onions

- 2 tablespoons vegetable oil or butter
- 2 medium-sized onions, thinly sliced
- ½ cup ketchup*
- Salt and pepper to taste

Heat oil or butter in a skillet large enough to hold onions. Sauté for 5 minutes or until tender. Add ketchup and salt and pepper. Cover and cook until onions are soft and tender. Serve on hot dogs or hamburgers.

**Barbeque sauce may be substituted to add more zip.*

Onion Au Gratin

1½ pounds thinly sliced onions
¼ cup butter
1 egg, beaten
½ cup sour cream
½ teaspoon Tabasco sauce
Salt and pepper to taste
1 (9-inch) pie pastry, unbaked
Shredded Parmesan cheese

Preheat oven to 350 degrees. Sauté onion in butter. Combine egg, sour cream, Tabasco and season with salt and pepper. Stir into onions and mix well. Bake pastry shell at 350 degrees for 8 minutes. Pour onion mixture into crust and top with Parmesan cheese. Bake at 350 degrees for 20 minutes. Reduce heat to 325 degrees and bake an additional 15 minutes or until lightly browned.

Serves 8

Creamed Onions

18-20 medium onions
⅓ cup vegetable oil
3 tablespoons all-purpose flour
1½ cups milk
1 cup shredded Cheddar cheese
Chopped walnuts or pecans

Peel onions and cook in large amount of salted boiling water until tender. Drain well. In a saucepan, combine oil and flour. Add milk and cook, stirring constantly, until thickened. Add cheese and stir until cheese melts. Stir in onions and heat thoroughly. Pour in a serving bowl and top with nuts.

Serves 6-8

Vegetable Topping

1 cup light mayonnaise
2½ teaspoons Worcestershire sauce
2 tablespoons olive oil
1 small onion, minced
2-3 hard-cooked eggs, finely sliced
¼ teaspoon dry mustard

Whisk together mayonnaise, Worcestershire sauce, oil, onion, eggs and mustard. Do not heat topping. Serve over cooked and drained hot mixed vegetables, green beans or English peas.

Serves 1½ cups topping

Pickled Peaches

1 (29 ounce) can peach halves, reserve juice
½ cup vinegar
¾ cup packed brown sugar
1 stick cinnamon
1 teaspoon whole cloves
1 teaspoon ground allspice

Combine peach juice, vinegar, brown sugar, cinnamon, cloves and allspice in a saucepan. Boil for 5 minutes. Reduce heat, add peach halves and simmer for 5 minutes. Marinate peaches in pickling syrup for several hours or overnight.

Serves 4-6

Pickled peaches are difficult to find in the grocery store and small, fresh canning peaches are not always available. This is a good, tasty substitute.

Quick and Easy Corn Relish

¼ cup sugar
1 teaspoon chopped onion
½ teaspoon dry mustard
½ teaspoon celery seed
¼ teaspoon salt
¼ cup white vinegar
1 (12 ounce) can Mexican corn

In a small saucepan combine all ingredients except corn. Bring to a boil. Stir in corn and simmer 10 minutes. Put in a jar, seal and refrigerate until ready to use.

Serves 1½ cups

Last Minute Tartar Sauce

½ cup sour cream or yogurt
2 tablespoons chili sauce
2 tablespoons chopped dill pickle
2 tablespoons chopped onion
2 tablespoons chopped bell pepper
2 tablespoons chopped parsley
1 tablespoon fresh lemon juice
½ teaspoon dry mustard

Mix all ingredients together and serve on your favorite fried fish.

Desserts

Under the Magnolia Brunch

Brennan's Bloody Marys, page 52

Assorted Bagels/Schmears

Christmas Morning Pie, page 66

Whole Wheat Sausage Bread, page 70

Fresh Fruit Fantasy, page 27

Baked Ham with Bourbon Glaze, page 128

Layered Vegetable Soufflé, page 181

Fig Cake, page 58

Cream Cheese Mints

- **1 (16 ounce) package powdered sugar**
- **1 (3 ounce) package cream cheese, softened**
- **Small amount food coloring of choice**
- **Candy flavoring of choice**

Cream powdered sugar and cream cheese. Add coloring and flavoring of choice. Mix thoroughly. Press mixture into small rubber molds. Let stand until firm. Gently punch out mints.

Serves 60 small mints

Great for making roses and leaves for wedding and showers.

Praline Sauce

- **1½ cups chopped nuts**
- **7 tablespoons butter, divided**
- **1¼ cups packed brown sugar**
- **3 tablespoons all-purpose flour**
- **¾ cup light corn syrup**
- **1 (5 ounce) can evaporated milk**

In a skillet, toast nuts in 3 tablespoons butter. Cool and set aside. Place 4 tablespoons in a large glass bowl. Microwave on high for 55 seconds or until butter melts. Stir in brown sugar and flour. Add corn syrup and stir well. Microwave on high for 3 to 4 minutes, stirring every 2 minutes, until mixture comes to a boil. Stir well. Microwave for an additional 3 to 4 minutes. Cool to lukewarm. Gradually stir in milk. Add nuts. Serve over cheesecake, vanilla ice cream or pound cake.

Serves 3 cups sauce

Lisa's Luscious Lemon Curd

- **½ cup butter**
- **⅔ cup sugar**
- **6 eggs, well beaten**
- **1 (6 ounce) can frozen lemonade concentrate, thawed and undiluted**
- **Juice and zest of one lemon**

Melt butter in the top of a double boiler. Stir in sugar. Add eggs and lemonade. Cook and stir until glossy and thick. Add juice and zest and mix well. Cool completely. Serve in mini phyllo shells or to top sugar cookies. Refrigerate unused portion.

Serves 2 cups lemon curd

Barbie's Bread Pudding with Amaretto Sauce

1 loaf stale French bread
4 cups milk
1 cup sugar
7 eggs, beaten and divided
1½ cups raisins
1 tablespoon vanilla
½ cup chopped pecans
1 teaspoon cinnamon
1 cup sifted powdered sugar
½ cup butter
¼ cup amaretto

Preheat oven to 350 degrees. Cut bread in half lengthwise and break into small pieces into a large bowl. Whisk together milk and sugar. Pour over bread and let stand for 5 minutes, stirring gently several times. In a separate bowl, combine 6 beaten eggs, raisins, vanilla and pecans. Add to bread mixture and stir gently. Pour mixture into a buttered 13 x 9 x 2-inch baking dish. Sprinkle with cinnamon. Bake at 350 degrees for 45 minutes or until lightly browned. Meanwhile, cook powdered sugar and butter over low heat, stirring constantly. Stir in amaretto. Add 1 beaten egg and cook 1 minute until slightly thickened. Pull pudding away from sides of pan. Pour half of sauce over warm pudding, allowing sauce to run down sides. Pour remaining sauce over top. Serve warm.

Serves 12

Bread Pudding

3 cups sugar, divided
4 eggs, divided
11 tablespoons butter, divided
1-2 tablespoons whiskey
1 loaf French bread, cubed
1 quart milk
2 tablespoons vanilla
1 cup raisins

Cream 1 cup sugar and 1 egg until well mixed. Melt 8 tablespoons in a saucepan. Add to creamed mixture. Stir in whiskey until smooth. Set sauce aside. In a large bowl, soak bread in milk. Stir until well mixed. In a separate bowl, combine 3 eggs, 2 cups sugar and vanilla. Add raisins and bread mixture and stir well. Add 3 tablespoons melted butter to a 13 x 9 x 2-inch baking dish. Pour bread mixture into dish. Bake at 350 degrees until slightly puffed and firm. To serve, spoon pudding into individual dessert dishes. Top with whiskey sauce and heat under broiler until bubbly. Serve additional sauce on the side.

Serves 8

Cinnamon-Almond Cookies

1 (6 ounce) package almond paste
1¼ cups all-purpose flour
1¼ cups powdered sugar
½ cup milk
6 egg whites
1 tablespoon vanilla
1 tablespoon cinnamon

Process paste, flour, sugar and milk in a food processor for 5 minutes. Add to egg whites in a bowl. Add vanilla and cinnamon. Drop batter by teaspoonfuls onto a greased and floured baking sheet. May also use a cookie template for a desired shape. Bake at 325 degrees for 6 minutes or until golden browned.

Serves 80-90 cookies

Praline Cookies

1 cup packed light brown sugar
2 tablespoons all-purpose flour
¼ teaspoon baking soda
Dash of salt
1 tablespoon amaretto
1 egg white, beaten
2 cups pecans

Sift together brown sugar, flour, baking soda and salt. Stir in amaretto. Fold in egg white and pecans. Drop by teaspoonfuls on a greased baking sheet. Bake at 350 degrees for 10 to 15 minutes.

Serves 12

Cold Crunch Dessert

2½ cups crisp rice cereal
1 (3½ ounce) can flaked coconut
1 cup chopped pecans
½ cup butter, melted
⅔ cup packed brown sugar
½ gallon vanilla ice cream, softened

Combine rice cereal, coconut, pecans and butter. Mix to evenly coat. Spread in a rimmed baking sheet. Bake at 300 degrees for 30 minutes. Stir every 10 minutes for even browning. Remove from oven and stir in brown sugar. Spoon half of mixture in the bottom of a 13 x 9 x 2-inch baking dish. Spread ice cream evenly over mixture. Top with remaining rice mixture. Cover and freeze. Prior to serving, cut into squares. May drizzle chocolate or caramel sauce over each square.

Serves 10-12

Walnut Biscotti

- ¾ cup walnuts, chopped
- ½ cup butter, softened
- ¾ cup sugar
- 2 eggs
- 1 teaspoon vanilla
- 1 tablespoon cognac or brandy
- 2 cups plus 2 tablespoons all-purpose flour
- 1½ teaspoons baking powder
- ¼ teaspoon salt

Preheat oven to 325 degrees. Toast walnuts in the oven for 10 minutes until browned. Do not scorch nuts. Cream butter and sugar until smooth. Add eggs, one at a time, beating well after each addition. Stir in vanilla and cognac. Whisk together flour, baking powder and salt until blended. Fold flour mixture and nuts into creamed mixture. Divide dough in half. Shape dough into two long rolls, 1½-inches wide and 12-inches long. Place on baking sheet two inches apart. Bake at 325 degrees for 25 minutes. Cool slightly. Slice crosswise into ½-inch thick slices. Place flat on baking sheet. Bake an additional 5 to 10 minutes until lightly browned.

Serves 24

Laura's Banana Fritters with Chocolate Hazelnut Sauce

- 1½ cups biscuit baking mix
- ⅓ cup plus 4 tablespoons milk
- 1 egg
- 1½ tablespoons butter, divided and melted
- 2 ripe bananas, mashed
- ½ teaspoon vanilla
- Vegetable oil for frying
- 1 cup chocolate hazelnut spread
- Sliced bananas and chopped hazelnuts for garnish

Combine baking mix, ⅓ cup milk, egg, ½ tablespoon butter, bananas and vanilla. Pour oil into a deep fryer or deep heavy stockpot to a 3-inch level. Heat oil to 375 degrees. Drop heaping spoonfuls of batter into hot oil. Turn once and fry until puffed and golden browned. Drain on paper towels. To make sauce, heat hazelnut spread, 4 tablespoons milk and 1 tablespoon butter in the top of a double boiler. Cook over low heat until melted and smooth. Add milk to thin as necessary. Place fritters on dessert plate and drizzle with sauce. Garnish with bananas and hazelnuts.

Serves 12 fritters

Peppered Strawberries Dessert

- 2 cups halved strawberries
- Freshly ground pepper
- 2 teaspoons sugar
- 1 teaspoon anisette
- 1½ cups Grand Marnier (optional)
- ⅓ cup heavy cream
- Vanilla ice cream

Place strawberries in a serving bowl. Grind lots of pepper from a pepper mill. Add sugar, anisette, Grand Marnier and cream. Mix lightly. Spoon strawberries over individual dishes of ice cream.

Serves 6

Chocolate Pâté

- 1 (8 ounce) package cream cheese, softened
- 4 ounces German chocolate, melted
- ¼ cup sugar
- 1 egg yolk
- 1 tablespoon unsweetened cocoa
- Sugar cookies or shortbread

Blend cream cheese, chocolate, sugar, egg yolk and cocoa in a food processor. Shape mixture into a log. Refrigerate until set. Serve with sugar cookies or shortbread. May also place in a mold.

Serves 6-8

Zabaglione Over Fruit

- 6 egg yolks, room temperature
- 3 tablespoons sugar
- ⅛ teaspoon cinnamon
- 1 teaspoon vanilla
- ½ cup Marsala
- Galliano or your favorite liqueur
- Fresh berries and fruit
- Whipped cream and flavored sugar for garnish

Cook egg yolks, sugar, cinnamon and vanilla in the top of a double boiler over low heat. Beat with mixer or whisk until frothy and pale yellow. Slowly add Marsala, beating constantly. Do not boil mixture. Beat until sauce reaches a thick consistency. Serve over liqueur marinated berries and fruit. Garnish with whipped cream and flavored sugar.

Serves 6

English Oranges

- 2 cups water
- 1 cup sugar
- 4 large naval oranges
- ½ pint whipping cream

Spray cooking spray in bottom and up sides of a saucepan. Add water and sugar and boil gently for 30 to 45 minutes until mixture is a golden amber color. Cool slightly. Remove peel and white membrane of oranges and section. Place orange sections in a bowl. Pour sugar mixture over oranges. Refrigerate for several hours or overnight. To serve, spoon mixture into individual bowls and pour in a small amount of whipping cream.

Serves 8

Sissy's Ice Cream

- 3 cups sugar
- 3 cups whole milk
- 3 cups heavy cream or half-and-half
- Juice of three lemons, about 9 tablespoons
- Juice of three oranges, about 1½ cups
- 3 bananas, mashed

Combine sugar, milk, cream, lemon juice, orange juice and bananas in an ice cream maker. Prepare ice cream, according to manufacturer's directions, freezing until hard.

Serves 8-10

Lemon Meringue Ice Cream

- 3 cups sugar
- 1⅓ cups lemon juice
- 1 (14 ounce) can sweetened condensed milk
- ½ pint whipping cream
- 1 pint half-and-half
- Milk

Combine sugar, juice, condensed milk, whipping cream and half-and-half. Pour into an ice cream maker. Pour enough milk to fill maker. Prepare according to manufacturer's directions until frozen.

Serves 1 gallon

Cool Lemon Dessert

- 2 cups crushed vanilla wafer cookies
- ½ cup butter, melted
- 1 cup chopped pecans plus additional for garnish
- 1 (8 ounce) package cream cheese, softened
- 1 cup powdered sugar
- 1 (8 ounce) package frozen whipped topping, divided
- 4 egg yolks
- 2 (14 ounce) cans sweetened condensed milk
- ¾ cup lemon juice

Combine cookie crumbs, butter and pecans. Press into the bottom of a 13 x 9 x 2-inch baking dish. Beat cream cheese and powdered sugar until smooth. Fold in 2 cups whipped topping. Spread over crust. Beat egg yolks until smooth. Add milk and juice and mix well. Pour over cream cheese filling. Top with remaining cup of whipped topping and nuts.

Serves 10-12

Orange Sherbet Homemade Ice Cream

- 6 (12 ounce) cans orange soft drink
- 1 (14 ounce) can sweetened condensed milk
- 1 (8 ounce) can crushed pineapple

Combine soft drink, milk and pineapple in an ice cream maker. Prepare sherbet according to manufacturer's directions and freeze until firm.

Serves 8-10

Food Memories: Summer meals with watermelon seed battles at the bungalow. Roasted corn on the cob made on an outdoor fireplace with a thick iron plate covered with wet blankets and steamed. Some kernels would be burned!

~Pat Eckenrode, Tupelo, MS

Frozen Lemon Mousse

- 1 (12 ounce) can evaporated skim milk, chilled
- 1 cup sugar
- 1 teaspoon lemon zest
- Juice of three lemons
- 1¾ cups crushed vanilla wafer, divided
- Sliced strawberries (optional)

Whip milk in a chilled bowl. Gradually add sugar and beat well. Add zest and juice. Beat until thick. Press 1½ cups crumbs into a 13 x 9 x 2-inch baking dish. Pour lemon mixture over crumbs. Sprinkle remaining crumbs on top. Cover and freeze for several hours. To serve, garnish mousse with strawberries.

Serves 8-10

Strawberry Squares

- 1 cup all-purpose flour
- ¼ cup packed brown sugar
- ½ cup finely chopped pecans
- ½ cup butter, melted
- 2-3 egg whites
- ⅔ cup sugar
- 2 cups frozen strawberries, thawed
- 2 tablespoons lemon juice
- 1 cup heavy cream, whipped

Combine flour, brown sugar, pecans and butter. Press mixture into a 13 x 9 x 2-inch baking dish. Reserve a small amount of crumbs for topping. Bake at 350 degrees for 20 minutes. Cool completely. Combine egg whites, sugar, strawberries and juice in a bowl. Beat on high speed with an electric mixer for 10 minutes. Fold in whipped cream. Spread filling over crust. Sprinkle with reserved crumbs. Cover with foil and freeze at least 7 hours.

Serves 12

Pineapple/Peach Cobbler

- 1 (18 ounce) package yellow cake mix
- 1 (20 ounce) can crushed pineapple, undrained
- 1 (16 ounce) package frozen peaches, thawed
- ¼ cup sugar
- ½ cup chopped pecans
- ½ cup butter

Spread pineapple in bottom of a 13 x 9 x 2-inch baking dish. Layer with half each peaches and cake mix. Repeat layers. Sprinkle with sugar and pecans. Drizzle with butter. Bake at 350 degrees for 45 minutes.

Serves 8-10

Strange Tastes

In Traceway's weekly care planning sessions, we tried to meet with families for insight as we addressed resident problems and issues. We were talking with a family member who seldom attended. The resident was unable to take part, so having her daughter attend was a real bonus. We discussed some weight loss and asked for some food likes and dislikes. The daughter shook her head and had no suggestions. We asked about breakfast, favorite foods, accompaniments, etc. Still no suggestions, but as an after thought, the daughter shared with us that her mother had always had buttermilk on her daily cereal. Buttermilk did not sound very good to the team, but we decided to try this approach. The dietary staff sent out the buttermilk with her cornflakes. A Hit! From that day this is what the resident received with cereal. Buttermilk was the solution! There's no accounting for peoples' tastes.

~Dolores Rose
Belden, MS

Tiramisu

1½ tablespoons instant coffee granules
¾ cup warm water
1 (10¾ ounce) frozen pound cake, thawed
1 (8 ounce) package mascarpone or cream cheese, softened
½ cup powdered sugar
½ cup chocolate syrup
1 (8 ounce) package frozen whipped topping, thawed and divided
2 (1.4 ounce) chocolate-covered toffee candy bars, frozen and crushed

Stir coffee granules and water until granules are dissolved. Cool. Cut cake into 14 slices, then each slice in half diagonally. Arrange cake triangles in bottom and up sides of a 9-inch deep dish pie plate. Drizzle coffee mixture over cake. Beat cheese, sugar and syrup at medium speed with an electric mixer until smooth. Add 2½ cups whipped topping. Beat until fluffy. Spread cheese mixture over cake. Dollop remaining topping around pie edge. Sprinkle with candy pieces. Refrigerate at least 8 hours.

Serves 8-10

Crème Brûlée

- 1 pint heavy cream
- 3 tablespoons packed brown sugar plus more for topping
- 3 tablespoons cognac plus more for topping
- 4 egg yolks, beaten

Preheat oven to 250 degrees. Scald cream in the top of a double boiler. Do not boil. Add brown sugar and cognac. Stir until sugar is dissolved and blended. Fold mixture into a bowl containing egg yolks. Pour into an 8-inch round glass ovenproof dish. Place dish in a 13 x 9 x 2-inch baking dish and place in oven. Pour hot water into dish to a depth of 1-inch. Bake at 250 degrees for 1 hour, 30 minutes or until custard is set. Sprinkle with brown sugar to ½-inch depth. Broil custard until sugar starts to bubble, turning bowl to avoid burn spots. Refrigerate. At least 1 hour before serving, pour a thin layer of cognac on top.

Serve 4-6

Caramel Pots De Crème

- 6 large egg yolks
- 1 cup sugar
- ¼ cup water
- 1 cup milk
- 2 cups heavy cream

Preheat oven to 300 degrees. Whisk egg yolks in a large bowl. Set aside. In a large saucepan, stir sugar and water over low heat until sugar dissolves. Increase to high heat and cook until mixture is a golden amber color. In a separate saucepan, stir together milk and cream. Scald mixture over medium-high heat. Slowly whisk hot milk mixture into sugar mixture until well blended. Whisk caramel cream into egg yolks. Refrigerate custard until cool, skimming off any air bubbles. Pour custard into six 6-ounce ovenproof ramekins. Place ramekins in a baking dish and put into oven. Fill dish one-third to one-half full with hot water. Bake at 300 degrees for 50 minutes or until edges are set and center not completely firm. Refrigerate for several hours or overnight.

Serves 6

Black Bottom Pie

- 14 gingersnap cookies, crushed
- 5 tablespoons butter, melted
- 4 egg yolks, beaten
- 2 cups scalded milk
- 1 cup sugar, divided
- 1¼ tablespoons cornstarch
- 2 squares unsweetened chocolate, divided
- 1 teaspoon vanilla
- 1 (¼ ounce) package unflavored gelatin
- 2 tablespoons cold water
- 4 egg whites
- 1 teaspoon cream of tartar
- 2 tablespoons whiskey or 1½ tablespoons rum flavoring
- 1 cup heavy cream, whipped

Combine crumbs and butter. Press evenly into a greased 9-inch pie plate. Bake at 300 degrees for 10 minutes. Cool. In the top of a double boiler, slowly add egg yolks to hot milk. Mix together ½ cup sugar and cornstarch. Whisk into milk mixture. Cook, stirring constantly, over low heat for 20 minutes, until mixture coats back of a spoon. Remove from heat and transfer 1 cup of custard to a bowl. Add 1½ squares chocolate to custard. Stir until chocolate melts. Stir in vanilla. Pour chocolate custard into pie crust and refrigerate. Mix gelatin with cold water until dissolved. Add to remaining custard. Cool custard but do not allow to thicken. Beat egg whites until stiff. Add ½ cup sugar, cream of tartar and whiskey. Fold into reserved custard. Spread over chocolate custard. Refrigerate. Spread whipped cream over custard. Shave remaining ½ chocolate square on top.

Serves 8-10

Cappuccino Pie

- 1 cup water
- 1 tablespoon instant coffee granules
- 1 tablespoon butter
- 30 large marshmallows
- 1 cup heavy cream
- 1 teaspoon vanilla
- 1 chocolate crumb pie shell
- ½ cup chopped pecans
- Whipped cream and chocolate-covered coffee beans for garnish

Boil water in a heavy saucepan. Add coffee granules and stir to dissolve. Add butter and marshmallows. Cook, stirring occasionally, over low heat until marshmallows melt. Cool completely. Whip cream and vanilla until soft peaks form. Fold into coffee mixture. Spoon into pie shell. Sprinkle with pecans. Cover and refrigerate at least 8 hours. Top with whipped cream 1 hour before serving. Refrigerate until ready to serve. Garnish with chocolate coffee beans.

Serves 6-8

Buttermilk Pie

- 2 cups sugar
- ¼ cup self-rising flour
- 3 eggs, beaten
- 2 teaspoons vanilla
- ½ cup butter, melted
- ¾ cup buttermilk
- ½ teaspoon ground nutmeg
- 1 (9 inch) pie shell, unbaked

Combine sugar and flour. Add eggs, vanilla, butter and buttermilk and mix well. Sprinkle with nutmeg. Pour into pie shell. Bake at 350 degrees for 45 minutes or until lightly browned and set in center.

Serves 6-8

Four-Minute Brownie Pie

- 2 eggs
- 1 cup sugar
- ½ cup butter, softened
- ½ cup all-purpose flour
- 4 tablespoons cocoa
- 1 teaspoon vanilla
- Pinch of salt

Combine eggs, sugar, butter, flour, cocoa, vanilla and salt in a bowl. Beat for 4 minutes with an electric mixer until smooth. Pour into a greased 9-inch pie plate. Bake at 325 degrees for 30 minutes. Serve with ice cream or whipped cream.

Serves 8-10

Jill's Lemon Pecan Pie

- 3 eggs
- 3 tablespoons butter, melted
- 1½ cups sugar
- 1 teaspoon lemon extract
- Juice of one-half lemon
- 1 (9-inch) pie crust, unbaked
- 1 cup pecans

Combine eggs, butter, sugar, extract and juice. Mix until just blended. Do not overmix. Pour filling into pie shell. Top with pecans. Bake at 350 degrees for 10 minutes. Reduce heat to 300 degrees and bake an additional 25 minutes or until set.

Serves 8

Dutch Apple Pie

6 Granny Smith apples, unpeeled and cored
1 teaspoon cinnamon
½ cup sugar
Pastry for 9-inch double crust pie
1 cup packed brown sugar
¼ cup butter, softened
1 tablespoon heavy cream

Grate apples in a food processor. Combine sugar and cinnamon. Layer a third of apples in unbaked pie pastry. Sprinkle with a third of sugar mixture. Continue to layer apples and sugar mixture until gone. Top with lattice of remaining pastry. Bake at 375 degrees for 15 minutes. Reduce heat to 350 degrees and bake an additional 50 minutes. Blend brown sugar, butter and cream until smooth. During last 10 minutes of baking, top with brown sugar mixture. Serve warm.

Serves 6-8

This recipe originally came from a restaurant in Laurel, MS. It has been the number one favorite in our family for years. The restaurant owner was a friend of my mother's and after the restaurant closed, she shared this recipe.

~ Alma Wright Poland, Tupelo, MS

Dried Peach or Apricot Custard Pie

2 cups dried peaches or apricots
3 egg yolks, beaten
1¼ cups sugar
3 tablespoons all-purpose flour
2 cups milk
1 teaspoon vanilla
1 (9 inch) pie shell, baked
3 egg whites, room temperature

Cook peaches or apricots in water until tender. Drain and mash. Sweeten to taste and set aside. Place egg yolks in top of a double boiler. Combine sugar and flour in a bowl. Gradually whisk into egg yolks until smooth. Add milk and cook over low heat, stirring constantly, until custard thickens. Stir in vanilla. Arrange peaches in pie crust. Pour custard over peaches. Beat egg whites until frothy and sweeten with sugar. Spread meringue over custard. Bake at 400 degrees until browned.

Serves 6-8

Winner's Circle Pie

1 cup sugar
½ cup all-purpose flour
2 eggs beaten
½ cup butter, melted
½ cup chopped pecans
½ cup chopped English walnuts
½ cup semi-sweet chocolate chips
1 teaspoon vanilla
2 tablespoons bourbon (optional)
1 (9-inch) pie crust, unbaked

Combine sugar and flour. Stir in eggs and butter. Mix well. Add nuts, chocolate chips, vanilla and bourbon. Pour filling into pie shell. Bake at 350 degrees for 30 minutes or until set and browned.

Serves 8

Coconut Cream Pie

¾ cup sugar, divided
¼ cup cornstarch
2 cups half-and-half
4 egg yolks, beaten
3 tablespoons butter
1 cup flaked coconut
2 teaspoons vanilla, divided
1 (9 inch) pie shell, baked
1 cup heavy cream
¼ cup sugar

Combine ½ cup sugar and cornstarch in a heavy saucepan. Gradually whisk in half-and-half and egg yolks. Bring to boil. Cook 1 minute, stirring constantly. Remove from heat. Stir in butter, coconut and 1 teaspoon vanilla. Cover tightly with plastic wrap and cool to room temperature. Spoon custard into baked crust and refrigerate for 30 minutes or until set. Beat cream on high speed with an electric mixer until foamy. Gradually add ¼ cup sugar and 1 teaspoon vanilla, beating until soft peaks form. Spread whipped cream over pie. Refrigerate until ready to serve.

Serves 6-8

Sugar Plums

1 cup blanched almonds
¾ cup raisins
¾ cup dried apricots, chopped
¾ cup pitted dates, chopped
¾ cup walnuts, chopped
¼ cup frozen orange juice concentrate, thawed
Sugar for coating

Combine almonds, raisins, apricots, dates and walnuts in a food processor. Pulse until blended. Add orange juice and pulse until mixture sticks together. Shape mixture into 1-inch balls. Roll in sugar and place in paper liners. Store in airtight container in the refrigerator.

Serves 24-30 cookies

Melting Moments

- 1 cup butter, softened
- 2 cups powdered sugar, divided
- 1¼ cups all-purpose flour
- ¾ cup cornstarch
- 1 tablespoon orange zest
- 3 tablespoons orange juice
- 1 teaspoon orange zest

Cream butter and ½ cup powdered sugar until light and fluffy. Beat in flour, cornstarch and 1 tablespoon zest. Mix well. Wrap dough in plastic wrap and refrigerate at least 2 hours.

Roll dough into 1-inch balls. Place on an ungreased baking sheet. Bake at 325 degrees for 8 to 10 minutes or until firm but golden. Cool slightly on baking sheet and remove to rack to cool completely. Combine remaining 1½ cups powdered sugar with orange juice and 1 teaspoon zest. Place waxed paper under racks with cookies to catch drips. Drizzle glaze over cookies. Let set on racks.

Serves 3½ dozen cookies

Delta Cookies

- 1 (16 ounce) package brown sugar
- 2 cups sugar
- 2 teaspoons vanilla
- 2 cups vegetable oil
- 4 eggs
- 4 cups all-purpose flour
- 2 teaspoons baking soda
- 1 teaspoon salt
- 1½ cups dry old-fashioned oats
- 4 cups cornflakes cereal
- 1 cup chopped pecans

Cream together brown sugar, sugar, vanilla, oil and eggs. Combine flour, baking soda and salt. Add dry ingredients to creamed mixture. Fold in oats, cornflakes and pecans. Roll dough into small balls. Place on greased baking sheet. Bake at 350 degrees for 6 to 8 minutes until edges are lightly browned.

Serves 8 dozen cookies

Miss Lois' Butter Pecan Cake

- 1 (18 ounce) package butter pecan cake mix
- 3 large eggs
- ¼ cup vegetable oil
- 1 cup water
- 1 container coconut-pecan frosting

Beat cake mix, eggs, oil and water with an electric mixer until smooth. Fold in frosting with a wooden spoon. Pour batter into a well greased Bundt pan. Bake at 350 degrees for 55 to 60 minutes.

Serves 15

Black Bottom Cup Cakes

- 1 (8 ounce) package cream cheese, softened
- 1 egg
- 1⅓ cups sugar, divided
- ⅛ teaspoon salt
- 1 (6 ounce) package semi-sweet chocolate chips
- 1½ cups sifted all-purpose flour
- ¼ cup cocoa
- 1 teaspoon baking soda
- ½ teaspoon salt
- 1 cup water
- ⅓ cup vegetable oil
- 1 tablespoon vinegar
- 1 teaspoon vanilla
- 1 cup chopped nuts

Blend cream cheese, egg, ⅓ cup sugar and salt until smooth. Stir in chocolate chips. Set aside. Sift together 1 cup sugar, flour, cocoa, baking soda and salt. Stir in water, oil, vinegar and vanilla. Beat until smooth. Pour batter into baking cups, filling one-half full. Spoon cream cheese mixture on top of each cup. Sprinkle with nuts. Bake at 350 degrees for 30 to 35 minutes.

Serves 24 cup cakes

Cameron's Toffee Cherry Crisps

- 1 cup butter
- ¾ cup sugar
- ¾ cup packed brown sugar
- 1 egg
- 1 tablespoon vanilla
- 1½ cups all-purpose flour
- 1 teaspoon baking soda
- Dash of salt
- 1½ cups dry old-fashioned oats
- 1 cup crushed chocolate-covered toffee candy bar
- 1 cup semi-sweet chocolate chips
- 1 cup dried cherries

Preheat oven to 350 degrees. Cream together butter, sugar and brown sugar. Add egg and vanilla. In a separate bowl, combine flour, baking soda and salt. Slowly add flour mixture to creamed mixture, beating well after each addition. Add oats, toffee pieces, chocolate chips and cherries, beating well after each addition. Drop by spoonfuls onto greased baking sheet at least 2 inches apart. Bake at 350 degrees for 14 to 16 minutes or until golden browned.

Serves 3 dozen cookies

Mary Nell Haskell's Plum Pudding Cake

- **1½ cups buttermilk, divided**
- **½ cup butter**
- **2½ cups sugar, divided**
- **1 teaspoon corn syrup**
- **1 teaspoon vanilla**
- **2 cups all-purpose flour**
- **1 teaspoon ground nutmeg**
- **1 teaspoon ground allspice**
- **1 teaspoon cinnamon**
- **2½ teaspoons baking powder**
- **½ teaspoon salt**
- **3 eggs**
- **¾ cup vegetable oil**
- **1¼ teaspoons baking soda**
- **1 cup cooked chopped prunes**
- **1 cup chopped pecans**

To make glaze, combine ½ cup buttermilk, butter, 1 cup sugar, corn syrup and vanilla in a saucepan. Cook, stirring constantly, over low heat until sugar dissolves. Keep warm. Sift together flour, nutmeg, allspice, cinnamon, baking powder and salt in a large bowl. Stir in 1½ cups sugar, eggs, oil and 1 cup buttermilk until well blended. Add baking soda. Stir in prunes and pecans. Pour batter into a greased 13 x 9 x 2-inch baking dish. Bake at 350 for 40 to 45 minutes. Pour glaze over warm cake in pan.

Serves 10-12

Karma-Chocolate Cakes

- **20 tablespoons butter**
- **¾ cup semi-sweet chocolate chips**
- **4 extra large eggs**
- **½ cup sugar**
- **¾ cup sifted all-purpose flour**
- **12 caramel candies**
- **4 tablespoons evaporated milk, divided**

Preheat oven to 325 degrees. Melt butter, 2 tablespoons milk and chocolate chips in top of a double boiler. Cook, stirring often, over low heat until chocolate melts. Cool slightly. In a bowl, beat eggs and sugar for 5 minutes. Gradually beat in flour on low speed until well blended. Beat in chocolate mixture for 3 minutes or until thick and glossy. Pour batter into 12 greased muffin cups. Bake at 325 degrees for 5 minutes. Meanwhile, melt caramels with 2 tablespoons milk. Spoon 2 teaspoons caramel mixture in the middle of each cake. Bake 8 minutes longer. Invert cakes onto serving platter.

Serves 12 small cakes

Banana Cake

- **1 (18 ounce) package yellow butter cake mix**
- **1 cup sugar, divided**
- **¾ cup vegetable oil**
- **1 (8 ounce) container sour cream**
- **4 eggs**
- **2 teaspoons vanilla, divided**
- **½ cup butter**
- **1 cup sweetened condensed milk**
- **3-4 bananas**

Beat cake mix, ½ cup sugar, oil, sour cream, eggs and 1 teaspoon vanilla with an electric mixer until smooth. Divide batter among three greased 9-inch round cake pans. Bake at 350 degrees for 20 minutes or until cake tester comes out clean. Cool completely. To make icing, combine ½ cup sugar, butter, sweetened condensed milk and 1 teaspoon vanilla in an iron skillet. Cook, stirring constantly, over low heat with a flat edge spatula until thickened. Spread a layer of icing over cake and top with bananas slices. Repeat for next cake layer, stacking on top of each other. Ice top cake layer, not sides.

Serves 8-10

Meringue-Swirled Chocolate Cake

- **1 (18 ounce) package chocolate fudge cake mix**
- **1⅓ cups water**
- **½ cup vegetable oil**
- **3 whole eggs**
- **3 egg whites**
- **¾ cup sugar**

Preheat oven to 325 degrees. Generously grease and flour a 9-inch springform pan. Prepare cake according to package directions using water, oil and 3 eggs. Beat egg whites until soft peaks form. Add sugar, 1 tablespoon at a time, beating well after each addition until stiff and glossy. Spread ⅔ of meringue three-quarters of the way up the side of the pan. Do not spread on the bottom. Pour cake batter into pan. Top with remaining meringue. Using a knife, swirl meringue through batter.

Bake at 325 degrees for 1 hour, 30 minutes or until cake tester comes out clean. Cool 10 minutes on a rack. Run a metal spatula along the side of the cake to loosen. Remove sides. Cool completely. Store loosely covered at room temperature.

Serves 10

Bourbon Pecan Pound Cake

- 2 cups sugar
- 1 cup whipped solid vegetable shortening
- 5 eggs
- 3½ cups sifted all-purpose flour
- ½ teaspoon ground nutmeg
- 2 teaspoons baking powder
- 1 teaspoon salt
- ½ cup milk
- ½ cup plus 1 tablespoon bourbon
- 1 cup chopped pecans
- 3 cups sifted powdered sugar
- 3 tablespoons water

Cream sugar and shortening. Add eggs, one at a time, beating well after each addition. In another bowl, sift together flour, nutmeg, baking powder and salt. Whisk together milk and ½ cup bourbon. Add dry ingredients and liquid ingredients alternately, to creamed mixture starting and ending with dry ingredients. Fold in pecans. Pour batter into a 10-inch tube or Bundt pan. Bake at 350 degrees for 1 hour. Cool completely. Stir together powdered sugar, 1 tablespoon bourbon and water until well blended. Pour icing over cake.

Serves 16

For me, the cinema is not a slice of life, but a piece of cake.

~Alfred Hitchcock, filmmaker

~from The New Food Lover's Tiptionary

White Chocolate Cheesecake

- 1½ cups crumbled pound cake
- 3 (8 ounce) packages cream cheese, softened
- 1 cup sugar
- 1 (12 ounce) package white chocolate chips, melted and cooled
- 1 (16 ounce) container sour cream
- 1 tablespoon vanilla

Press cake crumbs in the bottom of a 9-inch springform pan. Bake at 300 degrees for 5 minutes. Beat cream cheese until fluffy. Add sugar and mix well. Beat in white chocolate on high for 1 minute. Beat in sour cream and vanilla for 3 to 5 minutes. Pour mixture into pan. Bake at 300 degrees for 40 to 50 minutes. Cool completely. Cover with plastic wrap and refrigerate at least 8 hours.

Serves 12

Holiday Charlotte Russe

Christmas at my husband's home always included wonderful homemade candies, cookies, cake, pies, ambrosia and Charlotte. My mother-in-law, Ione McGuire Vaughn, made fabulous, never-fail desserts. This recipe is shared in memory of a bright and lovely Southern Belle.

~Barbara Vaughn, Tupelo, MS

1 tablespoon gelatin
2½ cups milk, divided
½ cup sugar
⅛ teaspoon salt
4 egg yolks
1 teaspoon vanilla
4 egg whites, room temperature
1 (10 ounce) jar maraschino cherries, chopped
1 (8 ounce) can crushed pineapple with juice
1 cup chopped pecans
1 pint heavy cream

Soak gelatin in ½ cup milk. Cook 2 cups milk, sugar, salt and egg yolks in a saucepan over low heat until sugar dissolves. Stir in gelatin and vanilla. Beat egg whites until stiff. Fold into milk mixture. Add cherries, pineapple with juice and pecans. Whip heavy cream until soft peaks form. Fold in fruit mixture. Refrigerate for several hours, gently stirring occasionally. May add 1 to 2 teaspoons cherry juice for color. This dish freezes well.

Serves 10

Brides Chocolate Cake

16 ounces semi-sweet chocolate squares
10 tablespoons butter, sliced
1 tablespoon sugar
1 tablespoon all-purpose flour
4 egg yolks, beaten
4 egg whites, room temperature
Dash of salt

Preheat oven to 425 degrees. Lightly butter and flour an 8-inch springform pan. Melt chocolate in top of a double boiler, stirring constantly. Add butter and stir until well blended. Remove from heat. Stir in sugar and flour. Add egg yolks and mix well. Set aside. Beat egg whites with salt until soft peaks form. Fold into chocolate mixture. Pour batter into prepared pan. Bake at 425 degrees for 15 minutes. Cool in pan for 10 minutes. Gently remove sides. Serve cold or room temperature.

Serves 8-10

For a prettier appearance, substitute cocoa powder for flour when preparing pan.

Pecan Pie Cake

- 4 eggs
- 2 cups sugar
- ½ cup butter, softened
- 1 teaspoon vanilla
- 1¼ cups self-rising flour
- 2 cups chopped pecans
- Ice cream, whipped cream, whole pecans for garnish (optional)

Beat eggs and sugar until well blended. Add butter and vanilla. Beat in flour until incorporated. Stir in pecans. Pour batter into two greased 9-inch pie pans. Bake at 350 degrees for 30 minutes or until browned. Cool slightly. Slice and serve warm or cold. May garnish with ice cream, whipped cream and whole pecans.

Serves 12-15

This recipe came from Bobbie Gentry's grandmother, Mrs. Streeter, who raised Bobbie and is known by friends as Miss Maude. In the folksinger's biggest hit, "Ode To Billy Joe", Miss Maude was the Mama to whom this and other songs refer. I met Miss Maude, a widow, 20 years ago and she served coffee and fresh-from-the-oven Pecan Pie Cake. She and her husband were known for their hospitality. Hundreds attended her 100th birthday celebration. She welcomed all kinds of people from the famous and influential to the ordinary folk.

~Phyllis Harper, Tupelo, MS

Cranberry-Caramel Cake

- 1 (18 ounce) package yellow cake mix with pudding
- 2 teaspoons pumpkin pie spice
- 1 cup eggnog
- ⅓ cup vegetable oil
- 4 eggs
- 1½ cups fresh or frozen cranberries, coarsely chopped
- ½ cup chopped walnuts
- ½ cup butter
- 1¼ cups packed brown sugar
- 2 tablespoons light corn syrup
- ½ cup heavy cream

Preheat oven to 350 degrees. Grease and lightly flour a 12-cup fluted tube pan. Beat cake mix, pie spice, eggnog, oil and eggs with an electric mixer on low speed for 30 seconds. Beat 2 minutes at medium speed. Stir in cranberries and walnuts. Pour batter into prepared pan. Bake at 350 degrees for 45 to 55 minutes or until cake tester comes out clean. Cool in pan for 10 minutes. Invert onto a wire rack. Cool completely. To make caramel sauce, melt butter in a saucepan over medium-high heat. Stir in brown sugar and syrup. Bring to boil. Cook, stirring constantly, for 1 minute or until sugar dissolves. Stir in cream and return to boil, stirring constantly. Remove from heat. Serve warm over cake.

Serves 16

Mountain Dew Cake

I remember the wonderful foods my grandmothers cooked; fried chicken, dumplings, vegetable soup, cornbread, peach cobbler. Never tasted anything like this before!

~Teresa Camp, Mantachie, MS

- **1 (18 ounce) package orange supreme cake mix**
- **1 (3 ounce) package coconut cream pudding mix**
- **¾ cup vegetable oil**
- **4 eggs**
- **1 (10 ounce) bottle Mountain Dew beverage**

Icing

- **1 cup sugar**
- **3 tablespoons cornstarch**
- **1 (20 ounce) can crushed pineapple with juice**
- **¼ cup butter**
- **1 (3½ ounce) can flaked coconut**

Beat cake mix, pudding mix and oil with an electric mixer. Add eggs, one at a time, beating well after each addition. Add Mountain Dew. Pour batter into three greased and floured 9-inch pans. Bake at 325 degrees for 30 minutes. Cool completely.

To make icing, combine sugar, cornstarch and pineapple with juice in a saucepan. Cook and stir over low heat until thickened. Remove from heat. Stir in butter and coconut. Frost cake with hot icing. Frost between layers, stacking one on another. Frost top and sides.

Serves 10-12

Easy Chocolate Torte

- **8 ounces unsweetened chocolate**
- **1 cup unsalted butter**
- **5 eggs, slightly beaten**
- **1 cup sugar**
- **1 tablespoon all-purpose flour**

Preheat oven to 400 degrees. Combine chocolate and butter in a microwave bowl. Heat on low for 2 to 3 minutes or until melted. Beat eggs and sugar with an electric mixer until smooth. Add flour and chocolate mixture. Beat until well blended. Pour batter into a nonstick 9-inch round cake pan. Bake at 400 degrees for 20 minutes or until cake tester comes out moist with batter. Cool. Serve with fresh berries or vanilla ice cream.

Serves 6-8

Orange Date and Nut Cake

- 1 cup butter, softened
- 4 cups sugar, divided
- 4 eggs
- 4 cups all-purpose flour
- 1 teaspoon baking soda
- ⅓ cup buttermilk
- 3 tablespoons orange zest, divided
- 1 pound dates, chopped
- 1 cup pecans, broken
- 1 cup orange juice

Cream butter and 2 cups sugar until light and very fluffy. Add eggs, one at a time, beating well after each addition. Combine flour and baking soda. Add alternately with buttermilk in about three batches, mixing well after each addition. Fold in 2 tablespoons zest, dates and nuts. Pour batter in a 10-inch tube pan. Bake at 325 degrees for 1 hour, 30 minutes.

While cake is baking, prepare sauce. Combine 2 cups sugar, 1 tablespoon zest and juice in a saucepan. Cook over low heat until sugar dissolves but do not boil. Let stand in pan until cool. Pour over hot cake just out of the oven.

Serves 10-12

Chocolate Almond Cake

- 1 cup plus 1 tablespoon butter, softened and divided
- 1⅔ cups sugar
- 2 eggs
- ¾ cup sour cream
- 2 teaspoons vanilla, divided
- 1½ teaspoons almond extract, divided
- 2 cups all-purpose flour
- ⅔ cup cocoa powder
- 2 teaspoons baking soda
- ½ teaspoon salt
- 1 cup buttermilk
- 2½ cups powdered sugar
- 3-4 tablespoons milk
- Sliced almonds, toasted for garnish

Cream ¾ cup butter and sugar. Add eggs, one at a time, beating well after each addition. Stir in sour cream, 1 teaspoon vanilla and 1 teaspoon almond extract and mix well. Combine flour, cocoa, baking soda and salt. Add to creamed mixture alternately with buttermilk. Mix well. Pour batter into a greased 10-inch tube pan. Bake at 350 degrees for 50 to 55 minutes or until cake tests done. Cool in pan for 10 minutes. Invert onto serving platter and cool completely. To make almond frosting, cream 5 tablespoons butter, powdered sugar, 1 teaspoon vanilla and ½ teaspoon almond extract until smooth. Add 1 tablespoon milk at a time, beating well, until frosting reaches desired spreading consistency. Frost cooled cake and decorate with toasted almonds.

Serves 12-15

To toast almonds, spread in a glass pie plate and bake at 325 degrees until lightly browned. Watch closely so nuts do not burn.

Mother-In-laws Coming Now No Bake Truffle Pie

17 caramels, unwrapped
¼ cup evaporated milk
1 chocolate cookie pie crust
½ cup chopped toffee bits*
1½ cups semi-sweet chocolate chips
1 cup heavy cream

In a medium saucepan melt caramels with the evaporated milk until smooth. Pour into the pie crust and cover with toffee bits; set aside. In another saucepan melt chocolate chips and heavy cream, forming smooth rich chocolate sauce called ganache.** Immediately pour over caramel layer. Cover and refrigerate at least 2 hours. Cut in thin slices and top with whipped cream. This pie is very rich but makes you hunger for more!

**Chopped nuts can be substituted for the toffee bits.*

**Chocolate ganache is a rich chocolate sauce used for glazing cakes, cookies or can be cooled to make fudge or truffle candies. If you make truffles they can be rolled in chopped nuts, coconut or sprinkles. They make great gifts.

Glenda's Caramel Cake

1 box yellow cake mix

Prepare cake according to package directions using 3 (9 inch) cake pans. Allow layers to cool while you make the frosting.

Frosting

3 sticks butter
1 teaspoon baking soda
1 cup buttermilk
3 cups sugar
1 teaspoon vanilla
3 tablespoons corn syrup

Melt butter over medium heat. Whisk baking soda into the cup of buttermilk. Add sugar to the melted butter and stir until sugar melts. Add the vanilla and corn syrup. Turn the heat up and add the buttermilk mixture. Cook until the mixture is a golden brown and forms a softball when a drop is added to a glass of cold water. Remove from the heat and place over a bowl of cold water. Beat mixture until frosting is creamy. Frosting may not look thick enough. Frost cake quickly as frosting sets up fast. Can be reheated if it gets too thick.

Cheesecake

1⅔ cups graham cracker crumbs
⅓ cup butter, melted
5 (8 ounce) packages cream cheese, softened
1½ cups sugar
3 eggs
2½ teaspoons vanilla

Combine crumbs and butter. Press in the bottom on a 9-inch springform pan. Bake at 350 degrees for 5 minutes. Remove and set aside. Beat cream cheese, one package at a time, until smooth. Gradually add sugar. Beat in eggs, one at a time, beating well after each addition. Add vanilla. Beat until well blended. Pour batter over crust. Bake at 350 degrees for 40 minutes. Turn off oven leave door ajar, leave cheesecake in oven for 30 minutes longer. Cool to room temperature. Cover and refrigerate.

Serves 10-12

May substitute gingersnaps or chocolate graham crackers for variation on crust. Add chopped walnuts or pecans also, however, use less crumbs.

**For clean cut slices, use plain or unflavored dental floss.*

Caramel Sauce

1 pint heavy cream
3 cups sugar
20 tablespoons water
3 tablespoons unsalted butter, softened
2 teaspoons vanilla

Heat cream to lukewarm in the microwave. Combine sugar and water in saucepan. Cook over medium heat, occasionally swirling, for 30 minutes. Do not stir. When sugar turns amber brown in color, slowly add warm cream; mixture will bubble. Cook, stirring constantly, over low heat until sauce is smooth. Add butter and mix well. Remove from heat and add vanilla. Pour into small microwave glass jars. Cool completely. Seal with lid and refrigerate. When ready to serve, reheat sauce and serve with cheesecake.

Serves 3 cups

Sauce is great served over ice cream, pound cake or with a spoon straight from the container. May store in the refrigerator indefinitely.

My Grandmother was the cook in our family. She cooked in mass quantities. I remember her calling our house to tell my mother to send my father over with a pot. That was her way of telling us she had prepared something good. Her love of cooking is the reason my brother and I went to culinary school.

~Joanne Golebiowski, Tupelo, MS

Nana's Chocolate Chip Cake

- 1 (8 ounce) package semi-sweet chocolate chips
- 3 tablespoons sugar
- 1 teaspoon cinnamon
- 1 (18 ounce) package yellow cake mix
- 1 (3¾ ounce) package instant vanilla pudding mix
- ½ cup vegetable oil
- 4 eggs
- 1 cup sour cream
- 1 teaspoon vanilla

Combine chocolate chips, sugar and cinnamon. Set aside. Beat cake mix, pudding mix, oil, eggs, sour cream and vanilla with an electric mixer on low speed for 1 minute. Beat for 2 minutes on medium speed. Batter will be thick. Pour half batter into a greased 10-inch tube pan or Bundt pan. Sprinkle half of chip mixture. Pour in remaining batter and top with remaining chip mixture. Bake at 350 degrees for 1 hour.

Serves 20

Fresh Apple Cake

- 1 cup vegetable oil
- 2 cups sugar
- 2 eggs
- 1½ teaspoons salt, divided
- 1 teaspoon baking soda
- 2 teaspoons baking powder
- 1 teaspoon vanilla
- 2½ cups all-purpose flour
- 1 cup pecans
- 3 cups peeled, chopped apples
- ½ cup butter
- 1 cup packed brown sugar
- 2 tablespoons evaporated milk
- Powdered sugar

Combine oil, sugar, eggs, 1 teaspoon salt, baking soda and baking powder and mix well. Add vanilla, flour and pecans. Fold in apples and mix well. Pour batter into a greased Bundt pan. Bake at 350 degrees for 50 minutes. Cool completely. To make caramel frosting, melt butter in a saucepan. Stir in brown sugar and ½ teaspoon salt. Cook over low heat until sauce becomes a golden amber color. Blend in evaporated milk. Add small amounts of powdered sugar until frosting reaches desired spreading consistency. Frost cooled cake.

Serves 12-15

Amalgamation Cake

- **4 cups all-purpose flour**
- **5 teaspoons baking powder**
- **Dash of salt**
- **2 cups butter, softened and divided**
- **4⅔ cups sugar, divided**
- **2⅓ cups milk, divided**
- **2 teaspoons vanilla, divided**
- **8 egg whites, stiffly beaten**
- **8 egg yolks, well beaten**
- **2 cups chopped pecans**
- **2 cups chopped walnuts**
- **2 cups raisins**
- **2 cups coconut**

Sift flour and measure 4 cups. Sift together flour, baking powder and salt. Cream 1 cup butter and 2⅔ cups sugar until light and fluffy. Add flour mixture and 1⅓ cups milk, alternately to creamed mixture. Beat until smooth. Add 1 teaspoon vanilla. Fold in beaten egg whites. Divide batter into four 9-inch round cake pans. Bake at 350 degrees for 30 minutes or until cake tester comes out clean. To make filling, combine egg yolks, 1 cup butter, 2 cups sugar and 1 cup milk in the top of a double boiler. Cook, stirring constantly, over low-medium heat until thickened. Stir in pecans, walnuts, raisins, coconut and 1 teaspoon vanilla. Stir until cool. Place a cake layer on a serving plate. Spread filling on top. Repeat layers of cake and filling.

Serves 10-12

This cake is better made a few days before serving. This is my family's Christmas Cake! We only have it at Christmas, so it was very special and we enjoyed it through the holidays. The first Christmas after my mother's death, we thought what would Christmas be without mother's cake? As the older daughter, I kept up the tradition and eventually my younger sister learned to make it as well.

~Frances Doler, Calhoun City, MS

Chocolate is good for you! Yes, it is combined with sugar and fat. That's why it tastes so good. It contains a high level of a chemical called pheno which has been shown to help decrease the risk of heart disease and lower LDL cholesterol–the bad kind...Now get this–it also affects the levels of brain chemicals including the three which are called the chemical of love. They are the same substances that are released in response to romance. Eat it in moderation. It's worth the indulgence. Pass the double fudge brownies, please.

~Reprinted from the book *Mama Said* by Martha Houston Reed Hammond

A Hospice Volunteer

In talking with my friend Kathy from Nashville, I mentioned Celebration Village and how it was the main source of raising money to build the Sanctuary Hospice House here in Tupelo. I also relayed to her that this house would be the first of its kind in the nation. Kathy said she could never say enough nice things about hospice and how helpful and caring they were during her dad's last days. The last weeks had been so exhausting for the family and feeling so drained physically and emotionally, Kathy went into the chapel to seek comfort. A hospice volunteer came into the chapel and sat with her. The volunteer took her hand and placed a cross in it and sat quietly for a few minutes. Kathy still has that cross and remembers with thankfulness the person who was so kind and compassionate.

Ann Womack
Tupelo, MS

Italian Cream Cake

12 tablespoons butter, softened and divided
½ cup vegetable oil
2 cups sugar
5 egg yolks
2 cups all-purpose flour
1 teaspoon baking soda
1 cup buttermilk
2 teaspoons vanilla, divided
1 (3½ ounce) can flaked coconut
1 cup chopped nuts
5 egg whites, stiffly beaten
1 (8 ounce) package cream cheese, softened
1 (16 ounce) package powdered sugar
1½ cups chopped pecans

Cream 8 tablespoons butter and oil. Add sugar and beat until smooth. Beat in egg yolks. Stir in flour and baking soda. Add buttermilk, 1 teaspoon vanilla, coconut and nuts. Fold in beaten egg whites. Pour batter into three 8-inch round cake pans. Bake at 350 degrees for 25 minutes. Cool completely. To make cream cheese frosting, beat cream cheese and 4 tablespoons butter until smooth. Add powdered sugar and mix well. Add 1 teaspoon vanilla and beat until smooth. Stir in nuts. Place cake layer on a serving platter. Spread frosting over layer. Repeat with remaining cake layers and frosting. Spread frosting over top and sides.

Serves 10-12

White Chocolate Christmas Cake

- ½ cup water
- 4 ounces white chocolate
- 1½ cups butter, softened and divided
- 3 cups sugar, divided
- 4 egg yolks, beaten
- 1 tablespoon plus 1 teaspoon vanilla, divided
- 2½ cups all-purpose flour
- 1 teaspoon baking soda
- 1 cup buttermilk
- 1 cup flaked coconut
- 1 cup chopped pecans
- 4 egg whites, stiffly beaten
- 1 (12 ounce) package frozen raspberries, thawed
- 1 teaspoon lemon juice
- 1 teaspoon cornstarch dissolved in 1 teaspoon water
- 1 (8 ounce) package cream cheese, softened
- 1 (16 ounce) package powdered sugar
- 1 tablespoon milk

Bring water to boil. Remove from heat and add chocolate. Stir until chocolate melts. Cool for 20 minutes. Meanwhile, cream 1 cup butter and 2 cups sugar until smooth. Add egg yolks and mix well. Beat in chocolate and 1 tablespoon vanilla. Combine flour and baking soda. Add to creamed mixture alternately with buttermilk. Mix well. Stir in coconut and pecans. Fold beaten egg whites into batter. Pour batter into three greased and floured 9-inch round cake pans. Bake at 350 degrees for 25 to 30 minutes or until cake tests done. Cool in pans for 10 minutes. Remove to wire racks to cool completely.

To make raspberry filling, blend raspberries in a food processor until smooth. Press berries through a strainer to remove seeds. Discard seeds. Combine raspberry puree, 1 cup sugar, lemon juice and cornstarch mixture in a saucepan. Bring to boil over low-medium heat. Boil, stirring constantly, until filling thickens. Cool completely. For cream cheese frosting, beat ½ cup butter and cream cheese until smooth. Gradually add powdered sugar, beating well after each addition. Stir in 1 teaspoon vanilla and milk.

To assemble, using a serrated knife, carefully slice each layer horizontally. Place one split cake layer on a serving platter. Spread with a third of raspberry filling. Stack with another split cake layer. Spread a third of frosting over cake. Repeat with remaining raspberry filling, cake layers and frosting, stacking one on top of each other ending with frosting.

Serves 10-12

Cake flour produces lighter cakes because it contains less gluten than all-purpose flour.

~from
The New Food Lover's Tiptionary

Coconut Cake with Lemon Filling

This was one of the Christmas cakes my mother-in-law, Ethel Hazel, always prepared. I can still remember her standing at her stove cooking the lemon filling. We cherish our memories of the delicious food this wonderful cook prepared for her family.

~Pat Hazel,
Tupelo, MS

1 (18 ounce) package white cake mix
1½ cups sugar
1 cup milk
2 cups grated coconut plus some for garnish
2 small lemons, seeded and chopped in food processor with peel
1 heaping tablespoon all-purpose flour
Small marshmallows for filling
2 cups powdered sugar
2-3 tablespoons water

Prepare cake according to package directions, using three 9-inch round cake pans. Combine sugar, milk, coconut and chopped lemon mixture in a saucepan. Bring to boil, stirring constantly. Add flour and cook until mixture becomes lumpy. Cool filling. Place cooled cake layer on a serving platter. Spread half of lemon filling over cake and top with a layer of marshmallows. Stack second cake layer and repeat with filling and marshmallows. Top with third cake layer. Combine powdered sugar and water. Stir until glaze reaches spreading consistency. Spread glaze over cake. Sprinkle with coconut. Keep refrigerated.

Serves 8-10

Cleoma's Boiled Custard

Cleoma was my Mother's cook and housekeeper for 60+ years. If custard begins to curdle, simply beat it strongly with a whisk. If that does not work, strain the custard.

~Dale Warrnier,
Tupelo, MS

2 eggs, slightly beaten
¼ cup sugar
⅛ teaspoon salt
2 cups whole milk, scalded
½ teaspoon vanilla

Beat eggs with sugar and salt until smooth not foamy. Scald milk in the top of a double boiler. Slowly add egg mixture to milk. Cook, stirring constantly, for 6 to 8 minutes. Reduce heat as custard thickens. Remove from heat and cool. Stir in vanilla and refrigerate. Serve cold.

Serves 2-4

Whipped Cream Pound Cake

3 cups sugar
1 cup butter, softened
7 eggs, room temperature
3 cups cake flour, sifted twice and divided
½ pint heavy cream
2 teaspoons vanilla

Cream sugar and butter until smooth. Add eggs, one at a time, beating well after each addition. Stir in half of flour. Add heavy cream and mix well. Stir in remaining half flour. Add vanilla. Pour batter into a buttered and floured 10-inch tube pan. Set in a cold oven and turn temperature to 350 degrees. Bake for 1 hour to 1 hour, 10 minutes or until cake tester comes out clean. Cool in pan for 5 minutes. Invert onto serving plate and cool completely. Cover in plastic wrap and store cake for several days.

Serves 12-15

A friend, who knew Elvis when he was two years old, is a lady who really knows how to cook. She would bake this pound cake for his birthday and every Christmas. This is a classic cake, moist, dense and buttery, yet simple and totally satisfying. A scoop of ice cream is the only way to improve this cake. The cake maker, who prefers to remain anonymous lest she be deluged by Tupelonians requesting her cakes for birthdays and special occasions, shared her recipe with us. It was her mother's and grandmother's recipe. It makes the ultimate pound cake. All the more fun to eat when you know it was Elvis Presley's favorite.

~Northeast Mississippi Daily Journal

Celebration Lemon-Cheese Filled Cake

Cake

1 package butter flavored yellow cake mix
¾ cup apricot nectar
¼ cup butter, softened

Heat oven to 350 degrees. Grease and flour a 10-inch Bundt pan. Combine the cake ingredients in a mixer bowl and beat as directed on the package. Pour into the prepared pan.

Filling

2 (8 ounce) packages cream cheese, softened
½ cup sugar
2 tablespoons lemon juice
1 cup flaked coconut

In a small bowl combine all the filling ingredients. Beat until smooth. Spoon the filling over the batter in the Bundt pan, being careful not to let the filling touch sides of the pan. Bake for 50 to 55 minutes. Cool upright in the pan for 1 hour.

Glaze

2 cups powdered sugar
2 tablespoons lemon juice
2 tablespoons apricot nectar

Remove cake from pan after cooling. Make the glaze and drizzle over the cake.

Prize Surprise

Everyone old enough to remember "Miss Nelle" Reed will be able to appreciate this story and those who do not remember her will surely enjoy a chuckle from the story! This is a true story and happened when I was a senior at Tupelo High School. Miss Nelle lived in a house designed after a World's Fair showcase home and the house was located at the site of the present Ballard Park.

As a graduation party, Miss Nelle invited a group of senior girls from the Class of 1948 to her home for an afternoon of bridge. The most any of us knew about playing was what we may have heard from our parents and we certainly did not know the rules of the game. Therefore, it came as a real surprise when they announced that I had won the high prize. Imagine my excitement when Miss Nelle handed me a beautifully wrapped package. I could hardly wait to tear open the box, but my excitement soon turned to amazement and I must say a great deal of disappointment when I discovered the prize was an old, much worn and not too clean bra. What do you say? Finally my sense of humor took over and we all had a big laugh.

Just so you know that she was not all fun and games, I want to add that a few years later when the announcement of my engagement and upcoming wedding appeared in the Daily Journal, Miss Nelle sent me an eight-place setting of very pretty china. This was a very generous gift that I really appreciated. You never knew what Miss Nelle would do next and there certainly will never be another!

Jo Anne Stallings Harris
Tupelo, MS

Food Memories: Pound cake sliced with butter – put under broiler and toasted – then chocolate syrup on top after sledding when I was a child in North Carolina Mountains.

Judy Jones, Belden, MS

Sour Cream Coconut Cake

- 1 (18 ounce) package white cake mix
- 1 (8 ounce) container sour cream
- ¼ cup vegetable oil
- 3 eggs
- 1 (8½ ounce) can cream of coconut
- 1 (3¾ ounce) package instant vanilla pudding mix
- 1½ cups milk
- ½ cup heavy cream
- 2 tablespoons powdered sugar
- ½ teaspoon vanilla
- 1 (7 ounce) package frozen coconut, thawed
- 3 egg whites
- ½ cup light corn syrup
- ¾ cup sugar
- Dash of salt
- ⅛ teaspoon cream of tartar

Beat cake mix, sour cream, oil, eggs and coconut cream with an electric mixer at medium speed for 2 minutes. Pour batter into four 8-inch round cake pans. Bake at 350 degrees for 25 minutes or until cake tester comes out clean. Cool completely. Place in refrigerator until ready to stack. Whisk together pudding mix and milk. Cover and refrigerate for at least 2 hours. Combine cream, powdered sugar and vanilla. Mix until stiff. Fold in coconut and refrigerate for 2 hours. Combine pudding and coconut mixture. Return filling to refrigerator for at least 1 hour.

To make icing, combine egg whites, syrup, sugar, salt and cream of tarter in top of a double boiler. Cook and beat with mixer for 4 minutes or until soft peaks form. Remove pans from water and beat 2 minutes until thickened.

To assemble, place cake layer on serving plate. Spread a third of filling over cake. Repeat with remaining cake layers and filling, ending with cake layer on top. Frost cake with icing and sprinkle with coconut. Cake must be refrigerated.

Serves 10-12

For better volume in your cakes, use room temperature ingredients.

~from The New Food Lover's Tiptionary

Fudge Delight

- 30 saltine crackers, crushed
- ¾ cup crunchy peanut butter
- 3 cups sugar
- 1 cup milk

Mix together cracker crumbs and peanut butter until smooth. Combine sugar and milk in a heavy saucepan. Bring to boil. Cook, stirring constantly, for 5 to 8 minutes. Pour over cracker mixture. Beat with an electric mixer until smooth. Pour mixture into a buttered 8 x 8 x 2-inch baking dish. Let fudge set. Cut into squares. Store in refrigerator.

Serves 15-20

Nightgown Gardening

I have found that the most pleasant kind of gardening is in my nightgown. Nightgown gardening can only be done in the early morning. It is the very best time for picking off dead blooms, cutting a few blossoms for the house, inspecting plants, turning a few pots around for different light, and watering those on the deck or patio.

No one can see me. I feel "loose" and cool. Water always runs down my arms as I reach to water the hanging plants. I do not like it but am not tall enough to prevent it. Well, I could stand on something, but it's too much trouble, so part of my gown and me are always wet by the time I go inside. Also, leaves and sometimes dirt are stuck to my gown, but still puttering around in my nightgown early in the morning is utterly delightful. Sometimes I venture out front to get the paper because no neighbors or cars are up and out - but yesterday our neighbor caught me as he went (fully dressed) to get his morning paper. "Morning Martha" he said as he reached in his box, turned and went back toward his house with his head down scanning the news. I could have been in a Halloween costume wearing a mask, for all the attention he paid. He might have noticed if I had been naked, but I am not sure. Anyway - I was in my cool, comfortable nightgown and loving the morning.

P. S. Sometimes a bug gets on my back or crawls up my leg. Then I do the "bug-boogie". It's not very graceful but very energetic and brief (until the bug is off).

~Reprinted with permission from
Mama Said by Martha Houston Reid Hammond
Corinth, MS

Apple Dumplings

2 Granny Smith apples, cut into 8 slices each
2 (8 ounce) packages refrigerated crescent rolls
1 cup butter, melted
1½ cups sugar
1 (12 ounce) bottle lemon-lime carbonated beverage

Roll 1 apple slice in a crescent roll and place seam-side down in an 11 x 7 x 2-inch baking dish. Combine butter, sugar and soda. Pour over rolls. Bake at 350 degrees for 30 to 45 minutes.

Serves 8-10

At Your Service–
Recipes from Professionals

Holiday Homecoming

(Heartwarming ideas to serve those you love at those special holidays.)

Miss Becky's Breakfast Eggs

~ Bay Breeze Bed & Breakfast ~

- **6 eggs**
- **2 tablespoons all-purpose flour**
- **¼ cup butter, melted**
- **2 cups cottage cheese**
- **1 (8 ounce) package shredded sharp Cheddar cheese**
- **1 (4½ ounce) can chopped green chilies, drained**
- **Dash of salt**

Combine eggs, flour, butter, cottage cheese, Cheddar cheese, green chilies and salt and mix well. Pour egg mixture into a 10-inch quiche dish. Bake at 375 degrees for 35 to 40 minutes or until set.

Serves 6

Probably our most asked for recipe. So easy, yet they will think you fussed and fussed. May serve sausage on the side.

Our Delicious Orange French Toast

~ Bay Breeze Bed & Breakfast ~

- **4-5 eggs**
- **⅔ cup orange juice**
- **⅓ cup milk**
- **Vanilla to taste**
- **¼ cup sugar**
- **French bread, sliced 1-inch thick (3 slices per person)**

Beat eggs, juice, milk, vanilla and sugar. Pour egg mixture into a 13 x 9 x 2-inch baking dish. Place bread slices in egg mixture. Let stand for a few minutes. Turn bread over to coat in egg mixture. Cover and refrigerate overnight. Before baking, allow bread to come to room temperature. Place bread on a well greased baking sheet or jelly-roll pan. Bake at 400 degrees for 10 minutes. Turn bread and bake an additional 10 minutes.

Serves 3 slices per person

To make ahead, wrap egg soaked bread in foil and freeze overnight. Place frozen slices in individual freezer bags and return to freezer. To serve, brush both sides with melted butter and bake at 500 degrees for 8 to 10 minutes. May need to double egg mixture depending on number of bread slices to coat on both sides.

At Bay Breeze B & B, this is served on a bed of heated apricot or boysenberry syrup, dusted with powdered sugar, garnished with strips of orange rind and accompanied by a thin slice of ham.

A recipe calling for 1 shallot typically means 1 clove, not the whole head.

~from The New Food Lover's Tiptionary

Red Pork with Coconut Milk

~ Mississippi University for Women Culinary Arts Institute ~

- **2 tablespoons vegetable oil**
- **½ pound ground pork**
- **1½ tablespoons ground New Mexico chili or paprika**
- **½ teaspoon cayenne pepper**
- **6 garlic cloves, thinly sliced**
- **1 large shallot, thinly sliced**
- **3 tablespoons sugar**
- **1 cup unsweetened coconut milk**
- **1 tablespoon fish sauce**
- **¼ cup peanuts, chopped**
- **Hot cooked rice**
- **Fresh cilantro for garnish**

Heat oil in a skillet. Cook pork, chili and cayenne over medium-high heat. Stir to break up meat. When pork is browned, add garlic and shallot. Cook until tender. Add sugar, coconut milk and fish sauce. Cook for 10 minutes longer to blend flavors. Add peanuts. Serve over a bed of rice and garnish with cilantro.

Serves 4

Baked Chicken with Sage and Salt Dough Crust

~ Martha Rutledge Catering ~

- **2 (3½-4 pound) whole chickens**
- **2-4 bunches fresh sage leaves**
- **30 garlic cloves**
- **Ground white pepper**
- **4 cups all-purpose flour**
- **4 cups kosher salt**

Preheat oven to 425 degrees. Rinse chicken with cold water. Pat dry inside and out. Carefully loosen skin from chicken flesh. Insert 3 to 4 sage leaves on the chicken breast. Add equal amounts of garlic, white pepper and remaining sage leaves to each bird cavity. Combine flour and salt. Add enough cold water to make dough. Divide dough and spread all over each chicken. Chicken should be encased in dough. Bake at 425 degrees for 45 minutes or until dough is golden browned. Let chicken set for 10 minutes. Remove crust with a sharp knife. Discard crust. Serve whole chicken on a bed of sage leaves.

Serves 4-6

Clambake In A Crust

~ Martha Rutledge Catering ~

- 1½ pounds round or oval loaf of French or Italian bread
- 3 (6½ ounce) cans chopped clams, reserving liquid
- 2 (8 ounce) packages cream cheese, softened
- 3 tablespoons dry white wine
- 2 green onions, chopped
- 1 teaspoon fresh lemon juice
- ½ teaspoon salt
- ½ teaspoon Tabasco sauce
- Raw vegetables for dipping

Preheat oven to 250 degrees. Using a serrated knife, slice bread horizontally. Set top aside. Remove ½-inch of center bread to form a hollow shell. Cut center bread into cubes and reserve. Measure ¼ cup clam liquid and combine with cream cheese, wine, green onion, juice, salt and Tabasco. Beat until well blended. Fold in clams. Pack clam mixture into bread shell and cover with top bread piece. Wrap tightly with foil. Bake at 250 degrees for 3 hours. Serve hot with reserved bread cubes and raw vegetables.

Serves 6-8

Grouper with Horseradish Crust

~ Buckhorn Inn ~

- 2 tablespoons chopped shallots
- 1 garlic clove, chopped
- 1 tablespoon butter
- 2 tablespoons all-purpose flour
- ½ cup white wine
- ½ cup chicken broth
- 1 cup heavy cream
- 1 tablespoon Dijon mustard
- 8 (6-8 ounce) grouper fillets
- 2 cups bread crumbs
- ½ teaspoon salt
- ½ teaspoon pepper
- 1 tablespoon horseradish

Sauté shallots and garlic in butter. Whisk in flour, stirring for 2 minutes. Add wine, broth, cream and mustard. Cook, stirring frequently, until slightly thickened. Season with salt and pepper. Keep sauce warm. Dust fish in flour and dip in egg wash (mixture of milk and egg). Combine bread crumbs, salt, pepper and horseradish. Dredge fish in breading mixture. Brown in olive oil for 4 to 5 minutes on each side or until done.

Serves 8

May substitute mahi-mahi, red snapper or halibut for grouper.

BBQ Shrimp and Black Bean Cake

~ Park Heights Restaurant ~

For the Black Bean Cake

- 6 cups black beans, cooked
- 3 eggs
- 2 teaspoons garlic powder
- 2 teaspoons onion powder
- 1 cup bread crumbs
- Salt and pepper to taste
- 1 tablespoon olive oil

In a food processor, puree half of the beans with the eggs, garlic, onion, bread crumbs, salt and pepper. Mix in the remaining whole beans. Mold into cakes about 3 inches in diameter. Heat oil in a skillet over medium heat. Add bean cakes and warm on each side for 4 to 5 minutes.

For the Shrimp and BBQ Sauce

- 30 shrimp, peeled and deveined with tails attached
- Olive oil
- 5 tablespoons paprika
- 1 tablespoon dried rosemary
- 2 tablespoons lemon juice
- 1 cup beer
- 2 tablespoons Worcestershire sauce
- ¼ cup butter
- Salt and pepper to taste
- Rosemary sprigs for garnish

Toss the shrimp in the paprika and rosemary. Heat olive oil in a skillet over moderate to high heat. Add the shrimp and sauté until opaque. (This may be done in batches.) Remove shrimp and, in the same skillet, add the beer, lemon juice, Worcestershire sauce and bring to a boil. Reduce the mixture by one fourth. While the mixture is boiling, add the butter, stirring constantly. Reduce the heat and simmer for 4 to 5 minutes.

Assembly

To assemble, arrange a bean cake in the center of a shallow bowl. Stack 5 shrimp on top and ladle sauce over and around shrimp. Garnish with a rosemary sprig.

Serves 6

Crespelle Lasagna

~ Basic Kneads ~

Crêpes (double recipe)
Meat Sauce
Parmesan Béchamel Sauce
⅛ teaspoon freshly grated nutmeg
1 cup freshly grated Parmesan cheese
1 tablespoon chopped fresh Italian parsley

Crêpes

1 cup all-purpose flour
1 cup cold water, divided
½ cup cold milk
2 eggs
3 tablespoons butter, melted
2 tablespoons olive oil
¼ teaspoon salt

Measure flour, ¾ cup water, milk, eggs, butter and salt into a blender. Blend until smooth. Refrigerate, covered, for 15 to 30 minutes. When ready to cook the crêpes add the remaining water and mix until the consistency of heavy cream. Spray a 10-inch non-stick fry pan and heat over a medium flame. Add ¼ cup of crêpe batter to center of the pan and tilt pan to spread out batter. Cook until edges curl and are light brown. Turn out onto a pan and continue with the rest of the batter.

14-16 (8 inch) crêpes

Meat Sauce

¾ pound ground beef
¾ pound ground pork or veal
3 cups tomato sauce
½ cup tomato paste
1 cup beef or chicken stock
Salt and pepper to taste

Brown the ground meats and drain. Add the rest of the ingredients to the pot and simmer for 45 minutes, covered. For a thicker sauce, remove the lid after 30 minutes and simmer uncovered until rich and concentrated.

Parmesan Béchamel Sauce

3 tablespoons unsalted butter
2 tablespoons all-purpose flour
2 cups whole milk
5 peppercorns, crushed
1 dried bay leaf
¼ teaspoon salt
¼ teaspoon freshly grated nutmeg
1 cup freshly grated Parmesan cheese
¼-½ cup thinly sliced fresh basil
Salt and pepper to taste

In a medium saucepan melt butter. Sprinkle in the flour and stir with a wooden spoon until blended. Cook, stirring 2 to 3 minutes to form a thin roux. In a separate saucepan, heat the milk, peppercorns, bay leaf, salt and nutmeg until steaming. Return the roux to the heat and add the steaming milk mixture, whisking to prevent lumps. Continue whisking for 3 to 6 minutes until the mixture thickens. Remove from the heat and add the Parmesan and basil. Season with salt and pepper to taste.

To Assemble Lasagna

Lightly grease a lasagna pan with olive oil and pour in 1 cup of Meat Sauce. Top with Crêpes to cover. Spread with a thin layer of Béchamel Sauce (about ¼ cup). Sprinkle with grated cheese and top with another layer of Crêpes, then a thin layer of Meat Sauce. Repeat layering to the top of the pan. Keep each layer thin. Finish with a layer of Crêpes and Béchamel Sauce, and sprinkle with cheese and parsley. Bake for 25 to 30 minutes or until light brown and bubbly. Let rest 10 minutes before cutting into generous servings.

This lasagna does not leave you with a heavy feeling. It is really light, yet filling. Clients I have served it to absolutely love it.

Thanksgiving Dinner

When our children were very young, we were transferred from Virginia to northeast Pennsylvania with my husband's job. We moved in the July heat but a cool spell came in August. Soon we became acclimated to the area and enjoyed a gorgeous fall. For Thanksgiving we planned to go to the grandparents in Virginia. Since we suspected that the Christmas weather would be "iffy", we planned to take Christmas gifts on our Thanksgiving trip. I baked pumpkin pies (even preparing pumpkins for the pies). We packed the car before going to bed. When I went to bed the weather was cold but clear. When we arose at 4:30 a.m. to hit the road, we expected to be lunching with family, turkey and all the trimmings.

When we pulled the station wagon out of the garage, it was snowing. We got stuck, then slid as we went down the driveway. My husband straightened the car and tried again, several times. It continued to snow. I went inside to call the highway patrol. We planned to head down Interstate 81 toward family. The dispatcher replied that the interstate was closed due to snow and low visibility. "Go back to bed, lady!" We followed his advice. For the rest of the day it snowed, a total of thirty-six (36) inches! For Thanksgiving Dinner we ate canned Ravioli and pumpkin pie. Memories are made with adventures such as these. When Thanksgiving arrives, we are thankful for happy times and laugh and enjoy the "Ravioli Memories"!

~Delores B. Rose
Belden, MS

About how many feathers do turkeys have at maturity?

A. *3,499*
B. *5,005*
C. *1,003*
D. *Turkeys have feathers?? I thought they came in plastic wrap.*

TurkeyTrivia.com

Answer: A.

Dr. John Evans

Dr. John Evans delighted in calling the office to talk with Dr. Bill Wood and hearing an unfamiliar voice answer the telephone. Like so many after me, I fell prey to his antics. He would ask to speak with "Bill" and identify himself as "Dr. Fuddpucker." Naturally, you would never question a physician. A page would be heard overhead, "Dr. Wood, line whatever for Dr. Fuddpucker." For everyone who had already been victimized by his sense of humor, laughter was instantaneous-he had done it again!! For the twenty-plus years I worked for Drs. Murphy and Wood and the subsequent merger and creation of Internal Medicine, I cannot count the times I heard that page. Having that experience was a right of passage for any new receptionist; no one ever forewarned them. I always said there was madness in his method. His constant joking and prank pulling were part of the physician he was. He was caring and used his sense of humor as part of the treatment. When he sensed a patient's apprehension or fear, he used humor to provide a calming effect-it worked.

Mary Williams Randle
Tupelo, MS
Permission granted by family of Dr. John Evans

Halibut Oscar

~ Woody's Restaurant ~

1 teaspoon vegetable oil
1 teaspoon minced shallot
2 teaspoons lemon juice
2 cups heavy cream
¼ cup sweet sherry
3 ounces lump crabmeat
Kosher salt and pepper to taste
⅓ cup shredded Asiago cheese
2-4 (8 ounce) halibut fillets, 1-inch thick and skinned
Salt and pepper to taste
Fresh parsley or chives for garnish

Stir together oil, shallot and juice in a saucepan. Add cream and sherry. Bring to boil. Reduce heat to medium-high. Cook, stirring frequently, for 2 minutes until sauce is reduced by half. Stir in crabmeat, salt and pepper. Stir in cheese and keep warm. Season fillet with salt and pepper. Brush a metal baking sheet with melted butter. Place fillets on baking sheet, vein side down. Bake at 450 degrees for 4 to 6 minutes or until fillet flakes. To serve, drizzle cream sauce over fillets. Garnish with fresh parsley or chives. For added appeal, top with crabmeat.

Serves 2-4

Maverick Grits

~ Slightly North of Broad ~

- **4¼ cups water, divided**
- **½ teaspoon salt**
- **¼ cup unsalted butter, divided**
- **1 cup old-fashioned stone-ground grits**
- **¼ cup heavy cream**
- **1½ chorizo links (spicy pork sausage), cut into ¼-inch thick slices**
- **4 ounces country ham, cut into julienne strips**
- **8 medium sea scallops**
- **12 medium shrimp, peeled and deveined**
- **2 tomatoes, peeled, seeded and chopped**
- **½ cup sliced green onion**
- **¼ teaspoon minced garlic**
- **Dash of Cajun seasoning**
- **Salt and pepper to taste**

Bring 4 cups water, salt and 1 tablespoon butter to boil in a 3-quart heavy saucepan. Whisk in grits. Slowly simmer, covered, stirring frequently, for 1 hour until grits are tender and thickened. Stir in cream and remaining 1 tablespoon butter. Remove from heat. Make topping 15 minutes before grits are done. Cook chorizo and ham in ½ tablespoon butter in a heavy skillet for 3 minutes until ham is golden. Transfer chorizo and ham to a plate with a slotted spoon. Add ½ tablespoon butter and heat until foam subsides. Sauté scallops for 2 minutes until golden on both sides and just cooked through. Transfer to plate with slotted spoon. Add ½ tablespoon butter to skillet. Sauté shrimp, turning occasionally for 3 minutes, until just cooked through. Add back chorizo, ham, scallops and remaining ½ tablespoon butter. Stir in green onion, garlic, Cajun seasoning and ¼ cup water. Cook, stirring and scraping browned bits in skillet, until heated thoroughly. Season with salt and pepper. Serve over grits.

Serves 4

Food Memories: We celebrated every occasion with a meal – Sunday lunch at my grandmother's and special dinners during holidays and birthdays.

Rose Anne Parker, Tupelo. MS

Grilled Shrimp and Corn Shiitake Ragoût with Basil and Tomato Oils

~ Park Heights Restaurant ~

- ½ cup basil leaves
- Olive oil
- ½ cup sun-dried tomatoes
- 2 shallots, minced
- 3 garlic cloves
- 2 tablespoons ground thyme
- 4 cups corn kernels, uncooked
- 2 cups shiitake mushrooms, chopped
- Salt and pepper to taste
- ½ cup heavy cream
- 20 large shrimp or prawns, peeled, deveined with head and tails attached
- 1 tablespoon minced garlic

To make basil oil, drop basil leaves in boiling water for less than 1 minute. Plunge leaves into cold ice water to stop cooking. Drain leaves. Place in a blender and add enough oil just to cover. Puree basil and oil. Force the oil through a fine mesh strainer, discarding the basil solids and saving the oil. For tomato oil, place tomatoes in blender and add enough oil just to cover. Puree mixture and force oil through a fine mesh strainer, discarding tomato solids and saving oil. Set both oils aside.

To make ragoût, sauté shallots, garlic and thyme in a hot, well oiled skillet until shallots are clear. Add corn, mushrooms and season with salt and pepper. Add cream and cook until corn is tender. Keep warm. Toss shrimp with garlic, oil, salt and pepper. Grill to desired degree of doneness. To serve, place a mound of ragoût in center of four plates. Surround ragoût with five shrimp each and drizzle with both oils.

Serves 4

Brown Beer Bread

~ Mississippi University for Women Culinary Arts Institute ~

- 3 cups all-purpose flour
- 3 cups whole wheat flour
- 3 tablespoons baking powder
- 1 tablespoon salt
- ⅔ cup packed brown sugar
- 2 (12 ounce) bottles brown beer (ale or bock)

Stir together flour, whole wheat flour, baking powder, salt and brown sugar. Pour in beer and mix until thoroughly blended. The batter will be very stiff. Divide dough into 2 lightly greased 9 x 5 x 3-inch loaf pans. Bake at 350 degrees for 50 minutes or until firm and browned.

Serves 2 loaves

Dr. P.K. Thomas

Dr. Thomas was a beloved Tupelo obstetrician-gynecologist, who delivered more than 5,000 babies during his 37-year career. When he wasn't busy seeing patients, Dr. P.K. loved working in his yard. Years ago, when Thomas Street was considered on the fringe of Tupelo, Dr. P.K., dressed in work clothes, was strolling the property gathering fallen limbs and tending his flowers. A woman driving by was admiring the lovely yard. She pulled over and rolled down her window. "Excuse me, sir," the woman said to Dr. P.K., "do you work here?" Dr. P.K. replied, "Yes ma'am." "I was wondering how much do you charge?" the woman said. "Well," Dr. P.K. said, "The woman of this house lets me sleep with her." Word is the woman couldn't roll up her window fast enough and left the "yardman" standing in a cloud of dust.

Glenn and Mary Thomas
Tupelo, MS

Rosemary Scones

~ Martha Rutledge Catering ~

1¾ cups all-purpose flour
2¼ teaspoons baking powder
2 tablespoons sugar
½ teaspoon salt
¼ cup cold butter
2 eggs
⅓ cup half-and-half
2 tablespoons finely chopped fresh rosemary or ½ teaspoon dried
Sugar for garnish

Preheat oven to 450 degrees. Sift together flour, baking powder, sugar and salt in a large bowl. Cut in butter using a pastry blender until mixture resembles small peas. In a separate bowl, beat eggs. Reserve 2 tablespoons egg for brushing scones. Add half-and-half to remaining eggs and mix well. Make a well in center of dry ingredients. Pour egg mixture into well. Add rosemary. Combine with a few swift strokes. Do not overmix. Turn dough onto a lightly floured surface. Pat down dough to ¾-inch thickness. Cut diamond shapes or rounds with a knife. Brush with reserved egg and sprinkle with sugar. Bake at 450 degrees for 15 minutes.

Serves 8

Basic Biscotti

~ Mississippi University for Women Culinary Arts Institute ~

3 eggs, divided
3 egg yolks
1 cup plus 2 tablespoons sugar
1¾ cups all-purpose flour
1 tablespoon baking powder
⅛ teaspoon orange oil
⅛ teaspoon salt
3 tablespoons slivered almonds, toasted

Beat 2 eggs and egg yolks with sugar. Add flour, baking powder, oil and salt. Beat until well blended. Stir in almonds. Shape dough into 1-inch high and 3-inch wide logs. Place on a paper lined baking sheet. Beat remaining egg and brush over dough. Bake at 375 degrees for 15 minutes. Remove from oven. Cut 1-inch diagonal slices. Lay slices flat on baking sheet and return to oven Bake an additional 10 minutes until golden browned and dry.

Serves 12

For variations, try adding dried cherries or cranberries, anise seeds or extract, coarsely chopped pistachio nuts, 1 teaspoon finely grated orange zest or dipping one side in melted tempered chocolate.

Bread Pudding Soufflé with Whiskey Sauce

~ Martha Rutledge Catering ~

1½ cups plus 2 tablespoons sugar, divided
¾ teaspoon cinnamon
Dash of nutmeg
1 whole egg plus 1 egg white, lightly beaten
1 cup half-and-half
1 teaspoon vanilla
¼ cup raisins
4-5 cups cubed French bread
1½ teaspoons cornstarch
1 tablespoon water
½ cup heavy cream
2 tablespoons bourbon
8 egg whites

Preheat oven to 350 degrees. Combine 1 cup sugar, cinnamon and nutmeg. Beat in egg mixture until well blended. Stir in half-and-half and vanilla. Add raisins and cubed bread; stir. Pour batter into a greased 8 x 8 x 2-inch baking dish. Bake at 350 degrees for 45 minutes or until tester comes out clean. Cool bread completely. To make sauce, whisk together cornstarch with water. In a small saucepan, heat cream to boil. Whisk in cornstarch and continue to boil. Remove from heat. Stir in 2 tablespoons sugar and bourbon. Cool and refrigerate. In a large bowl beat egg whites until foamy. Add ½ cup sugar and beat until shiny and glossy. In a separate bowl, break half of cooked bread pudding into small pieces. Reserve other half for another use. Gently stir in half of meringue with bread. Spoon mixture into six individual buttered 6-ounce custard cups. Top each with a swirl of reserved meringue. Place cups in a large baking dish. Place in a 350 degree oven. Pour hot water around cups. Bake for 20 minutes until golden browned. Warm whiskey sauce in double boiler. Pierce tops of soufflés and spoon sauce on top.

Serves 6

Luscious Coconut Cream Pie

~ Beverly Blaylock Caterer ~

This recipe was given to me from my mother-in-law, Donis Sullivan Blaylock. She was known for her coconut pie. I asked her to help in making her pie. She explained the importance of measuring correctly, having egg whites at room temperature, adding 1 tablespoon of sugar per egg white, one spoonful at a time, and using only a glass bowl. The meringue was about 4-inches high making the pie absolutely beautiful. As she held the pie, I exclaimed that I was going into labor. She became so excited that she dropped the pie. She cried and I laughed. Pie was everywhere. Everytime I bake this pie, I think about that lesson.

1 cup plus 3-4 tablespoons sugar
⅓ cup all-purpose flour
2 cups milk
¼ cup butter
3-4 egg yolks
2 cups flaked coconut, divided
Dash of salt
1 teaspoon vanilla
1 (9-inch) deep dish pie shell, baked
3-4 egg whites, room temperature

Combine sugar and flour in the top of a double boiler. Add milk, butter, egg yolks. Cook, stirring constantly, until thickened. Remove from heat. Add 1½ cups coconut, salt and vanilla. Pour filling into baked crust. Beat egg whites and 3 to 4 tablespoons sugar in a glass bowl until stiff peaks form. Spread meringue over filling. Top with remaining ½ cup coconut. Bake at 350 degrees until lightly browned.

Serves 6-8

White Chocolate Bread Pudding

~ The Palace Cafe ~

3⅓ cups heavy cream, divided
18 ounces white chocolate, divided
1 cup milk
½ cup sugar
2 eggs
8 egg yolks
1 loaf French bread, cut into ¼-inch slices and dried in the oven
2 tablespoons chocolate shavings for garnish

Warm 3 cups cream in top of a double boiler. Add 10 ounces chocolate and stir until chocolate melts. Remove from heat. In a double boiler, heat milk, sugar and egg yolks until warm. Blend egg mixture into chocolate mixture. Place bread slices in 13 x 9 x 2-inch baking dish. Pour half chocolate mixture over bread. Let bread soak up liquid. Top with remaining chocolate mixture. Cover with foil and bake at 275 degrees for 1 hour. Remove foil and bake an additional 15 minutes until top is golden browned. Meanwhile, melt 8 ounces white chocolate in double boiler. Remove from heat and stir in ⅓ cup cream. Spoon over warm bread pudding. Garnish with chocolate shavings.

Serves 8

Mascarpone Cheesecake with Pecans and Dulce de Leche Sauce

~ Buckhorn Inn ~

8 ounces shortbread cookies
1/3 cup pecans
2 tablespoons unsalted butter, melted
4 (3 ounce) packages cream cheese, softened
2 (8 ounce) packages mascarpone cheese
1 1/3 tablespoons all-purpose flour
1 1/4 cups sugar
1 teaspoon vanilla
1 teaspoon lemon juice
4 large eggs, room temperature
1 cup heavy cream
1 cup packed brown sugar
1/2 cup sweetened condensed milk
Pecans for garnish

Preheat oven to 350 degrees. Wrap outside of 9-inch, 2¾-inch high side springform pan with 3 layers heavy duty foil. Finely grind shortbread cookies and pecans in food processor. Add butter and process until crumbs are moistened. Press crumb mixture onto bottom of pan. Bake at 350 degrees for 5 minutes or until golden browned. Cool completely on rack. Reduce oven to 325 degrees.

Beat cream cheese until smooth. Add mascarpone and flour. Beat until smooth. Gradually add sugar. Beat in vanilla and juice. Add eggs, one at a time, beating well after each addition. Pour filling into crust. Place springform pan in large roasting pan. Pour enough hot water into roasting pan to reach halfway up side of springform pan. Bake at 325 degrees for 1 hour, 15 minutes or until top is golden and cake is almost set. Cool cake on rack for 1 hour. Refrigerate, uncovered, overnight.

To make sauce, combine cream and brown sugar in heavy saucepan. Stir over medium heat until sugar dissolves. Boil, stirring occasionally, for 5 minutes until reduced to 1 cup. Stir in milk. Cool completely. Arrange pecans decoratively atop cake. Cut into wedges. Serve with sauce.

Serves 14

Pressed for time? Turn on the oven the moment you walk in the house so it can be preheating while you prep for dinner.

~from
The New Food Lover's Tiptionary

Warm Pear and Ginger Dumpling with Crème Anglaise

~ Park Heights Restaurant ~

- **1⅔ cups all-purpose flour**
- **½ teaspoon salt**
- **½ cup unsalted butter, chilled and cut into small pieces**
- **1 egg, lightly beaten**
- **2 teaspoons water**
- **2 tablespoons finely minced ginger**
- **3 tablespoons packed brown sugar**
- **3 Bosc pears, or canned pears, halved and poached in white wine, sugar and lemon juice**
- **1 vanilla bean**
- **2 cups heavy cream**
- **½ cup sugar, divided**
- **½ cup egg yolks**

Sift together flour and salt. Add butter pieces and beat with an electric mixer until bread crumb consistency. Beat in egg and water. Roll dough into a ball, wrap in plastic wrap and refrigerate for 30 minutes. Preheat oven to 400 degrees. Combine ginger and brown sugar. Add pears and toss to coat. Place pears in 13 x 9 x 2-inch baking dish. Bake at 400 degrees for 15 minutes. Cool completely.

To make sauce, scrape seeds from bean into a saucepan. Add pod and cream. Bring to simmer. Stir in ¼ cup sugar until dissolved. Meanwhile, whisk egg yolks and remaining ¼ cup sugar until blended. Whisk in one-third of hot cream mixture into yolks. Add egg mixture to cream mixture. Stir custard over low heat until it thickens and coats back of wooden spoon. Immediately pour custard into a bowl set in an ice water bath and stir to cool. Strain and refrigerate.

For assembly, cut dough in half. Roll each piece to ⅛-inch thick. Place pear halves on one sheet of dough. Take second sheet and place over the pears, covering completely. Trim the dough around each pear half. Pinch sides and trim off excess dough. Score top of each dumpling. Bake at 400 degrees for 20 minutes or until golden browned. Serve warm with crème anglaise.

Serves 6

Teresa's Limoncello

~ Teresa Del Giudice ~

- **8 lemons**
- **1 liter of pure alcohol (Everclear)**
- **1 liter of water**
- **1 kilo of sugar (2 pounds)**

Peel the rind of 8 lemons, taking care to cut the rind as thinly as possible. Place the peel in a large jar with pure alcohol and close the jar (should be airtight). After 4 or 5 days, boil the water and sugar together for a few minutes and leave to cool. When cooled, put into the jar with lemon rinds and alcohol. The mixture should then be filtered and bottled. Limoncello is best when served very cold!

Serves 24-30

Pineapple Dessert

~ Atlanta Catering Company ~

- **2 cups all-purpose flour**
- **¼ teaspoon salt**
- **2½ tablespoons cocoa powder**
- **2½ cups sugar, divided**
- **¾ cup unsalted butter, chilled and cut into pieces**
- **2 eggs**
- **1 tablespoon water**
- **2 cups unsalted butter**
- **½ cup vanilla sugar**
- **1 tablespoon honey**
- **1½ cups heavy cream, divided**
- **Juice of six lemons**
- **2 tablespoons corn syrup**
- **¼ cup unsalted butter plus cold cubed butter for layering**
- **2 large ripe pineapples, peeled and cored, sliced very thin**
- **Coconut Gelato**

To make chocolate sweet dough, sift together flour, salt cocoa powder and sugar. Using a stand mixer with paddle attachment, mix dry ingredients with ¾ cup butter on low speed until resembles sand. Add eggs and mix until dough forms into a ball. Add water if necessary. If dough is too moist, add more flour. Wrap dough in plastic wrap and refrigerate overnight. Dust surface with flour and powdered sugar. Roll dough out to ⅛-inch thickness. Cut dough with favorite cookie cutter. Bake at 375 degrees for 7 minutes or until done. Store cookies.

For lemon-vanilla brown butter sauce, brown 2 cups butter in a non-reactive saucepan. Transfer to a bowl to cool. In a small saucepan, combine sugar, honey, lemon juice and 1¼ cups cream. Bring to boil, stirring often. Remove from heat and cool. Pour cream mixture into a blender. Blend on low speed while adding browned butter in a steady stream. Sauce will thicken as it emulsifies. Set aside.

To caramelize pineapples, cook 1½ cups sugar and corn syrup over medium-high heat until a dark amber color. Whisk in ¼ cup butter until blended. Remove from heat and add ¼ cup cream. Stir until smooth. Pour half caramel sauce into a 13 x 9 x 2-inch baking dish. Cool slightly. Layer with pineapple slices. Sprinkle with sugar and cold cubed butter. Repeat layers until pineapple is gone. Pour remaining caramel sauce on top. Cover with foil and place on baking sheet. Bake at 375 degrees for 45 minutes until golden browned and tender.

To assemble, ladle brown butter sauce in the center of a plate. Place one cookie in sauce. Place a generous scoop of gelato on cookie, pressing lightly to flatten the top. Place another cookie on top, pressing to anchor. With same cookie cutter, cut out a section of warm pineapple. Place atop cookie. If not warm, heat in microwave, then top cookie. Serve immediately.

Serves 12-15

To make vanilla sugar, store 2 dry vanilla beans with sugar in airtight container. If you cannot prepare this, just add ½ teaspoon vanilla to brown butter sauce.

Pier House Key Lime Pie

~ Pier House Restaurant ~

1¼ cups graham cracker crumbs
¾ cup plus 2 tablespoons sugar, divided
¼ cup butter, softened
5 egg yolks
1 (14 ounce) sweetened condensed milk
½ cup Key lime juice
½ teaspoon finely grated lime zest
5 egg whites, room temperature
¼ teaspoon cream of tartar
¼ teaspoon salt
¼ teaspoon vanilla

Combine cracker crumbs, ¼ cup sugar and butter until crumbly. Press into a 9-inch pie pan. Bake at 350 degrees for 5 minutes. Cool on wire rack. Beat egg yolks until light and fluffy. Gradually add milk, juice and zest. Pour filling into cooled crust. Bake at 350 degrees for 15 minutes. Cool slightly. Increase oven to 425 degrees. Combine egg whites, cream of tartar, salt and vanilla. Beat with electric mixer until frothy. Add ½ cup and 2 tablespoons sugar, a little at a time, beating well after each addition. Beat until sugar dissolves and mixture is not grainy. Continue to beat until stiff peaks form. Spread meringue over pie all the way up to edges. Bake at 425 degrees for 5 to 6 minutes or until nicely browned. Cool on wire rack. Serve cold.

Serves 6-8

Shrimp and Tabasco Cheese Grits

~ City Grocery ~

1 cup quick grits
¼ cup unsalted butter
¾ cup shredded sharp Cheddar cheese
½ cup Parmesan cheese
1 teaspoon cayenne pepper
1½ tablespoons paprika
1 tablespoon Tabasco sauce
Salt and pepper to taste
2 cups chopped smoked bacon
3 tablespoons olive oil
1½ pounds 26-30 count shrimp
3 tablespoons minced garlic
3 cups sliced white mushrooms
3 tablespoons white wine
2 tablespoons lemon juice
2 cups sliced green onion

Cook grits according to package directions. Whisk butter into grits. Add Cheddar cheese, Parmesan cheese, cayenne, paprika and Tabasco. Season with salt and pepper. Set aside. Cook bacon until browned. Remove bacon and set aside. Reserve bacon drippings. Heat a large skillet until very hot. Add 2 tablespoons bacon drippings and oil. As oil begins to smoke, add shrimp covering bottom of pan. Season with salt and pepper. Stir shrimp until turns pink. Reduce heat and add garlic. Add mushrooms and coat in oil. Add wine and juice. Stir for 30 seconds. Add green onion and stir for 20 seconds. Serve immediately over grits.

Serves 8

An Unforgettable Delmonico's Experience

A few days before we were scheduled to leave for our yearly trip to Las Vegas with our best friends John and Dee, Jay received a phone call while we were running errands. It was a regular patron of the sports bar that Jay manages who coincidentally has a brother who is a chef at Delmonicos, our favorite restaurant in Las Vegas.

Delmonico's is the best steak house that I have ever eaten in and I am not just saying that because the famous Emeril Lagasse owns it. The steaks are to die for with side dishes that leave you pleasantly satisfied after each dining experience. We have dined there on at least three different occasions but after this particular phone call we were in for the ultimate dining experience. Our connections landed us in the kitchen of Delmonico's on Sunday evening. How could anyone pass up that opportunity? After our knee jerk response of excitement and a hearty yes, we started to wonder how much this might actually cost us. Jay called his friend back and was assured that there was no room fee, just the cost of dinner. The room itself is hard to reserve due to the fact that there are only two seatings a night. That is what made the opportunity so rare. Needless to say we were already looking forward to dinner.

Sunday finally came, we decided to arrive early and treat ourselves to a few cocktails in the bar area while we waited for our table. Right away we felt like royalty. After telling the hostess our name, she replied with "I will let the kitchen know you have arrived." I immediately turned to Jay and said, "I never thought anyone would ever be waiting our *arrival*." As we sat at the bar we discussed what we were about to experience. Three of us did not like to take chances with our food so we were a bit worried about what we might be forced to eat. Dee doesn't eat seafood but has such a southern charm and she would never hurt anyone's feelings so we felt she would probably try it anyway. Jay said that he was willing to dabble in a few things just to see how they tasted. John eats anything so no worries there, but I am a bit picky. Let's just say that I was a master at feeding the dog secretly under the table as a kid without my parents finding out. No mom, I never really ate the lima bean casserole, but the dog loved it.

As we were led back to our table I wanted to stick my tongue out at the others in the restaurant so they would know that I got the better table, but I refrained. I do have to admit though we were watched closely as we were led

continued on next page

through the restaurant and through the white door right by the kitchen. The room was all white with floor to ceiling windows on one whole wall exposing the well oiled machine that makes Delmonico's superb. The kitchen was a wonderful tango of people moving and cleaning and cooking and prepping, sending out tray after tray of silver covered dishes just waiting to be devoured. Right away we were greeted by Albert who "would be assisting us throughout the night with anything that we needed". After Albert, came J.D., who introduced himself as our sommelier for the night. Thank goodness I watch the food network otherwise; I would have never known what that means. J.D. explained that we would be served anywhere between five and six courses and that we should pace ourselves. He also offered a wine pairing that would compliment each dish. Since Jay isn't a big wine drinker he stuck to his bourbon, but for John, Dee and myself we thought that sounded like a great idea. After J.D left, in came Octavia the head chef. After introducing himself in his thick Spanish accent he asked if we had any food allergies. That should have clued me in right away, but again with the excitement of it all I was along for the ride. We all answered "no", but John spoke up for the group. He said "Well, we don't have a lot of seafood eaters here so if we could stay away from fish that would be great." Octavia said there would be little seafood so not to worry.

Course One: Fried potato chips topped with garlic and grated cheese. My kind of food! It was paired with champagne that was a mix of several different white wines with champagne. Wonderful!

Course Two: Blue Crab cakes with a light white wine. This is as far as I usually go with seafood and let me tell you it was wonderful. I would say it was the best I ever had but that would eliminate the one that my Uncle Bob made me at his restaurant and honestly I have never had a better one since his, this one was a close second. Dee was a little nervous but I was proud of her for trying it and she did like it. It was getting better as we went along.

Course Three: Arugula salad with a creamy rosemary dressing, paired with a very light white wine. Yes, the third glass of wine so far. Unfortunately we weren't counting. I don't think I could pick arugula out of the produce section in the grocery store but it was fantastic and I was glad that Octavia thought to serve it. The dressing was unbelievable. I wish they bottled it. Then I could ask the produce guy where to find the arugula.

Course Four: Here is where we decide that Octavia wanted to teach us a lesson in fine cuisine. Foie Gras pan seared and served over marinated tomatoes with pancetta. I tried to wipe the look of horror off my face because there was no dog under the table to feed. It didn't help that the big window in front of me made it seem like everyone was staring at us just to see if we would actually eat it. I looked to Jay and he had the same look on his face. John just smiled. Dee politely asked me after Octavia left the room "What is foie gras?" I blurted out loudly "its duck liver!" John told me to hush because now Dee was never going to try it because I told her what it actually was. I couldn't let her dive in to something that I have seen them use multiple times on Iron Chef. Jay whispered, "I don't think I can do this", and I said, "I think we have to." By this time John was already finished and Dee had picked out the tomatoes and eaten them. The bonus was that we had gotten another glass of wine so I could wash anything down, or swallow it whole like I used to do with my peas and milk. I put on my brave face and tried it. It was more of a texture thing but honestly it wasn't bad at all. Jay just chopped his up a lot to make it look like he ate it and thank goodness it was time for the next course.

Course Five: Sea Bass in a creamy butter sauce with asparagus. Okay, now he was definitely messing with us. What happened to the no seafood rule? Apparently they love to torture anyone in the big fishbowl who thinks they can sit in the kitchen and choose what they get to eat. I have to admit though this was a step above the foie gras. It was very good, not fishy at all, but I ate all the asparagus. With yet another glass of wine, a Riesling, my favorite. Wine count: 5 glasses.

Course Six: Rib-eye steak with a homemade barbeque sauce on the side and potatoes. (I think.) The wine count was getting up there. Give me a break. Now this is my kind of dinner. Call me a meat and potatoes gal because I was in heaven. Although I am a filet fan it was very tender, just the way I like it. Yes, served with another glass of wine. This time Shiraz, a red wine. Whew. Switching is not a good thing.

Course seven, yes seven: An ice cream pie that had more of an ice minty cinnamony taste to it. Great description I know but all I know is that it was stinkin' good.

After our seven-course meal we all sat in our food/wine comas and talked to our lovely service staff. We had them sitting at the table with us by the end of the night answering all our crazy questions. All three treated us like old friends, letting us in on their dreams of opening their own restaurants, the most famous people they have served, and who was the craziest party they served so far, besides us of course. Soon it was time for the bill! By this time we had been eating and drinking for two and a half hours. Needless to say we were past our

continued on next page

prime for the night. Now we have a running joke between the four of us. John has always promised to take Jay out to Morton's, the nicest steakhouse in St. Louis as payback for the work Jay has done around John's house. The offer had been promised for about a year now so John decided to pick up the bill. Not looking at the bill, John slides a credit card inside the sleeve and Octavia takes it away. We thanked Octavia, J.D, and Albert and told them how much we enjoyed the experience. We decided that we would have never tried some of the things that had been placed in front of us if it hadn't been for them. They had truly opened our taste buds to new things. I can't say that I am going to prepare foie gras for dinner one night, but now I have tasted it.

We left the restaurant and wandered into the casino of the Venetian. Dee and I wandered ahead and Jay and John lagged behind as usual. Little did I know this whole time Jay was trying to get John to tell him the amount of the bill. Next I notice Jay is gone and John and Dee are laughing hysterically. I asked Dee what happened and she told me that they let Jay know the grand total and he flipped out. I asked her "Well, how much was it, $300?" She just laughed and said, "No, it was $800." I guess it was the fact that we had guzzled down seven glasses of wine that made the $800 dinner bill so funny but again we agreed it was a once in a lifetime experience, but next time we go to Delmonico's we'll take the table **next** to the kitchen, not in it!

~Allyson Golebiowski
Webster Groves, Mo.
Ally is the daughter of Cookbook Chair Joanne Golebiowski, who takes the blame for Ally having a "Champagne taste on a beer salary."

Professional Contributors

Atlanta Catering Company – Atlanta, Georgia

Basic Kneads Catering – Tupelo, Mississippi

Bay Breeze Bed and Breakfast – Mobile, Alabama

Beverly Blaylock Caterer – Tupelo, Mississippi

Buckhorn Inn – Gatlinburg, Tennessee

City Grocery – Oxford, Mississippi

Martha Rutledge Catering – Mobile, Alabama

Mississippi University for Women Culinary Arts Institute – Columbus, Mississippi

Park Heights Restaurant – Tupelo, Mississippi

Pier House Restaurant

Slightly North of Broad – Charleston, South Carolina

The Palace Café – New Orleans, Louisiana

Woody's Restaurant – Tupelo, Mississippi

Contributors

Gay Abney
Betsy Abraham
Amanda Adams
Louise Adams
Jima Alexander
Judy Armentrout
Audra Armistead
Cecelia Armstrong
Pamela Morris Atkins
Emily Atkinson
Kathy Bailey
Betty Barnes
Jean Beasley Barnes
Joyce Barnett
Evelyn Baxley
Lottye Betts Beasley
Wilma Beasley
Rachel Becker
Jean Beasley Beggs
Rita Bell
Hilda Bell
Betty Black
Sheryl Blackburn
Amy Blackmon
Beverly and Steve Blaylock
Amy Paxton Blossom
Pat Bobo
Jay Boehlow
Gail Boland
Charles Bradley
Ruby Bradley
Sandra Bridges
Barbara Briscoe
Linda Britta
Marty Brown
Marty Massey Brown
Esther Brown
Charlotte Busby
Linda Butler
Adrian Caldwell
Debi Caldwell
Renee Cameron
Teresa Camp
Judy Beasley Cappel
Missy Carter
Peggy Carter
Betty Cayson
Karen Chambers
Sarah Chancellor
Mary Ann Chiles
Alma Chishlom
Glenda Clanton
Elna Clark
Jane Beasley Clark
Syble Clark
Karen Clayton
Hugh C. Cobb
Tish Coleman
Nancy Collins
Becky Cook
Mabel Crawford
Martha Dale
Mary Margaret Dale
Alice Virginia Daniels
Judy Daniels
Beulah Davis
Ellie Decker
Jane A Denton
Romaine Dickson
Nancy Diffee
Martha Tate Dodge
Frances Doler
Sandra Dossett
Reta Doughty
Pat Eckenrode
Carol Elliott
Mary Elliott
Celeste Ellis
Kim Ensmann
Ruth Epps
Cindy Faucette
Dennis Faulkner
Lela Finney
Martha Fleming
Anna Fortner
Lucy Gaines
Gretchen Geisey
Ann K. Gibbs
Sally Gillentine
Mary Faye Gillham

Virginia Goddard
Joanne Golebiowski
Claudia Gore
Cathy Grace
Whit Grace
Sarah Graham
Theresa Graham
Pat Gray
Mary Green
Nina Grice
Patsy Griffin
Nancy Grisson
Betty Guin
Anne Haire
Deborah Woodrick Hall
Jane Hammond
Martha Houston Reid Hammond
Nita Hamric
Elaine Hancock
Anna Jean Hanson
Katy Hardin
Caroline Harmon
Cherie Harris
Jo Anne Harris
Louise Harris
Paige Harris
Sara Hartley
Aimee Hawkins
Lisa Hawkins
Pat Hazel
Waurene Heflin
Deborah Henn
Pat Henson
Ann Bryant Herring
Kim Hester
Georgie Lou Holley
Kim Hopmann
Elaine Hudson
Merrie Hughes
Antony Jacobs
K.K. Jacobs
Tracey Jefferys
Delores Keenan
Glenda Keenan
Melissa Kingsley
Gayle Klauser
Carol Kloac
E.L. Koonce
LaNelle Lacey
Frances Ladd
Pat Lamar
Nell Lamberson
Faye Lann
Barbara Lawhon
Shirley Lawrence
Bess Leathers
Jean Leech
Jean Lollar
Cindy Lombardo
Brandi Long
Ona Lowery
Pamela Morris Lowery
Emily Maddox
Missy Malone
Agnes Martin
Fran Carter Massengill
Jackie Massey
Jeannie Massey
Virginia Mathews
Bill & Lynn McAllily
Beatrice McBryde
Rett McCarthy
Lou Ann McCarty
Amy McClellan
Sylvia McCurdy
Karen McFerrin
Posey McGraw
Susan T. McGukin
Marilyn Megginson
Lisa Megginson
Laura Potts Melvin
Betty Merrit
Ellen Miller
Gail Molari
Mary Claire Moncrief
Sally Monroe
Judy Moore
Debbie Morris
Kim Mosley
Edie Muse
Sally Muzii
Kristi Napier
Mary Nell
Pamela Morris Nichols
Darlene Oliver
Nan Parker
Rose Anne Parker

continued on next page

Sarah Parker
Ginna Parsons
Lauren Patterson
Sharon Phillips
Susan Phillips
Margaret Pickard
Alma Wright Poland
Joy Potts
Jane Powell
Evelyn Pritchard
Angie Ramage
Doris Ramage
Gretchen Ramsey
Carolyn Rasberry
Jane Rather
Cindy Rials
Liz Rice
Prisscilla Robinson
Nan Rogers
Eloise Rollins
Bobbie Rosato
Delores Rose
Lynn Russell
Nell Russell
Eloise Scott
Gail Scoville
Amanda Scruggs
Virginia Shannon
Mrs. Charles Sheffield

Sandra Shaepard
Kathryn Taylor Short
Jim Simmons
Mary Ann Simpson
Amanda Sisk
Amelia Smith
Delores Smith
Lisa Smith
Sarah Smith
Laura Sneed
Allison Spencer
Brenda Spencer
Lisa Springer
Ann Stafford
Stephen Stanford
Cherry Stone
Linda Stone
Bama Strawn
Myron Suchanick
Trice Warriner Sumner
Brenda Swords
John Swords
Altha Tackett
Barbara Taft
Holly Temple
Daintry Thomas
Shirley Thomas
Linda Thompson
Molly Thompson

Carolyn Todd
Frances Todd
Barbara Tyre
Dody Vail
Barbara Vaughn
John Vaughn Jr.
Shirley Waddell
Dale & Richard Warrnier
Jean Webb
Ann Weir
Kristina Weir
Elizabeth Whitenton
Bette Whitenton
Mary Morgan Whitfield
Cathy Wikle
Will Wikle
Sherry Wilemon
Debbie Wiley
Beverly Williams
Jo Anne Williams
Margaret Williamson
Tomicene Monts Wilson
Susan Winkler
Ann Womack
Dessie Woods
Sandra Wright
Paige Yarbrough

Index

E

Celebrating Hospice-tality

Sanctuary Hospice House, Inc.
P.O. Box 192, Tupelo, MS 38802
662/844-2111 • FAX 662/844-2354
www.sanctuaryhospicehouse.com
email: office@sanctuaryhospicehouse.com

Please send me:

______copies of *Celebrating Hospice-tality* (tax included)	@ $25.00 each	________
Shipping and handling for first copy	@ $ 5.00 each	________
Shipping and handling for each additional copy to same address	@ $ 3.00 each	________
	TOTAL	________

Name ______________________________

Address ______________________________

City ______________ State ________ Zip ________

Make check payable to *Sanctuary Hospice House, Inc.*

Charge to *(circle one)* Visa MasterCard American Express Signature ______________

Account number ______________ Expiration Date ________

Proceeds from the sale of this book will be used to aid in the day to day operations of the Sanctuary Hospice House, Inc. of North Mississippi.

Celebrating Hospice-tality

Sanctuary Hospice House, Inc.
P.O. Box 192, Tupelo, MS 38802
662/844-2111 • FAX 662/844-2354
www.sanctuaryhospicehouse.com
email: office@sanctuaryhospicehouse.com

Please send me:

______copies of *Celebrating Hospice-tality* (tax included)	@ $25.00 each	________
Shipping and handling for first copy	@ $ 5.00 each	________
Shipping and handling for each additional copy to same address	@ $ 3.00 each	________
	TOTAL	________

Name ______________________________

Address ______________________________

City ______________ State ________ Zip ________

Make check payable to *Sanctuary Hospice House, Inc.*

Charge to *(circle one)* Visa MasterCard American Express Signature ______________

Account number ______________ Expiration Date ________

Proceeds from the sale of this book will be used to aid in the day to day operations of the Sanctuary Hospice House, Inc. of North Mississippi.